TENNESSEE

NAMES

TENNESSEE
PLACE
NAMES

LARRY L. MILLER

INDIANA UNIVERSITY PRESS   BLOOMINGTON & INDIANAPOLIS

This book is a publication of

Indiana University Press
601 North Morton Street
Bloomington, IN 47404-3797 USA

http://iupress.indiana.edu

Telephone orders   800-842-6796
Fax orders   812-855-7931
Orders by e-mail   iuporder@indiana.edu

© 2001 by Larry L. Miller

The paper used in this publication meets the minimum requirements
of American National Standard for Information
Sciences—Permanence of Paper for Printed Library Materials, ANSI
Z39.48-1984.

Manufactured in the United States of America

Library of Congress Cataloging-in-Publication Data

Miller, Larry L., date
Tennessee place-names / Larry L. Miller.
p. cm.
ISBN 0-253-33984-7 (cloth : alk. paper) — ISBN 0-253-21478-5 (paper : alk. paper)
1. Names, Geographical—Tennessee. 2. Tennessee—History, Local. I.
Title.
F434 .M54 2001
917.68'001'4—dc21
2001001542

1 2 3 4 5   06 05 04 03 02 01

To
Harry J. Miller
and
Grace V. Miller

CONTENTS

ix   Preface

I Place-Names

231   County Names

243   Acknowledgments

Preface

This volume has been designed as an aid in historical or geographical research, as well as to satisfy the curiosity of general readers. Among those who may find it of interest or utility are librarians, library patrons, members of historical and genealogical societies, and laypersons.

While the book contains a certain amount of secondary or ancillary data, its primary purpose is to provide the "reasons" for naming Tennessee's hamlets, towns, and cities. The compiler has striven diligently to meet this primary goal even when little else could be found regarding the place.

With any project of such an ambitious nature, it is necessary to circumscribe its bounds, designating what is within the purview of the work as well as distinguishing that which is outside its scope. Not to do so is to blur the aims of the undertaking and allow it to get out of hand. When that occurs, a danger exists that the undertaking will become a lifelong, all-consuming task instead of a doable assignment with a reasonable expectation of culminating in a timely manner in a volume that will be made available to the public. For it is only by finally placing this work in the hands of readers and searchers that it can serve its purpose of answering questions and satisfying interest.

Notwithstanding that the book has been purposely designed to have distinct bounds and limitations, it may rightfully be claimed to possess by far the best and broadest coverage of any similar work on Tennessee's populated places—not that there have been many books with the sole aim of addressing this niche.

The volume you are holding contains close to 2,000 place-name entries, and in virtually all of them the certain or probable name rationale is set forth. (In a minority of the entries, the explanation is speculative to a lesser or greater degree, since no authoritative documentation exists or could be unearthed using reasonable investigative means.)

Wherever possible, in addition to a reason for or explanation of the place-name, an attempt has been made to flesh out the entry with the year the place was founded, surveyed, or platted. And, although current names are the primary focus, previous names are provided and discussed where such information was available. Where applicable and convenient to do so, incorporation dates are provided.

The entries include Tennessee cities, towns, villages, hamlets, and communities of every size and stature having their own distinct identities. No importance has been placed on the legal aspect of this terminology, and no fine distinctions have been attempted. Cities and villages, technically, have legal definitions. Even the word *hamlet* at one time was not generically applied—as I have taken the liberty to do here— to virtually any tiny community, but instead had its own defined, legal application. Becoming overly concerned with geopolitical entity status was deemed a distraction from the primary goal of this compilation; so little attention should be paid to those terms as employed herein.

As a bonus, the names of Tennessee's ninety-five counties have been included, with brief origins, in a separate listing.

Outside the parameters of this work are ghost towns and other places that no longer exist at their original location. Admittedly, one might have a difficult time discerning between some of the places included in this volume and those deemed ghost towns. The judgment to include places was often arbitrary; frequently it was based on being able to locate them on maps in current use.

Neighborhoods and developments fall outside the scope of the coverage. Developments are not in any sense towns or cities, and while neighborhoods often possess many of the distinctions that identify places as towns, they usually do not have defined boundaries, are unincorporated, and have never been laid out. In urban areas, neighborhoods may well be sections of cities or villages.

A high value has been placed on anecdotal material relating to the naming of towns. Consequently, wherever interesting stories regarding the naming process existed and could be located, a capsule account has been included for its human interest value. In some instances, the veracity of the account is suspect. But such stories do add an element of humor to an often dry recitation, and so it was decided to incorporate them and let the reader judge how much credence to place in them. No attempt was made to become the final arbiter between or among place-name explanations focusing on the same community. All accounts that were found are presented.

Nowadays, if a town were being founded and a name was required, no doubt it would be left to a computer to spit out unused possibilities, perhaps even to make the final selection. But few Tennessee towns are being founded at the dawn of the twenty-first century. Most were spawned from the late 1700s through the nineteenth century.

So what were the most common sources for town names in Tennessee? Probably the surnames (in some cases the given names) of individuals—persons who were directly involved with founding the places, or persons whom the namers desired to honor. Entries that fall into this category will be of special note to readers interested in onomastics.

In earlier years, the U.S. Post Office Department was tremendously influential in deciding on place-names. If a place wanted to obtain a post office, the department often dictated its name or a name change. The department preferred short names and ones that would not be confused with other Tennessee post office names. In many instances, the name of the postmaster became the name of the place.

Names recycled from other states or counties now designate many Tennessee places. Often the original name came from a city, region, state, or nation that the settlers had left behind.

The penetration of railroads through the state's countryside had a profound effect on the place-names. Equally influential was the Native American presence in Tennessee; numerous towns were named after prominent Indians or carry names that derive from Indian terms.

Judging by the number of place-names incorporating the term "springs," the state must have more natural springs than most other states. Numerous entries in this book end in "Springs." In fact, many other place-names including "Springs" were left out, since an explanation for the rest of the name could not be found.

A great many sites took on a name that included the type of timber prevalent at that locale. Oak Ridge and Poplar Hill typify such entries.

Mining or minerals found locally, geophysical or aesthetic features, local flora, battle sites, and biblical names were other frequent inspirations for Tennessee place-names.

The compiler takes pride in the vital role that lay consultants played in bringing this volume to fruition. In fact, their role is probably unique for books on this subject. These consultants are listed in an acknowledgments section at the end of the book.

Many local newspapers around the state published the compiler's plea for input from readers. Those who replied, gratifyingly, often had firsthand knowledge of the naming of a town in question; some were descendants of the founders and were able to furnish rich accounts of the town's formation.

The compiler also sent out letters to county historical and genealogical societies, some of whom contributed information directly or disseminated the request for data to members who possessed such information. A few who received the plea passed it on to third parties in other states; so information on the naming of tiny Tennessee hamlets arrived from states hundreds or even thousands of miles distant.

Thousands of hours of arduous library research also went into the volume, with the compiler tapping the holdings of at least a dozen libraries in two states.

It should be emphasized that virtually nothing "new" is to be found in this volume; its main accomplishment is centralizing between two covers data that were widely scattered. Often the bits of information relevant to this work were deposited within verbose, wide-ranging contexts and had to be diligently separated out for presentation here.

Credit and gratitude are owed to the chroniclers whose work made this book possible. Some place-names were discussed at length in early works, while others were accorded only the briefest of mentions. But whether terse or detailed, such passages, when taken collectively, made up a rich repository without which this volume would not have been possible.

Is the volume comprehensive? Not at all. While the reader will find more Tennessee town and city names covered here than in any other extant work, there are still many place-names whose rationales could not be located despite assiduous sleuthing. If there is one consolation, it is that nothing brings forth corrections or additions so much as the publication of a book. The author encourages such feedback, since it could well prove the foundation for an expansion or updating of this volume.

TENNESSEE
PLACE
NAMES

Place-**Names**

Acton *McNairy County.* This name is believed to have been inspired by a site in England of the same name. Tradition has it that a Lucy Castleberry had visited the English locality and was impressed by it. Apparently, she assigned the label to this spot, and it was adopted.

Adams *Robertson County.* At one time, the real estate on either side of the Edgefield & Kentucky Railroad was held by Reuben Adams. (One source identifies him as James Reuben Adams.) The rail line concluded its push through the locality in 1858, and two years later the depot was finished. It was designated Adams Station. The store and post office were in the same structure. When the town itself was still called Red River, incorporation took place (1869). The name Adams was not applied to the community as a whole until 1898. Reincorporation occurred in 1908, and the city of Adams was incorporated in 1963. There were some periods between the first and last incorporation when the town was not incorporated at all.

Adamsville *McNairy County.* The community was incorporated in 1870. According to one source, at an earlier time—in the 1840s—a stagecoach stop and inn were operated here by George D. Adams, after whom the site is undoubtedly named. An alternate source states that the Adams family came on the local scene in 1833 and that a George G. Adams opened a post office and store, calling the site Adamsville.

Aetna *Hickman County.* The reference is to the Sicilian volcano Mount Etna. This place-name was often applied to sites where there were forges, hot springs, flour mills, or geological evidence of early volcanic activity.

Aetna *Marion County.* See preceding entry.

Afton *Greene County.* This place-name is usually inspired by Robert Burns's song "Flow Gently, Sweet Afton," a reference to the River Afton in Scotland.

Alamo *Crockett County (seat).* In 1847, this town was still referred to as Cageville. The name traces to Licurgus Cage, the first merchant. The community had been laid out in about 1845. Twenty-four years later, the name Alamo was conferred upon it as a memorial to the Texas site where Davy Crockett and others died at the hands of Mexican General Santa Ana and his troops in 1836. A frontiersman, Crockett was a native of Tennessee. The Spanish word *alamo* translates as "poplar." The town was incorporated in 1911.

Alanthus Hill *Hancock County.* This promontory may have been labeled Alanthus by settlers emigrating from the Alanthus, Virginia, area, or for a prevalent type of tree. *American Place-Names* believes "Alanthus" to be "a simplified spelling of *ailanthus,* for the tree." Supporting the second theory, a native of the area writes, "Alanthus Hill is where I got what . . . education I have. It was a four-room building built about 1900. I do not know why it was called Alanthus Hill unless it was because of the large alanthus trees growing nearby on the top of the river cliff above Powell River."

Alcoa *Blount County.* The community takes its name from the acronym for Aluminum Company of America: Alcoa. The "company town" arose around the manufacturing plant and served as a base of operations while a major dam was being constructed nearby. Alcoa was incorporated in 1919.

Alder *Campbell County.* See following entry.

Alder Springs *Campbell County.* The hazel alder grows in this section of the state and undoubtedly flourished near these springs.

Alder Springs *Union County.* Alder bushes grew in profusion at a wetland near where a Baptist church was built of logs and dubbed Alder Springs Baptist Church. Later, the church was rebuilt of improved materials about a mile away. Unaware that the alder bushes had inspired the name of the site, subsequent owners had them cut.

Alexander Springs *Lawrence County.* Absalom Alexander arrived in the county in 1853, purchasing a little over an acre of real estate surrounding the local springs, which assumed his name.

Alexandria *DeKalb County.* Dr. Daniel Alexander laid out the community in 1820 and named it after himself. He was born in Maryland in 1773. The first settler arrived at the site in about 1801. (Dr. Alexander may have been that first settler.) A conflicting source claims that the site takes its name from the renowned Egyptian city. Still another source differs in several respects from the preceding account. It claims Alexander founded the town in about 1815, naming it after his "native town" in Virginia, not Maryland. Presumably, that place would have the name Alexander, or Alexandria, Virginia. The community was incorporated in 1846 but surrendered its charter in 1879. (Another source gives the year of incorporation as 1831.)

Algood *Putnam County.* Although no additional details have been located, it appears this hamlet took the surname of an individual named Joel Algood, who had purchased a tract of land here. For a period, it was referred to as Algood's Old Fields. The town was incorporated in 1901.

Allandale *Hawkins County.* Strangely enough, the name of this town is said to trace back to a horse! Mr. and Mrs. Harvey Brookes were prominent early residents, their domicile becoming known as the Brookes Farm (or Mansion). But Mr. Brookes had a Tennessee walking horse named Roan Allen (or Roan Allan), which he loved dearly and of which he was very proud. So he changed the name of the estate to Allandale, after the equine. The surrounding community eventually assumed the name, as well. Mr. Brookes died in 1969.

Allardt *Fentress County.* According to one source, this city is known by the surname of a landowner who toiled there in some early year. More specifically, *What's in a Name?* states that, sometime after 1880, Frederick Allardt and Bruno Gernt led a contingent of Germans from Michigan to this locality, where they settled. The town incorporated in 1964.

Allen's Chapel *DeKalb County.* In 1911, the Allen's Chapel Methodist Church was established here, near the home of Lemuel Allen. A nearby school assumed the same name.

Allen's Grove *Cocke County.* At an early time, the residents scattered around this area were served by a church and school, the land for which was contributed by Isaac Allen. Thus, the site took on his surname. Allen lived from 1817 to 1895.

Allons *Overton County.* An unnamed source claims that *Allons* means "to gather around." (*Allons,* or *Allons-y* is French for "Let us go [together].") A post office finally opened here in 1896. A nickname—or alternative name of the place—has long been Needmore. A volume entitled *Cracker Barrel Tales* recounts an incident when a customer entered the general store and requested a number of commonly carried items, only to be informed that the store was out of virtually all of them. Later, the customer told someone else about the sorry state of the store's inventory and added, "They really do need more." The store became known as the "needmore store," and presently the surrounding area took on the Needmore nickname.

Alloway *Cumberland County.* This place-name probably traces back to an individual named Archelus Alloway, who resided in White County in 1820. Later, portions of White County were taken to help constitute Cumberland County.

Almaville *Rutherford County.* According to a historical account, David Phaine operated a general store at this location. In 1879, the Post Office Department awarded the town a post office, which was installed in Phaine's store, but required a name. He is said to have chosen Almaville out of affection for a local lass named Alma.

Alpha *Hamilton County.* Judging by the meaning of the term, early settlers probably looked on taking up residence at this site as "a new beginning." Alpha is the first letter of the Greek alphabet.

Alpine *Overton County.* A school was established on Alpine Mountain here in 1810 by Christopher Organ and John L. Dillard, who were young Presbyterian ministers probably associated with the Cumberland Presbyterian Church. The name officially became Alpine in 1922. An earlier name of the site was Nettlecarrier, said to be the name of a Cherokee chief encamped locally in the early 1800s.

Altamont *Grundy County (seat).* This place-name was apparently composed by taking the French *mount* and prefixing *alta,* Italian or Spanish for "high." The site claims to occupy the county's highest elevation. Incorporation took place in 1853.

Alto *Franklin County.* This hamlet is probably situated at a relatively high elevation from its surroundings. *Alto* is Spanish for "high" or "tall."

Amherst *Knox County.* Although some U.S. places named Amherst trace back to Amherst, New Hampshire, most eventually trace back to Baron Jeffrey Amherst (1717–1797). Amherst was a British general serving during the French and Indian War. He ultimately commanded all British forces deployed in North America.

Amis *Hawkins County.* Several Amises resided locally at the time of the 1840 census, including Thomas G., Haynes, and James. One or more of them was probably associated with this community.

Anderson *Franklin County.* His great-grandson reports that John Fitzgerald Anderson was this community's namesake. Anderson is said to have arrived at the place in the early 1800s, organizing and building the town.

Anderson *Overton County.* William, Thomas, Dicy, Jacob, Christopher, and John Anderson resided in the vicinity when the 1850 census was taken. Quite likely the place-name is associated with their family or families.

Andersonville *Anderson County.* A former name of the site was Wallace Crossroads. Like the county, it takes its name from Joseph Anderson. Anderson served from 1792 to 1797 as judge of the Territory South of the River Ohio. From 1797 until 1815, he was a senator.

Angeltown *Sumner County.* Eliza, Francis, James, William, Mary, and Robert Angel resided in this vicinity when the 1850 census was recorded. They are probably connected, individually or as families, with the designation of this location.

Antioch *Davidson County.* Probably named by persons of strong religious convictions, the town bears the name of the biblical city in Syria.

Antioch *DeKalb County.* See entry for Antioch, Montgomery County.

Antioch *Haywood County.* See entry for Antioch, Davidson County.

Antioch *Jackson County.* See entry for Antioch, Montgomery County.

Antioch *Loudon County.* See following entry.

Antioch *Montgomery County.* This place-name was undoubtedly biblically inspired. At least two ancient cities bore the name—one in Syria and the other on the border between the Pisidian and Phrygian districts.

Apison *Hamilton County.* The town was given its name in honor of Cincinnatus Apperson, head of a section crew that built the first railroad line through the site. When the name was recorded, it was misspelled and came out Apison. A colonel in the Confederate Army, Apperson served under General Longstreet, fighting in many battles. He passed away in 1916 at the age of 74. Colonel Apperson's granddaughter provided this information.

Appleton *Lawrence County.* Wes Appleton founded a village here in 1817. But by 1830, a Kentuckian named Pinson Hooks settled here, opened a store, and changed the name to Pink Hook. In 1840, John Appleton opened his home to a post office and reassigned the name Appleton to it. The locale was best known for a landmark referred to as the "Big Red Store," which featured a wide array of merchandise that included everything from coffee to coffins. Appleton family members residing locally in 1850 included Hiram and Robert.

Archer *Marshall County.* This community is also sometimes referred to as Springplace. The accepted name traces back to an individual named Archer Beasley.

Arcott *Clay County.* This place-name is also seen styled as Arcot. The name may trace to about 1887 and refer to a town in Ireland. It seems settlement of this site was by a Colonel James McColgan, who may have been a native of Ireland, or at the very least, traced his ancestry to that country. Colonel McColgan arrived here in about 1810. Bennett's Ferry and Hix were previous names of the site.

Ardmore *Giles County.* This city borrows the name of an Atlantic coastal town in Ireland called Ardmore. It was first dubbed Austin, for Alex Austin, who in 1911 opened a store to provide supplies for the railroad builders coming through. When the railroad company erected a depot, they assigned it the name Ardmore, resulting in the town's current name. It straddles the Tennessee-Alabama line. Some feel it also straddles the Giles and Lincoln county lines. Ardmore was incorporated in 1949.

Arlington *Shelby County.* One source states that the community is believed to be named for Arlington, Virginia. It goes on to relate that the idea of naming this particular site Arlington may have come as early as 1778 from Captain Henry Pitman (or Pittman), who constructed a dwelling place here. However, another source claims that the site had other names before Arlington, including Withe Depot and Haysville. The Withe Depot designation came about in 1856 as a result of attempts by the Memphis & Ohio Railroad to attract shipping to the Fayette County community of Withe (now Hickory Withe). But real estate for the facility had been donated by General Samuel J. Hays; so eventually it became known as Haysville. Haysville was incorporated in 1878. The post office was unable to use that name; so in 1883 it was changed to Arlington. The town's second incorporation took place in 1900. The two sources agree in part, the second stating that Captain Pitman had visited Washington, D.C., and Arlington Cemetery, and was partial to the name Arlington.

Armona *Blount County.* Although unlikely, an explanation from the *Maryville Daily Times* hypothesizes that the name is the result of a misspelling of Aroma strawberries. Such strawberries were grown and shipped from this community. Some, however, claim that the place was known as Armona long before strawberries became a major local crop.

Arp *Lauderdale County.* The first white settlers, Sam Jenkins and his wife, may have come to this location in 1850. In the 1880s, a mercantile enterprise was begun here by J. F. Morris. He also served as the postmaster. It is said that Morris named the site Arp in honor of Bill Arp, "or rather, Hon. Charles Smith, of Atlanta, Georgia, of whose writings he was very fond." The account is set forth in the volume *Lauderdale County from Earliest Times.*

Arthur *Claiborne County.* A developer named Alexander A. Arthur arrived in this area from Montreal, Canada, in 1870. Consolidating some land parcels purchased from settlers, he laid out a town. (The year is uncertain, but a map was made by the Rogers Syndicate Land Company.) In 1876, the place was known as Butcher Springs. The post office became designated as Arthur in 1890. Mr. Arthur was instrumental in having a rail line laid from Knoxville to Middlesboro (Kentucky), through Arthur. It was used primarily to ship coal, ore, and other minerals to other markets.

Asbury *Coffee County.* See entry for Asbury, Pickett County.

Asbury *Haywood County.* See entry for Asbury, Pickett County.

Asbury *Lauderdale County.* See following entry.

Asbury *Pickett County.* The name may have been brought to this area by settlers with ties to New Jersey, where one of the better-known Asburys is located. The New Jersey place-name derives from a pioneer of Methodism, Bishop Francis Asbury. In 1788, Bishop Asbury held the first Methodist Conference west of the Alleghenies.

Asbury *Washington County.* There was a building here called the Asbury Meeting House. (See preceding entry.)

Ash Hill *Williamson County.* The hamlet takes its name from the profusion of green ash timber that covered the hill at the time a place-name was needed.

Ashland City *Cheatham County (seat).* The Kentucky estate that belonged to Henry Clay was known as Ashland. Ashland City was named for that famous dwelling place, according to a source. Other authorities claim that the municipality was created by an act of the General Assembly in 1859, incorporating under the Ashland City name due to the many ash trees in nearby forests. It is believed to have first carried the name Ashland, due to the local ash trees, with "City" added when it became a city in 1859. The Adam Binkley family may have first settled the place, about 1780.

Ashwood *Maury County.* This designation is said to refer to the residence of Bishop-General Leonidas Polk. In turn, the dwelling name was probably inspired by a stand of ash timber at or near the site.

Aspen Hill *Giles County.* An elevated site and nearby aspen trees provided this place with its name. Families who settled in the vicinity as early as 1807 had surnames such as Kimbrough, Cox, Westmoreland, Reed, and Riggs. Soon afterward, John Butler, John Barnett, Baker Potts, and the Roger Simpson family settled nearby. The Reverend Aaron Brown settled the site later owned by his son, Governor Aaron V. Brown, referred to as Aspen Hill Place.

Athens *McMinn County (seat).* The adoption of classical names was popular for a period in America. This one refers to the Greek capital. Often, towns given this name had some sort of academy, school, or "seat of learning" that recommended the name. Incorporation came to this Athens in 1829.

Atkins *Anderson County.* In the 1830 census of West Tennessee, Jessee, William N., William S., Henry L., and George Atkins are identified as county residents. It is likely one or more of them resided at this locality and inspired, at least in part, the designation.

Atnip *DeKalb County.* At the time of the 1840 census, Joseph, Elex, and Gemmima Atnip resided in the area. The site name was adopted from their family name.

Atoka *Tipton County.* The *Illustrated Dictionary of Place Names* states that the Atoka in Oklahoma was named in honor of a Choctaw athlete. Possibly the Tennessee site with the same name owes its label to that individual. A second source claims that the term means "the ball field" in the Muskogee language. Possibly, it was a site where Native American children kicked a ball around an open expanse near their encampment. Atoka was founded in 1872 and incorporated in 1911.

Atpontley *Bledsoe County.* Three men who opened and worked a seam of coal in this mining town bore the surnames of Atkinson, Dupont, and Finley. When they decided the site needed a name, each man wanted the place to be named after himself. A compromise was struck: they would take "At" from "Atkinson," "pont" from "Dupont," and "ley" from "Finley," and form Atpontley.

Atwood *Carroll County.* The site retained the surname of an early resident, according to one source that is probably accurate. However, a second theory suggests that the name came about during railroad days, when the stop here was to take on fuel in the form of wood ("at wood"). Nineteen forty-one was the year of incorporation.

Auburntown *Cannon County.* This village is the namesake of the city of Auburn, New York. Emigrants from that section of New York may have settled in this area and brought the name with them. Some sources say, in fact, that for nearly a century it was known simply as Auburn, but that at some time the Post Office Department forced the change to Auburntown because there were too many Auburns. At one time, the site was identified as Poplar Stand, because of poplar trees there. Incorporation occurred in 1949.

Austin's Mill *Hawkins County.* Several Austins are mentioned in local records; however, all of them lived in the twentieth century. They include Elmer Pipkin Austin (1928–1984), Howard Earl Austin (1932–1970), and Sharon Kay Austin (1957–1974). Margaret Austin was born in 1921. The place-name may trace back to an ancestor or ancestors of one or more of these persons.

Austin Springs *Washington County.* One source states that two brothers, surnamed Austin, discovered a spring at this location. Later, they built a hotel at the site, in part to house visitors who sought the minerals-laden water of the spring. The water was believed to be conducive to better health. The hotel later burned down. A source close to Austin Springs writes that land was purchased in 1860 by Clisby Austin, and that he built a hotel overlooking the Watauga River. So Clisby was apparently one of the brothers who discovered the spring or springs.

Austin Springs *Weakley County.* The site derives its name from Chris Austin, who arrived from North Carolina and acquired considerable land here. The "Springs" portion of the name stems from pure mineral water springs that were discovered by two Austin brothers adjacent to Powell Creek, on Austin land. The Austins built a hotel (which later burned down) and developed the springs into an attraction that drew people from a wide area; the mineral waters were believed to impart health benefits.

Awalt *Franklin County.* In 1850, John Awalt resided nearby, no doubt inspiring this name that still appears on maps.

Aymett Town *Giles County.* An early settler here was Allen Aymett, from whom the community takes its name. A family named Maclin (MacLin?) donated two acres of land for construction of a school.

Baggettsville *Robertson County.* Local authorities confirm that the site retains the name of early Baggett families who resided here. Eli, J. B., Sally, and William Baggett were present here in 1850. Two others spelled the surname Bagget; their names were B. F. and Archable. Eighteen-seventy census records show the following Baggetts and their ages at that time: G. T., 17; B. F., 48; Eli, 41; Mildred, 70; A. B., 45; Burl, 34; J. B., 44; and A. C., 28. The aforementioned A. B. Baggett may have been Archer B. Baggett, who became the site's first postmaster in 1870.

Baileyton *Greene County.* Although the site was first designated Laurel Gap, it was settled at a very early time, 1776. Although many Baileys resided in the vicinity over the years, the first ones may have been a pair of brothers, Claudius and Thomas P. Bailey, twenty-four years before the turn of the century. Baileyton was incorporated in 1915.

Baird's Mills *Wilson County.* The name of this locality probably relates to an individual who was prominent in the area, Walter Jackson Baird. Baird was born in 1873 and died 107 years later.

Baker's Crossroads *Cumberland County.* This intersection probably derives its name from the family or ancestors of Mary Baker, 73, an 1880 resident of the area. At the same time, William, age 25, and John Baker, 19, were local citizens.

Baker's Station *Davidson County.* This locality became known by the Baker name in the mid-1800s. John Wesley Baker was a property owner through whose land a section of railroad track passed. The water tank and pump and the stationhouse were located on Baker property. A general store served the needs of the many travelers and local residents, and was operated by Connell Baker. The post office that opened in 1875 eventually became designated Baker's Post Office.

Bakerton *Clay County.* The designation probably traces to John Baker, who served as the local postmaster in 1904, and also operated a store in the same building until his retirement in 1906.

Bakertown *Moore County.* The *1880 Moore County Census* book lists eighteen Bakers residing in the county at the time. Some of them were John, Ben, Maggie, Alice, William, and Elizabeth. In all probability, the place-name relates to one or more of the families, which probably resided at this site.

Bakerville *Humphreys County.* The name of the site probably traces back to one of the local Baker families residing in the area during the nineteenth century. *Humphreys County, Tennessee Marriage Records, 1861–1888,* lists a number of Bakers repeating the vows. Included are W. H., Charley, J. B., John, James, L. D., S. B., W. T., J. D., D. K., and J. W. Baker. Another source, *1880 Humphreys County Census,* sheds additional light, listing no fewer than eighty Bakers. Some of the men included Ezekiel, a farmer; William H., a laborer; and S. B., age 44 at the time, a farmer. Some of the women included Betty, Jemima J., and Martha.

Bakerworks *Dickson County.* There were a great many Bakers calling Dickson County home when the 1850 census was taken, including the following: Absalom, Armstrong, Charles W., Elisabeth, Benjamin, Charles A., West H., William T., Carter, William J., Thomas, and Henderson. One or more of them probably contributed the surname to this site, which evidently had some type of shop or manufacturing facility, such as a wagonworks or ironworks.

Ball Play *Polk County.* This location is said to have been the site of a large playing field where early Native American inhabitants played ball games. Several Indian former residents of the place are believed to be buried in the Ball Play church cemetery.

Baltimore *Cocke County.* The community was named after Baltimore, Maryland.

Baneberry *Jefferson County.* A relatively "young" community, Baneberry had its genesis when a Mr. Anderson was seeking land from various farmers to be used for a recreational community. It was termed Lakeland Development Corporation, and was to be located on a peninsula bordering Douglas Lake. Tennis, swimming, golf, and other activities were offered. After the initial development, the project was purchased by the Butcher Brothers banking firm, which hired Buddy Pack as their developer. Mr. Pack sought a name change for the area, and noticed a lot of baneberry bushes on the land. He conceived the name Baneberry Resorts. Although the plant is a poisonous bush, the new owners liked the name and agreed to the change. Eventually, a homeowners' association was formed. Later, the possibility of annexation by a neighboring town arose, so the association incorporated, giving birth to the city of Baneberry. One of the first orders of business by the new mayor and council was a name for the entity. After a brief discussion, few could see any reason for a new name; so the Baneberry name was officially adopted.

Baptist Ridge *Clay County.* The former name of this location was Oak Grove. A correspondent who grew up locally states, "My father says before he was 21, a Baptist preacher (Jess Hooten, he thinks) held meetings for nine straight weeks [here, after which] everyone started calling it Baptist Ridge."

Barfield *Rutherford County.* It is likely that the place-name refers to Frederick Barfield, who served as a trustee of the nearby Bradley Academy and held real estate in this area.

Bargerton *Henderson County.* There were two Henry Bargers and an Elijah M. Barger in the county's 1870 census rolls. The family surname probably contributed to the place-name, appended with the common *ton* to indicate a town.

Barnardsville *Roane County.* John, age 67; Catherine, 15; Malinda, 44; Card, 32; and Johnathan Barnard, 49, were local residents in 1880 when the census was recorded. It is likely the place-name came about as a result of the commonality of this surname at the site, or due to Barnard predecessors who lived locally.

Barnes *Pickett County.* The census records of 1870 show a number of Barneses as citizens of nearby Overton County, which in 1879, with Fentress County, contributed land to form Pickett County. Some of these Barneses and their ages follow: Nathan, 43; T. H., 29; Sarah, 44; Thomas, 48; Thomas, 23; James, 23; John, 48; and Zaceriah, 39.

Barnesville *Lawrence County.* All that is known about this place-name is that it was suggested by the local residency of a Barnes family. Beginning in 1893, the site had a post office for a period, but it eventually closed and residents were served from the Summertown post office.

Barnett's *Sullivan County.* In the 1850 census rolls for the county, the names of all the residents having this surname are spelled with one *t* at the end. Included were William, Eliza, George, Henry, Malinda, and William Barnet. Still, the place-name probably refers to this family, or these families. Thirty years later, census records show several Barnetts, all spelling the name with two *t*'s at the end. They included William, age 32; Nancy, 78; James, 18; Calib, 23; and Jane, 37.

Barren Plains *Robertson County.* When the first of its future citizens arrived at this site, it was largely barren of trees. Settlement of the site began in about 1830. Surnames of some of the earliest residents and businesspersons included Ryan, Bagbee, Mason, Paige, Taylor, Scott, Farmer, and Benson.

Barretville *Shelby County.* An 1890 Civil War veterans census record shows that a person with this surname (Joseph Barret) had resided in the area. At the time of the 1870 census, several were on the rolls. Occasionally, the name was styled with one *t*, but most used the more common Barrett spelling. Included were A. R. Barrett, age 43; Henry, 36; J., 28; and Peter, 45. One family member was identified by the given name abbreviation of Michl.

Barron's Corner *Gibson County.* The designation at this intersection probably relates in some way to the family or families of local 1870 residents M. S. and William Barron. William was 28 at the time, while M. S. was 30.

Bartlett *Shelby County.* A Mrs. Rowena Bartlett was laid to rest in the Morris Cemetery in 1852. This is the sole Bartlett reference that can be readily tied to this area.

However, local citizens believe the place takes its name from a one-time businessman and plantation owner, Major G. M. Bartlett. The first label on the place was Union Depot, but when it was incorporated, in 1866, it was Bartlett. Bartlett is now a city.

Bates Hill *Warren County.* This elevation probably traces its name back to one or more of several Bateses residing in the area in 1830. Allen, James, Newton, and William Bates were Rhea County citizens at the time, but later, in 1855, part of Rhea contributed to the current area of Warren County.

Bath Springs *Decatur County.* Dr. Joel Handcock built a health resort here, where patients boarded on the premises. The sulfurous waters of the local springs were used for drinking and bathing and were believed to provide health benefits. The resort was started in the early 1800s. From that time on, the site was known as Bath Springs.

Baucom *Coffee County.* It is believed this designation leads back to Moses Baucom, who resided locally in 1840.

Baugh *Giles County.* The site traces its name to the family of Dr. John E. Baugh, who lived nearby. Sometime between 1911 and 1914, a railroad was constructed between Decatur (Alabama) and Nashville, and a depot was constructed here, after which some businesses and a post office sprang up. Long prior to this, in 1830, a Martin Baugh resided nearby. Forty years later, local Baughs included two named Thomas, James L., two named William, Archie, and James. They were probably ancestors of John E. Baugh.

Baxter *Putnam County.* This community is the namesake of the builder of the Tennessee Central Railroad, Colonel Jere Baxter. Mine Lick and The Lowland were earlier designations. The community was incorporated in 1915.

Beacon *Decatur County.* The location was first referred to as Moray. Once a thriving community, it is home to about 150 persons today. When the Tennessee Midland Railroad came through, the name was changed to Beacon for reasons not entirely clear.

Beans Creek *Franklin County.* This place-name traces to early Franklin County settlers having the Beans surname.

Bean Station *Grainger County.* According to one source, in 1787, the Bean brothers established a fort here to protect pioneers from Indian attacks. William and Robert became captains in the militia, while George was an artisan. The fourth brother was named Jesse. Other local Beans included Elizabeth, Stephen, John, and John H. A second source claims that Captain William Bean established a homestead here as early as 1768, although that year seems extremely early. This source mentions William, John, and Jesse as family members, and makes reference to a Major Russell Bean. The Bean surname continues to survive in the county.

Bearden *Knox County.* Numerous Beardens resided in the area when the 1850 Tennessee census was taken. Included were Ann, William, Caroline, Sarah, and Charles Bearden. Earlier still, in 1830, local Beardens included Nancy, Richard, Benjamin, and Marcus D.

Bear Spring *Stewart County.* The name may predate the year 1803. The story is told of a pioneer family whose cabin was near a large cave spring. One night, they were awakened from slumber by the barking of the dogs. The father took gun and lantern in hand and went to investigate. What he found was a large bear in the spring. He promptly shot it, and bears have been extinct in Stewart County since approximately that time. The hamlet thereafter took on the name Bear Spring.

Bedford *Bedford County.* An uncomplimentary first nickname was Fleaburg. It probably took its current name from the county name. (See Bedford entry in the Counties section of this book.)

Beech Bluff *Madison County.* According to a passage in *Historic Madison,* "the community was once called Homer, but its name . . . soon changed because of a large bluff surrounded by native beech trees."

Beech Bottom *Macon County.* The bottomland here was dotted with American beech trees.

Beech Grove *Anderson County.* A grove of American beech trees distinguished this site.

Beech Grove *Coffee County.* See preceding entry.

Beech Grove *Dyer County.* See entry for Beech Grove, Anderson County.

Beech Grove *Grainger County.* See entry for Beech Grove, Anderson County.

Beech Grove *Knox County.* See entry for Beech Grove, Anderson County.

Beech Grove *Trousdale County.* See entry for Beech Grove, Anderson County.

Beech Hill *Franklin County.* The American beech tree is found in all ninety-five counties of Tennessee, accounting for the name at this elevation.

Beech Hill *Giles County.* See preceding entry.

Beech Hill *Macon County.* See entry for Beech Hill, Franklin County.

Beech Hill *Maury County.* See entry for Beech Hill, Franklin County.

Beech Springs *Sevier County.* A cluster of beech trees shaded the natural springs at this location.

Beersheba Springs *Grundy County.* A local historian specializing in this area advises that the community owes its name to Mrs. Beersheba Porter Cain. Mrs. Cain has been credited with discovering a local chalybeate (iron water) spring, which became celebrated for its curative powers. She was the wife of John Cain of McMinnville, twenty miles north of this town. The Bible also refers to the waters of Beersheba.

Belfast *Marshall County.* Persons of Scottish-Irish descent settled here; so it is generally believed that the place was named for Belfast, Northern Ireland.

Belk *DeKalb County.* In about 1893, the post office was given this name by Nathan T. Wall (1843–1924), in honor of his wife, Mary L. Belk (1848–1914), of Georgia. Nathan served at various times as postmaster, and ran a store in the community. The local school also took the Belk name.

Bellamy *Montgomery County.* This place-name probably relates to an early Bellamy family in the area. John T. Bellamy was born in the county in 1840. His father, Robert, was born in Kentucky in 1818. John's mother's name was Sarah.

Bell Buckle *Bedford County.* At least two stories have been passed down in an attempt to explain this place-name. One holds that a cowbell and buckle were carved on a tree by Indians at this locality, to tell other Indians that settlers in the area had cows. Another account states that a cowbell and strap-buckle were found by a spring at this site.

Bell Eagle *Haywood County.* At first this location was called Brooklyn. One day, according to local lore, an eagle wearing a bell landed here, and ever since the place has been designated Bell Eagle.

Belle Meade *Davidson County.* Now a city, this site uses a name that translates as "beautiful meadow," probably describing the view in the days before settlement or development.

Belleville *Lincoln County.* John Bell and his family were instrumental in helping this community develop. A son, James Bell, became a village merchant. (At least one map styles the name as Bellville.) Earlier, the site was known as Norris Creek, taking the label from the man who stumbled upon the creek in 1806, Ezekiel Norris. In post–Civil War times, a school called Oak Hill Institution operated here; so the town assumed the Oak Hill name, until it eventually became Belleville. After Norris, early settlers here, in 1810, included three brothers from Virginia with the Dollins surname.

Bells' *Crockett County.* Two versions of the name rationale exist. One states that the name refers to William and John Bell, two South Carolinians said to have come here from Kentucky and to have purchased one thousand acres from Daniel Cherry of nearby Cherryville. The fertile land here is thought to have appealed to the Bells. A second version suggests that the name may have come about from the peal of local church bells.

Bellsburg *Dickson County.* Some believe the site's name traces back to Shadrach Bell, an early settler in the vicinity, who is mentioned in the census records of 1820. However, evidence strongly suggests that Montgomery Bell platted the site and named it Bellsville. He had purchased the land from the children of his nephew, John I. Bell, in the late 1820s. (John Bell is mentioned in the census records of 1850.) Only a few lots were sold; so the unsold parcels were returned to Montgomery's great-nephews and great-nieces. Many years later, the Post Office Department changed the name to Bellsburgh, because another Bellsville existed in the state. In 1884, the *h* was dropped. A ferry operated at the site as early as 1805. It was run by Caludius David'l (or Davidiel). Shadrach Bell is known to have sold slaves, and many of them took the Bell surname, in part accounting for many African Americans having the name Bell.

Bell Town *Cheatham County.* A number of Bells were present locally in 1870. Some of them were Alfred, Green, Miles, George, G. W., E. D., Fredrick, Patty, Alexander H., and John. One or more of these Bells probably influenced the naming of this town.

Belltown *Polk County.* A local historian reports that, in the late 1920s, there was such a concentration of Bell families inhabiting the tri-state (Tennessee-North Carolina-Georgia) section of eastern Polk County that everyone referred to it as Belltown. Years later, a researcher of the Bell family discovered court records of some litigation that took place in 1928. Reportedly, many pages of the record were required just to enumerate the many Bells involved.

Bellview *Lincoln County.* According to one correspondent, a school was constructed here in 1912. Apparently, the place-name can be construed as "in view of the bell," a reference to the schoolbell in the tower. A second source expands on this, saying that one of the men installing the bell paused, surveyed the surrounding area, and remarked, "We have a bell's-eye view from here." At an earlier date, the hamlet was known as The Towry Community, because of the many persons having the Towry surname.

Bellwood *Wilson County.* This name may have a connection with John Bell, a congressman who eventually became Speaker of the House.

Belmont *Anderson County.* Probably situated at an elevation, this place uses the French word for "beautiful mountain."

Belmont *Coffee County.* French for "beautiful mountain," this label referred to Belmont County, Ohio. It is said to have been named by William Workman Wiley, who with his wife, Eliza Jane Eckels, two small children, and father-in-law, emigrated from eastern Ohio in 1871 and purchased hundreds of acres here. Mr. Wiley had been a schoolteacher in other venues, and here operated a store and served as postmaster.

Belmont *Jefferson County.* (See explanation for Belmont, Anderson County.)

Belvidere *Franklin County.* The application of this term here may derive from the Italian term for "beautiful view" or "beautiful to behold," or perhaps from the French meaning "fine view," "place of beauty," or "terrace." A variant spelling would be Belvedere.

Bemis *Madison County.* Founded in 1899, this company town was controlled by the Bemis Brothers Bag Company, whose chief was Judson Bemis. It began to take shape the following year, on a plantation belonging to H. E. Jackson, south of Jackson, the city and county seat. A cotton mill was established, to support the Bemis bag industry.

Benjestown *Shelby County.* This label probably refers to William Benjes, born in Germany, who conducted business in Memphis and married in 1883. He operated Benjes Ginning Company and Benjes Cotton Mills & Carriages.

Benton *Polk County (seat).* In early times, the location was labeled Four Mile Stand, because traveling animals were fed and watered here before continuing the journey from Kentucky to Alabama and Georgia. The current name honors Thomas Hart Benton (1782–1858), a North Carolinian who resided in several Tennessee locations and served in the state legislature. Later, he found greater fame as a U.S. senator from Missouri. Incorporation took place in 1915.

Benton Springs *Polk County.* Apparently, springs were located here, and the basename of the site was for Thomas Hart Benton. (See preceding entry.)

Benton Station *Polk County.* (See immediately preceding entries.) The "Station" part of the name may have been for a railroad stop.

Berea *Giles County.* See following entry.

Berea *Warren County.* This is a biblical name inspired by a mention in Acts of the Apostles 17:10, which is sometimes styled Veria.

Berry *Dickson County.* In 1870, the lone representative of the Berry surname on census rolls for the year was identified only as M. Berry. He or she may have been responsible in some way for this geographical designation surviving on maps.

Berry Hill *Davidson County.* According to some historians, wild berries grew in profusion here, when settlers first decided to make the spot their home. However, others point out that the William Tyler Berry family once resided here, and attribute the name to them. Pre-1800 records show that a William Berry died in this area in 1789, but a second source states that he died in 1889 (the latter year is probably correct). His wife's name was Keziah and their daughter was named Mary. The incorporation of Berry Hill took place in 1950.

Berry's Chapel *Williamson County.* The label may relate in some way to a Tom Berry, who served on a jury here in 1810, or to his descendants. The "Chapel" part of the name suggests that a church was established here, and served as a landmark of sorts.

Beta *Meigs County.* It is not known why this site uses the designation for the second letter in the Greek alphabet.

Bethany *Warren County.* According to *American Place-Names,* this label usually traces back to an Old Testament village. The term was often used for a church, then transferred to the settlement around it.

Bethel *Anderson County.* See entry for Bethel, Giles County.

Bethel *Benton County.* See entry for Bethel, Giles County.

Bethel *Blount County.* See entry for Bethel, Giles County.

Bethel *Cheatham County.* See entry for Bethel, Giles County.

Bethel *DeKalb County.* See following entry.

Bethel *Giles County.* This term is often applied to a place of sanctuary or a sacred area. It is usually translated as "house of God."

Bethel *Hardin County.* See preceding entry.

Bethel *Haywood County.* See entry for the Bethel, Giles County.

Bethel *Maury County.* See entry for the Bethel, Giles County.

Bethel *Perry County.* See entry for the Bethel, Giles County.

Bethel Springs *McNairy County.* The initial segment of the name refers to the biblical term usually translated as "house of God." (A second source states that the "Bethel" part of the name comes from a biblical term meaning "hope.") The Bethel application here probably traces to the presence of the Bethel Presbyterian Church, organized in 1828. In the early 1860s, the site was known as Bethel Station, probably because the Mobile & Ohio Railroad had penetrated the site by 1858. "Springs" replaced "Station" in about 1866; the justification was the presence of large, natural springs nearby. The community incorporated in 1927.

Bethesda *Williamson County.* The name refers to a spring-fed pool in Jerusalem mentioned in the Bible as having healing properties.

Bethlehem *Bedford County.* See following entry.

Bethlehem *Campbell County.* Ultimately referring to the village where Christ was born, the label may have been assigned here by persons from the Bethlehem, Pennsylvania, area. Or it may have simply been given to honor the biblical Bethlehem, located about seven miles northwest of Nazareth. It means "house of bread."

Bethlehem *Hardin County.* See preceding entry.

Bethlehem *Wayne County.* See entry for Bethlehem, Campbell County.

Bethlehem *Williamson County.* See entry for Bethlehem, Campbell County.

Bethpage *Sumner County.* According to popular belief, the hamlet was so named in memory of Elizabeth ("Beth") Page Parker, by her surviving husband, Nathaniel Parker.

Betsy Willis *Coffee County.* The rolls of the 1850 census reflect such Coffee County names as John Willis, John G. Willis, and two persons named Elizabeth Willis. Peter Willis settled in the county at an early time. At one juncture, in the county seat of Manchester, there was a general merchandise business by the name of Willis & Wilkerson. One wonders if one of the women was nicknamed Betsy, and that some admirer dubbed this site "Betsy Willis" in her honor.

Beulah *Greene County.* A mention in Isaiah 62:4 and use of the name in *Pilgrim's Progress,* by John Bunyan, inspired this name to be adopted for towns and as a girl's name. (Also see following entry.)

Beulah *Union County.* Unless this hamlet was so designated in honor of a woman named Beulah, it is probably of biblical origin. The *New Westminster Dictionary of the Bible* states that Beulah refers to "the once forsaken land of Palestine when it was restored to God's favor and repeopled after the captivity."

Bible Hill *Decatur County.* At one time a thriving community, Bible Hill began to decline when better roads were built. A tornado in 1952 destroyed the school, after which the students were educated in Parsons. The place-name is not directly attributable, but chances are that revival meetings took place here, or an early church inspired the name.

Bidwell *Lincoln County.* John and Major Bidwell were listed as local citizens in 1830. The site probably assumed its label from the Bidwells.

Bigby *Maury County.* Joseph Bigby resided locally at the time of the 1840 census. In all probability, the place-name refers to him or his family. One map shows the site as Bigbyville.

Big Cherokee *Washington County.* Big Cherokee takes its name from Cherokee Creek, on which it is located. The Cherokee Indians were longtime occupants of this region. Gabriel Arthur and James Needham are said to have been the first European explorers of this vicinity, in 1673. In 1771, Jacob Brown built a cabin on the north side of the Nolachuckey River. He may have been among settlers who, in about 1780, started the Cherokee Meeting House for the purpose of worship. Big Cherokee denotes a larger branch of Cherokee Creek; Little Cherokee is further to the south.

Big Hill *McNairy County.* A local source states that the site was just that: "a big hill." The first white settler is believed to have been David Young, who established a ferry on the Tuscombia River.

Big Lick *Cumberland County.* The area became so known as a result of the presence of a large natural salt rock. Free-roaming cattle were attracted to the place to lick the salt rock. Originally, it was called Deer Lick. The first settlers began residing here between 1820 and 1830.

Big Piney *Loudon County.* The site owes its name to the Virginia pine, shortleaf pine, and pitch pine timber occurring in this area.

Big Rock *Stewart County.* A limestone rock one hundred feet in each dimension was discovered here. A large oak grew out of the rock, which had a crevice leading to an underground lake.

Big Sandy *Benton County.* Big Sandy arose in about 1860, due to railroad activity. It was chartered in 1903. The name is adopted from the Big Sandy River, which flows along the town's east side. The river probably was given that name from its appearance to early explorers or surveyors, who may have observed a sandy bottom or evidence of siltation. An alternate explanation of the town name is that it refers to the quality of the soil at the site.

Big Sinks *Union County.* Two stories are told to explain this place-name. One is that springs in this area would sink, reappearing at another location. According to another source, the settlement is situated in a natural sinkhole, with water runoff in the mile-long valley all disappearing into a cave.

Big Spring *Blount County.* The spring for which this site is named forms the source of Gallahar's Creek.

Binfield *Blount County.* According to a newspaper account, this Louisville & Nashville (L&N) Railroad station takes its name from a combination of a corn bin and cornfield situated near the station. The name is believed to date to the early 1900s.

Bingham *Shelby County.* According to the 1870 census, several Binghams populated this vicinity. Included were Mary, age 70; William and Famy, both 40; William, 24; and Frank, 12. The community name is undoubtedly associated with these individuals.

Bingham *Williamson County.* James J. Bingham was a local citizen in 1840, with the probable result that the place was assigned his surname.

Birchwood *Hamilton County.* When a post office went into operation here in 1854, the name was still spelled as two words (Birch Wood). Older local residents testify that the designation resulted from a birch tree situated near a spring at the site. Apparently, it stood near the intersection of Defriese Lane and Highway 60, and provided shade to a blacksmith and tannery shop. The current and longtime resident at the site states that the original birch tree has long since been gone and that the only one now there was planted by him. "It is just now big enough to start shedding its bark. . . . The big (original) birch was the only one in this community (and was) probably planted by Indians or someone passing through." Birchwood dates to before Civil War days and was the domain of the Cherokee.

Bird's Crossroads *Sevier County.* This place-name is seen in several forms, including Bird Crossroad and Bird's Cross Roads. A German community grew here at a very early date. Jacob Bird was one of the earliest of these settlers, in the 1780s. Surnames of other early families included Baker, Fox, and Derrick.

Bishop *Dyer County.* The 1870 census rolls reflect that a James Bishop resided near here. The label on the site probably refers to him or his family.

Bivens *Giles County.* According to the 1850 census records, several Bivenses resided in the area. Among them were Abraham, L. F., Nathaniel, Jesse F., Louisa, and Aly.

Black Fox *Bradley County.* Cherokees at one time inhabited this area. The place-name is believed to come from one of the principal chiefs, the nephew of Dragging Canoe, Black Fox.

Blackman *Rutherford County.* In 1870, a number of local citizens had the Blackman surname. Among them were Henderson, age 30; Allen, 73; Bradford, 55; Mattie, 18; Thomas, 45; Alfred, 24; and two named Charles, 30 and 45.

Black Oak *Knox County.* The black oak occurs throughout Tennessee; so the name was probably applied here for a prominent one—or many of them.

Black Oak *Scott County.* See preceding entry.

Blaine *Grainger County.* The community was incorporated in 1978. Around 1890, a general store opened here, operated by a Pennsylvania native, Robert Blaine. A variant spelling does not have the *e* on the end.

Blair *Roane County.* This hamlet took its name from one or more of the numerous Blairs residing nearby. In 1870, there were at least fifteen. Among them were Samuel T., Jerry, Richard, Charly, Dick, H. H., George, J. M., Jack, Kate, and John. Some of the Blairs were African Americans.

Blair Gap *Sullivan County.* Among county citizens in 1850 were John and Richard Blair. This family likely is connected in some way to the locality, the place-name being formed by the addition of a geographical feature. The "Gap" portion may refer to a passage between hills or mountains.

Blakeville *Lincoln County.* The site probably took on the surname of some of the Blake families residing locally. Some of those individuals were Adelia, John, G. W., M. H., and William F. Blake.

Blanche *Lincoln County.* At an earlier time, this area was designated Pleasant Plains, having been settled probably prior to 1845. Although Pleasant Plains had had a post office, when John J. Rawls became postmaster of the "new" post office in 1870, the site took on the name of his daughter, Blanche Rawls.

Blanche Chapel *Lincoln County.* A place of worship at the site, located a mile north of Blanche, undoubtedly contributed to this place-name. (See preceding entry.)

Blanton Chapel *Coffee County.* Several Blantons resided in this vicinity, according to the *Tennessee 1840 Census Index.* Among them were Charles, Smith, two named Thomas, Coleman, and Willis. Coleman was an early settler, while Willis was clerk of the circuit court from 1842 to 1850. There was also a William Blanton, whose daughter, Laura, married Stokely Jacobs in 1866. One or more of them are probably connected to this place-name. (It is possible different historians recorded "William" as "Willis," or vice versa.)

Bledsoe *Lincoln County.* The name of this site probably does not relate in any way to the namesake of Bledsoe County. The county took its name from a well-known military figure, Anthony Bledsoe, who died in 1789. However, several persons with this surname resided in Lincoln County at the time of the 1840 census. Lewis Bledsoe and Thomas H. Bledsoe were two of those. Although his name was styled differently, Harry M. Bledso also was an area resident at the time. One or more of these individuals may have influenced the naming of this locale.

Blevins *Carter County.* Numerous Blevinses were identified with this area in 1880. Some of them were Nancy, age 40; Willy, 40; Luna, 60; Adaline, 38; Allan, 55; Jerrimiah, 51; Nathan, 45; and two named William, 27 and 45.

Blockhouse *Blount County.* The name is a shortened version of Black's Block House. Dating to the 1780s, it may have been built by Samuel Black, one of the residents, who used the original building as a wilderness fort.

Blondy *Lewis County.* The pastor of a church in this community wondered about this name. "I was curious as to how this name . . . came into existence. After my father, a long-time Blondy resident, passed away, he left one surviving brother. I phoned him and asked him. Here is his answer: 'Many years ago when we were small boys, there was a train that came through the community, on its way to Hohenwald. It seems that when this train would come by, neighborhood boys would stand by the side of the tracks and ask the engineer to blow his whistle. The engineer was a blonde-haired gentleman and the children would shout to him, "Blow it, Blondy!" Evidently, the other people on the train began to call this place Blondy. As a matter of fact, the railroad company erected a railroad sign that still exists today in our community, reading simply *Blondy*.'"

Bloomingdale *Sullivan County.* The town took its name from the product of an iron foundry that operated locally. The large pigs of iron that were produced were known as "blooms"—thus, the term "blooming mill."

Blountville *Sullivan County (seat).* The town probably owes its name to William Blount, who served as governor of the Territory South of the River Ohio, which became Tennessee. Blount served in many important posts, including the Continental Congress, the North Carolina legislature, the U.S. Senate, and the Tennessee Senate.

Blowing Springs *Wayne County.* A source close to the area asserts that the name refers to a spring that periodically "blows out."

Blue Ridge *Sullivan County.* The well-known Blue Ridge Mountains in this area at times seem to have a bluish cast to them.

Blue Springs *DeKalb County.* There was a large spring on Sink Creek at this location. Having a blue appearance, it was dubbed Blue Springs. The nearby school also assumed this name.

Bluff City *Sullivan County.* Incorporation took place in 1880. Rocky bluffs along the Holston River suggested the name for this community, but earlier it was known by an intriguing series of labels. Possibly the first was Choate's Ford, followed by Middleton. When a railroad was built through the site, it became Union. But during the Civil War, General Felix Zollicoffer had the place named after himself. (It is unclear whether the designation was Felix or Zollicoffer!) Following the war, the name reverted to Union, with this designation holding until 1887, when the current name was adopted.

Bluhmtown *DeKalb County.* Phillip Bluhm (b. 1818 in Russia) arrived in this area from Iowa shortly after the Civil War with his wife, Charlotte (b. 1817 in Ireland). They had four children and the family operated a sawmill. Two of the sons, Phillip C. and Fremont, became postmasters at the local facility, which was called Bluhm and was established in about 1892. The surrounding hamlet became Bluhmtown.

Blythe Ferry *Rhea County.* An article in the *Chattanooga Free Press* by John Wilson sheds a great deal of light on this name. The first Blythes to arrive in America may have been William and Sarah, who came from England to York River, Virginia, in 1652, settling in Isle of Wight County. William died in 1663. A son, Christopher Blythe, moved to Chowan County, North Carolina. A second William Blythe, a descendant of Christopher, went to Greenville, South Carolina, and married Sarah Murphree in 1769. (He may have had an earlier wife, and his last wife was named Barbary.) William fathered twelve children. The Blythes who immigrated to Rhea County shortly after 1800 were believed to be children of William Blythe of Greenville, who passed away about 1837. In Rhea County in 1809, one of his sons, also named William Blythe, married Nancy Fields, daughter of a prominent Cherokee, Richard Fields. This William was among the Cherokee contingent who accompanied General Andrew Jackson in a campaign against the Creek Indians in 1814. He was in Captain John Brown's company, under Colonel Gideon Morgan. In 1817, he was allowed a 640-acre reservation "in the right of his wife," below what is known as Blythe's Ferry. In 1836, Blythe sold 310 acres straddling Sale Creek to William Clift. At about the time of the Indian Removal (1838), William went west with his wife's people, settling in McDonald County, Missouri. The ferry was operated continuously until well into the 1990s, until the Highway 60 bridge was constructed nearby. The ferry was located near the point where the Hiwassee River empties into the Tennessee River, near Jolly's Island, and took travelers across the Tennessee.

Bodenham *Giles County.* Eighteen-thirty census records for western Tennessee reveal what are probably clues to this place-name. In that year, in Giles County, a J. W. Bodenhamer, a William Bodenhammer, and an Elizabeth Bodenhanor are listed on the rolls. One—or even two—of these surnames may contain a typographical error that accounts for the variant spellings. In any event, by common verbal usage, the last syllable of the surname may have been dropped, the result being that the site where one or more of these individuals resided became known as Bodenham.

Bogota *Dyer County.* For uncertain reasons, this community was named for the capital of Colombia, South America. For some years, it was fashionable to name new towns for larger, well-known, faraway cities.

Bold Spring *Humphreys County.* A longtime area resident states that the place acquired its name because of a very fast moving stream issuing from a spring at the site.

Bolen's *Henderson County.* David Bolin was a local resident at the time of the 1850 census. By 1870, census records reflected the residency of John W. Bolin and Sion M. Bolin. In spite of the variant spelling of the place-name, it is likely the community takes its name from the Bolin family. The label is sometimes seen styled as Bolen's Chapel, suggesting that a family member may have donated land or materials for the building of a church.

Bolivar *Hardeman County (seat).* At first, this town was referred to as Hatchie (or Hatchie Town), but in 1825 it was changed to Bolivar to honor the man who liberated Colombia and Venezuela, Simon Bolivar.

Bolton *Shelby County.* An 1820–1824 county archives book makes reference to three Boltons—Charles, John, and Isaac—raising the probability that the place-name relates to this local surname. Reinforcing this assumption, two local "lay historians" surnamed Bolton refer to county ancestors named John C. and Sarah S. Bolton.

Boma *Putnam County.* In 1850, Andrew J. Boman lived near here, in what was then part of White County. Portions of White eventually went to make up Putnam County. The place-name may be a variant of Boman. It is well documented that early census takers often spelled residents' names phonetically and sometimes made spelling errors when recording the names.

Bon Air *Sumner County.* *Bon* meaning "good" in French, the air here must have seemed fresh and clean to early settlers.

Bon Air *White County.* See preceding entry.

Bon Aqua *Hickman County.* The intent was probably to name this community Bon Agua, the *bon* being French for "good" and the *agua* being Spanish for "water." However, someone mixed up the *q* with the *g,* and Bon Aqua was indelibly enrolled on the list of the state's inhabited places. The name undoubtedly stems from the existence here of a mineral spring, which led to the site becoming a summer resort of sorts.

Bon Aqua Junction *Hickman County.* This site occupies an intersection a little more than a mile southeast of Bon Aqua. (See preceding entry.)

Bond *Hickman County.* The name is believed to trace to an early settler, Joseph McRea Bond.

Bone Cave *Van Buren County.* During the War of 1812 and the Civil War, a large dry cave at this location was mined to supply nitrates used in gunpowder. During the Civil War period, the bones of a giant prehistoric ground sloth were unearthed in the cave, and the place became known as Big Bone Cave. The appellation became shortened over the years to its current form.

Bonnertown *Lawrence County.* Beginning in 1909, some families with the Bonner surname began moving to this location from Haleyville, Alabama.

Bonny Kate *Knox County.* Catherine Sherrill was the second wife of John Sevier. This community's name is an affectionate reference to her. It is sometimes seen styled Bonnie Kate.

Boone *Washington County.* As the tale is told, Daniel Boone passed through this area in 1760, stopping long enough to carve his name on a tree.

Boone's Creek *Washington County.* Tennessee's first town is said by some to have arisen at this site, taking its name from frontiersman and scout Daniel Boone, who frequented the area as early as 1760.

Booneville *Lincoln County.* Booneville lies in an area heavily frequented by Daniel Boone and his brother in frontier times, thus attracting this designation.

Boothspoint *Dyer County.* The 1870 census recorded a Richard Boothe in the county, as well as Andre and Henry Booth. One or more of these families was probably the source of this place-name.

Boring *Sullivan County.* The only individual with the Boring surname who could be placed in this locality was Elizabeth Boring, in 1870. She was 46 years of age at the time. Possibly she, or her family, gave this place its name.

Bowling *Cumberland County.* This label is the result of the 1820 residency near this spot of Rodney Bowling. Bowling was at the time a citizen of White County, but a portion of White County later went to help make up what is now Cumberland County.

Bowman *Cumberland County.* The explanation for this place-name is similar to the one immediately preceding. In 1820, Nathaniel Bowman was a White County citizen.

Boyce *Hamilton County.* Ker Boyce of Charleston, South Carolina, one of his state's wealthiest men, may be the individual to whom this name traces. Boyce was a merchant and investor in the railroads.

Boyd *Knox County.* Five Boyds are mentioned in the index of an early county tome. It is likely this place-name traces back to (the family of) one or more of them.

Boydsville *Weakley County.* Abner Boyd was a large landowner in this area; the site was named for him. Boyd served as the first postmaster for the town, which arose in 1832. On one map, this place appears to bisect the Kentucky-Tennessee line, although just south of this spot, within Weakley County boundaries, is a site labeled Boyd's Chapel.

Brackentown *Sumner County.* Among local citizens listed in the 1850 census rolls were Isaac, Granville, James, John, and Rhoda Bracken. The town takes its name from one or more of these individuals.

Braden *Anderson County.* The 1880 census rolls of East Tennessee place a number of Bradens in this vicinity. Among them were Edith (age 55 at the time); Bettie, 38; Spencer, 23; Silas, 31; Hiram, 52; Delilah, 90; Wiley, 33; James, 42; and Samuel, 29. One or more of these persons is probably the source of the place-name.

Braden *Fayette County.* Joseph P. Braden is the person for whom the community was named.

Braden *Union County.* The Braden family of Union County gave its name to this site, although few other facts about the family can be located. The community was cut off from much of the county when the Tennessee Valley Authority (TVA) flooded Norris Reservoir and there was no longer a bridge across the river. So Clayton Helms, superintendent of roads, had a ferry established at the narrowest point, which is known as Helms Ferry. (The first ferry sank, but Helms was instrumental in obtaining a second ferry.)

Bradford *Gibson County.* This town's namesake was Robert E. Bradford, who arrived from North Carolina in 1853 and acquired considerable influence and prestige. He may have had something to do with the IC (probably Illinois Central) Railroad. The previous name of the location was Kimball.

Bradyville *Cannon County.* The village is the namesake of early settler William Brady.

Branchville *Franklin County.* Twenty-four Branches are listed in the 1870 Franklin County census book. It is very likely that this site takes its name from one "branch" or another of this family tree. Among those listed were Wilburn, Bird, Millie, Joel, Martin, Mary, and Andrew Branch. Earlier, Jonathan Branch was listed as a county citizen in 1830.

Bransford *Sumner County.* At the time of the 1870 census, an 18-year-old named Bell Bransford was recorded on the rolls as a local citizen. It is not known if his—or her—family was somehow identified with this site.

Bratcher's Crossroad *Warren County.* This site is sometimes designated simply Bratcher. The name probably leads back to an 1830 resident of this locale, Benjamin Bratcher, or his family.

Bray *Hancock County.* In the 1830 census book covering the eastern portion of the state, Benjamin Bray is listed as a resident of Hawkins County, part of which later went to constitute Hancock County. In 1850, B. Bray is on the census rolls of Hancock County; these individuals may have been one and the same. The place-name likely derives from him or his family.

Braytown *Anderson County.* A family having the Bray surname settled this place at an early date, accounting for the town name. James and John Bray were listed as taxpayers in 1801.

Brazil *Gibson County.* The village was formally settled in about 1867 or 1868. However, as early as 1820, Colonel Solomon Shaw of North Carolina resided here. At some early date, the site was referred to as Pin-Hook, for an unknown reason. When the first businesses and houses were being erected, there was a good deal of local excitement over a proposed emigration to Brazil, South America, by a group of residents from this locality. Reportedly, some of the more daring did, indeed, move to the metropolis of the Southern Hemisphere. Others, however, opted to stay put. So in about 1869 or 1870, they dubbed their Gibson County settlement Brazil.

Brentwood *Williamson County.* A noted English estate called Brentwood inspired this place-name.

Briceville *Anderson County.* New York City financier Calvin Stewart Brice, who also served as a U.S. senator from Ohio, is the person to whom this place-name refers. He was also an attorney, and served on the board of the East Tennessee, Virginia & Georgia Railroad. Described in a book by Marshall McGhee and Gene White as "a short, heavy-set, impulsive, red-headed man of great energy," Brice was born in Ashtabula, Ohio, in 1845.

Brick Church *Giles County.* This locality was initially known as Richland Church. When a more pretentious brick structure was built as a place of worship, the community itself became known as Brick Church. The edifice fell victim to the Civil War. In 1870, a wood frame building was erected on the grounds of the Old Brick Church.

Bridgeport *Cocke County.* The first bridge in the county was erected here, spanning the French Broad River. The bridge washed away in a flood in 1867.

Brigham Hill *Stewart County.* Several Brighams resided in the county in 1830, according to the 1830 census rolls. Among them were Elizabeth, David, John, William, Thomas, Albert, and David. One or more of the individuals or families probably caused this elevation and community to be so named.

Brighton *Lincoln County.* The ultimate referent of this name is the resort city in England.

Brighton *Tipton County.* Although most U.S. places using this designation take it from Brightons in other states or, ultimately, England, this one is said to come from an individual with the Bright surname. He is believed to have been the conductor on the first train after the tracks were laid through this locale in 1873. The hamlet really didn't arise until about that time, needing the entry of the railroad to spur settlement. Land for the tracks was given by Augustus Washington Bright Sr. The line was named the Memphis & Paducah.

Brim's Corners *Crockett County.* P. R. Brim, age 54, was a Haywood County resident in 1870. Part of Haywood was annexed to help constitute Crockett County the following year.

Brimstone *Scott County.* It is likely early settlers noted the odor or presence of naturally occurring sulfur nearby, as *brimstone* is another word for sulfur.

Bristol *Sullivan County.* This town is the namesake of Bristol, England.

Brittontown *Greene County.* In 1840, James, John, Daniel, two Williams, Thomas, and Wallis Britton resided in the neighborhood. The name probably traces back to their family or families.

Britt's Landing *Perry County.* This place-name probably relates to William O. Britt, who is listed as residing in the county during the 1850 census.

Broadmoor *Dyer County.* This type of name falls into the "commendatory" category. The namer(s) may have desired to suggest a broad, open expanse.

Brockdell *Bledsoe County.* A former longtime resident of the town says that many early settlers of the place bore the surname Brock. Many of them were skilled carpenters, she adds, and two members of the founding family were Welkum Brock and Poly Brock. Berry (possibly Barry) Brock operated the first post office to serve the community. There are still persons with the Brock surname residing locally.

Browder *Loudon County.* This designation emanates from a common family surname of these environs. The 1880 East Tennessee census counted Joseph, age 18; John, 24; Anderson, 54; Patsey, 59; Tine, 23; and Samuel Browder, 43, as nearby citizens. Tine, Anderson, Patsey, and Joseph were African Americans. In addition, an F. V. Browder is mentioned in the *Inventory of the County Archives of Tennessee, No. 53*, as having resided in Loudon County. At an earlier time, Albert, Calvin, Edmond, John, Joseph, Robert, and Isham Browder resided in McMinn County in 1850. Nancy, Mason, Ann, John, and William D. Browder were Roane County residents, while William Browder was a Monroe County citizen. McMinn, Roane, and Monroe were three counties that gave up territory to form Loudon County.

Brownington *Franklin County.* Leoda, William, Rachel M., Silena M., Louis, and Margaret Browning are among the Brownings residing in the county at the time of the 1870 census. One or more of them, in all probability, lived at this site and lent their surname to the place.

Brown's *Macon County.* The names of Mary, James, Elizabeth, Samuel, Nancy, and Nelson Brown are in the 1850 census records as having resided in this area. It is likely the family was associated with this very site.

Brown's Crossroads *Lawrence County.* John Brown was among the earliest settlers here; so the site took his surname as part of its label. It is located just off the Lexington-Loretto Road.

Brown's Mill *Franklin County.* The name is sometimes styled Brown Mill. A researcher from the area writes only that "Brown's Mill was so called because a man named Brown operated a mill on Robinson Creek in the 1800s. . . . The road was Brown's Mill Road." In 1870, when George Brown was 36, he was a resident of this vicinity, joined by Nancy E. Brown, Elah Brown, and Stephan Brown. It is likely that one or more of them was associated with milling operations conducted here.

Brownsville *Haywood County (seat).* This city's name honors Jacob Jennings Brown. Brown was wounded during the War of 1812 near Niagara Falls, in the Battle of Lundy's Lane. Incorporation took place in 1826.

Browntown *Cumberland County.* The 1880 census of East Tennessee revealed numerous Browns populating the county, one or more of whom probably gave his or her name to the locality. John H., Jane, Martha, Clarence, Fenton, George W., N. C., James S., Marion, and Green Brown were some of those local Browns. In a census ten years earlier, three of the foregoing were listed as county citizens, plus Elizabeth, Nathaniel, Williamson, Larken, Ephraim H., and Gideon Brown. All were in their middle years at the time.

Broyles *Campbell County.* Seven persons with the Broyles surname lived in this neighborhood in 1870. Three were named Aaron, two were named Nancy, one was named George, and one was named William.

Broylesville *Washington County.* Adam Broyles may have been the namesake of this site. In 1825, he married Nancy Doak. Mention of them was located in *Eastern Tennessee Historical Society Publications.* Members of the Broyles family were among the first settlers of this locality, having purchased 840 acres on Little Limestone Creek. The occupations of family members included saddlers, millers, blacksmiths, carpenters, merchants, and innkeepers.

Bruceton *Carroll County.* In order to give the post office here a name, in about 1922 it was dubbed New One. A year or so later, it was renamed Junction City, due to the Nashville, Chattanooga & St. Louis Railway's presence. A few years later still, it was renamed Bruceton in honor of E. L. Bruce. Bruce was a Nashville resident who served as the railroad's president in the 1920s and is credited with assisting the young community a great deal. Bruceton was an extremely thriving place, thanks to the diversity of the rail travelers who disembarked during stopovers. One historian in the county holds a divergent opinion on the origin of the town's name. He states that Bruceton represents "Bruce Town" and traces back to Robert deBruce, an aide to William the Conqueror. The deBruce family included members who became kings of Scotland, the source adds.

Bryant *Sequatchie County.* At the time of the 1850 census, Mary and Jessa Bryant were Hamilton County citizens. They probably resided in the portion of Hamilton County that went to help form the new Sequatchie County. This place-name probably traces to these Bryants or their close relatives.

Bryant Station *Maury County.* There were several Bryants nearby at the time of the 1840 census, including Edward, James, Moses, Samuel, and Robinson. The site may have related to this family or these families. Later, a railroad may have served the site, and the "Station" part of the name may have been added then.

Bryson *Giles County.* This hamlet was first known as Bethany, a name of biblical origin. It was organized by the Reverend Duncan Brown in 1824. Among the earliest settlers at the time were the families of Neil Smith and Daniel McCallum. When a post office was authorized, the name Bethany was deemed too common. An individual identified only as Mr. Bryson, from Fayetteville, Tennessee, was given the honor of renaming the community, a change which took place in 1885. Mr. Bryson is believed to have been instrumental in acquiring the post office.

Brysonville *Cannon County.* In 1880, the Bryson surname was not an unusual one in these environs. J. A. and N. L. Bryson are known to have resided in the area. Their daughter, Miss M. A. Bryson, in 1880 married the editor of the *Cannon Courier,* W. T. Mingle.

Buchanan *Henry County.* At the time this locality was being settled—the first part of the 1840s—President James Buchanan held office. So residents applied his name to the hamlet.

Buckeye *Campbell County.* This hamlet likely was named for the local prominence of one or more yellow buckeye trees, which grow throughout the eastern half of Tennessee.

Buckner *DeKalb County.* By 1882, a church had been erected here, called Buckner's Chapel Methodist Church, on land thought to have been donated by descendants of Louisa Buckner (b. 1818 in Virginia). The Baptists shared the church until the 1920s. The community also was often called Walker's Chapel, from a school of that name established about 1904, probably on land given by John W. Walker and his wife, Cyrena Puckett.

Buckner Chapel *Putnam County.* William Buckner is listed in the 1820 census rolls as residing in Jackson County, one of the counties that later contributed to the composition of Putnam County. So it is possible he or his family was associated with a place of worship that now is listed as being in Putnam County, but which at the time was in Jackson County.

Bucksnort *Hickman County.* According to the county's historian, a merchant doing business here during the early years sold whiskey among his wares. Someone observed that his motto was, "For a buck, you can get a snort."

Bucktown *Hardin County.* Martha Buck may have inspired this place-name. She lived here in 1850.

Buena Vista *Carroll County.* The name translates from the Spanish as "good view." A battle or skirmish at a place called Buena Vista during the Mexican War may have inspired application of the name here.

Buford's *Giles County.* Charles and James Buford lived in this neighborhood in 1830, according to census data of those times. Another source confirms that several Buford families settled in the vicinity. The site was a stagecoach stop between Huntsville and Nashville, and eventually a railroad was constructed on the route. The resulting depot was referred to as Buford Station.

Bugscuffle *Bedford County.* The label was local slang for the place. It was probably known for a healthy population of mosquitoes or other insects.

Bullard's Creek *Jackson County.* In 1840, Lean Bullard was a county resident and probably gave his surname to the stream's designation.

Bull's Gap *Hawkins County.* A storekeeper and gunsmith, John Bull, was the first to send down roots at this locality. Subsequently, it became known by his surname.

Bumpass Cove *Washington County.* The community may have been named for Isaac Bumpass, although he apparently was not a landowner. (On at least one current map, the name is styled Bumpus Cove.) Three hundred-fifty acres of prime mineralized land here was owned by William Colyer, according to 1780 tax lists.

Bumpus Mills *Stewart County.* Harry and Andrew Bumpus were listed in Stewart County in the 1870 census rolls. At that time, Harry was 49 years of age and Andrew was 36. The place-name is said to honor Andrew Jackson Bumpus, one of the hamlet's earliest citizens, who served as its first postmaster. A mill was established in 1846, operated by Andrew's grandson, Joe Williams. It was a saw-, grist-, and flour mill; planing and turning operations were also performed there.

Bunker Hill *Giles County.* Indian Creek and Bull Killer were earlier names of this settlement. Later, Bunker Hill was the assigned designation, probably a reference to the Revolutionary War skirmish. Surnames of some of the town's earliest families include Nave, Brooks, Bass, Harris, Kennedy, Tucker, and Wells.

Buntyn *Shelby County.* Cemetery records mention a number of local Buntyns, although the entries are characterized by spelling variations. Eliza Buntyn and Spencer C. Buntyn both were buried in this county. Evie Buntin, Evie Byrd Buntin, and J. T. Buntin also are mentioned in burial records, as is Hugh Lawson Bunting.

Burbank *Carter County.* The town's namesake was John A. Burbank, who was born in Indiana and immigrated to this area, purchased land, and planted orchards.

Burem *Hawkins County.* The scant information that could be found on this community included only that it was probably named for a local physician having the Burem surname.

Burgess *Putnam County.* Four miles from here, on the boundary with White County, are the Burgess Falls Dam and the Burgess Falls State Natural Area. The Falling Water River runs through the area. The dam and natural area take their name from Tom

Burgess, who was deeded the land in 1793 by the U.S. government as partial payment for his services in the Revolutionary War. Probable descendants of Tom were Joel, J. W., Mary F., V. D., Washington, and Chalmers Burgess, who by 1870 called Putnam County home. One of the Burgess families once operated a gristmill on the Falling Water River.

Burke *Cumberland County.* A local historian advises that a man with the Burke surname opened a stand (or inn) for travelers crossing the mountain. Whether this individual was Robert Burke, once of Center, is unclear. In addition, the 1850 census records list Phoeba Burk and Sophia Burk as residing in Roane County, one of the counties that later formed Cumberland County. The spelling of the surname may have later evolved to the more common Burke.

Burlison *Tipton County.* The place-name is believed to be a misspelled version of William Lafayette Burleson's surname. In 1857, Burleson acquired a parcel of land here and settled in. Later, he signed over a small plot for use as a post office site. This occurred in 1870, and the office became known by Burleson's name, although it became misspelled in the transmission of information to Washington. The settlement may have begun to take shape sometime after 1850. Incorporation took place in 1966.

Burns *Dickson County.* This site was known for a time as Grade 42, referring to the mileage from Nashville via the railroad. Known locally as "The Grade," it was inhabited during Civil War days mostly by Union soldiers and railroad workers, according to the local newspaper. A detachment of black soldiers here had been commanded by a Captain Burns; so following the war, when local residents wanted a "proper name" for the place, they chose Burns Station. This was later shortened to Burns. The earliest permanent settler here is believed to have been "Captain" Billy Austin, in 1803. A second source disagrees, stating that the place took its name from the poet Robert Burns (1759–1796). The community incorporated in 1953.

Burristown *Jackson County.* At the time of the 1850 census, William, James, John, and Elijah Burris were nearby residents. The hamlet owes its name to the Burrises.

Busby *Lawrence County.* This label undoubtedly results from the circa 1850 local residency of Mahala, Rynie, Stephen, and Stephens Busby.

Busselltown *Decatur County.* This place-name may be in some way connected to Judah Bussell or Houston Bussell, local residents found on the rolls of the 1850 census. (One current map spells the name Busseltown.)

Busselltown *Loudon County.* Irvin and Phoebe Bussell, and two Bussells with the given name William, resided in this area when the 1880 census was taken, making it likely that the place-name resulted from the near residency of one or more of these persons, or an ancestor.

Busy Corner *Coffee County.* A source close to the scene advises, "when we moved here, in 1979, we were being shown homes on the outskirts of town by a State Farm agent . . . now deceased . . . who then lived near Busy Corner. He told us, 'I named Busy Corner, because it is.'"

Butler *Johnson County.* The rolls of the 1880 East Tennessee census disclose several Butlers residing in the county, among them William H., Rodrick R., age 53, and J. G., a 32-year-old male. It is likely this family, or these families, are somehow associated with the name of the site.

Butler's Landing *Clay County.* In Jackson County, one of the counties that later formed Clay County, the 1850 census rolls list thirteen persons spelling their surname Butlar and seven spelling it Butler. The latter include Abslom, Obadiah, Sarah, three Thomases. A Thomas J. Butler's Landing was previously called "Point," and at one time was designated Butler's Ferry. The ferry is believed to have been operated by Bailey C. and Thomas Butler, who were brothers. Other early records reveal that Bailey Butler became a postmaster near here in 1831. Other Butlers associated with this site included Franklin W. and W. B. Butler.

Bybee *Cocke County.* Bybee takes its name from the family of Tipton Bibee, whose father, Thomas, a Revolutionary War soldier, settled here in 1812. The place was once dubbed Lickskillet. (This information comes from data compiled by E. R. Walker III.)

Byrd Chapel *Knox County.* The origin of this place-name is vague. It may relate in some manner to Thomas Byrd, a local citizen in 1830.

Byrdstown *Pickett County (seat).* The community was incorporated in 1917. It is believed to trace its name to Colonel Robert Byrd, who strove to keep Tennessee in the Union during the Civil War and, when the state seceded, joined the Union army. Byrd hailed from Kingston. The town's name almost became Wrightsville, for Lem Wright, an individual who joined with Howell Pickett in leading a legislative effort to organize the county.

Cabo *Chester County.* This is a Spanish word usually used to designate an end point or terminus (as in the English *cape*). Perhaps it was used here for the end of Taylor Road.

Caffey *McNairy County.* See New Hope entry.

Cainsville *Wilson County.* The landowner, George I. Cain, platted and developed the town. It is thought to have been established in 1829.

Cairo *Sumner County.* General James Winchester is said to have named the site, in about 1800. Winchester purchased some land here with two other men, and as the riverfront town flourished in the early 1800s, he foresaw a bright future for it. Thus, he named it for Cairo, the riverport capital of Egypt.

Calderwood *Blount County.* I. G. Calderwood is the individual for whom this community was named. Calderwood was dispatched from Massena, New York, to this locality to ensure completion of a section of the Southern Railway.

Calfkiller *Putnam County.* One wonders if the namer(s) might have intended to assign the name of an Indian chief in the state, Pathkiller, to this location. Pathkiller at one time occupied a site in Loudon County. The name may have been "heard, not written," and consequently was misunderstood and recorded as Calfkiller.

Calhoun *McMinn County.* The town's namesake was a Southern political figure and prominent statesman, John C. Calhoun, who served as secretary of war. He was born in 1782 and died in 1850. Settlement of the community occurred in about 1819. A part Cherokee individual, John Walker, is credited with founding and naming the community. As a point of interest, the 1850 Tennessee census records show that a James Calhoun was residing in the county in that year, as well. It is not certain whether he was a relative of John C. Calhoun. Incorporation took place in 1961.

Call's *Coffee County.* Robert Call was a Franklin County resident in 1830, according to the Middle Tennessee census of that year. Coffee County was formed in part from Franklin County; so it is likely he resided at this locality. By 1850—again, according to the census—Daniel H. Call was a local resident. The surname was undoubtedly applied to the site.

Calvary *Dyer County.* This name was no doubt assigned by Christian settlers, who may have established a church here with "Calvary" in the name. Calvary (from the Latin *calva,* "skull"), a skull-shaped hill in Jerusalem (also known as Golgotha), was the site of Jesus's Crucifixion.

Camargo *Lincoln County.* According to a source, this name may have been borrowed from a town in north-central Mexico where some Tennesseans stayed in the early days of the Mexican War. However, according to a more popular story, the site was initially referred to as Come or Go, and the current label is an adaptation from that. One of those responsible for naming the community is believed to have been John Martin McFerrin. The hamlet arose about 1847.

Cambridge *Warren County.* An early school at this location was called Cambridge, probably for the famed British educational institution.

Camden *Benton County (seat)*. The city takes its name from the earl of Camden, Charles Pratt, by way of Camden, South Carolina, or Camden, New Jersey. Settlers were here at a very early date, perhaps 1768. Eighteen thirty-six is considered the year of founding. Two years later, a charter of incorporation was granted, but it was reincorporated in 1847 and 1903. The town landsite was owned by Charles M. Sarrett and John Jackson, but they relinquished their claims. Burrel Beard and John Daugherty did the surveying, in 1836. At some earlier juncture, it may have been dubbed Tranquility.

Campaign *Warren County*. The name is probably traceable to Joseph Campain (variant spellings include Campaign and Campen), a North Carolina native who came to this area in 1842. Mr. Campain operated a store adjacent to the railroad tracks, which became referred to as Campaign Stop. This was later shortened to simply Campaign. Another possible family member, Galvin Campaign, is mentioned in the Deed Book of 1884–1886.

Campbell Junction *Cumberland County*. A number of Campbells dot the census rolls for the county in 1880. Two named James lived in the area, plus William, John, W. C., and Moleon. The spelling of the given name of the last-named Campbell is questionable. "Junction" usually was appended to place-names because of a local railroad stop or highway intersection.

Campbell's Station *Maury County*. Probably the first to come to this locality, in about 1810, were John and Sarah Kimbrough Campbell. John's brothers settled nearby as well, at a place that became known as Campbellsville. The "Station" portion of the name refers to its site on the Nashville & Decatur Railroad. The company was given right-of-way by Andrew Jackson (Jack) Campbell, through his farmland. A station house and depot were erected, and the rail line designated it as Campbell Station, or Campbell's Station. Sometimes, this was shortened to simply Campbell's. A member of the Confederate Army, Jack Campbell rose to the rank of major and was captured at Fort Donelson. The son of John and Sarah Campbell, he was later freed in a prisoner exchange, and died in May of 1863. In county records of deeds transacted in 1813, "Philips and Campbell," probably a business endeavor of some sort, is mentioned.

Campbellsville *Giles County*. Several Campbells inhabited the vicinity in 1830 and are listed in census records from the times. H. C., Hugh, Jane, Joab, and Sara were among them. H. C. probably refers to Hamilton Crockett Campbell. Giles County sources state that the site takes its name from him. He married Mary Mitchell Dickey and in 1820 donated the land for a public square. Sixty years later, the community began to boom. The first airplane to land in Giles County did so at this locality.

Camp Creek *Greene County*. A resident of nearby Middle Creek explains that her community is situated between Horse Creek and Camp Creek. In school, she was told that Union soldiers camped in the Camp Creek area during the Civil War, and kept their horses in the Horse Creek area. "Between these two sites was a section that wasn't fit for either; that was Middle Creek," the correspondent writes.

Camp Ground *Weakley County.* Great revivals were held here at a Methodist camp-ground. As a result, the surrounding community became known as Camp Ground.

Canaan *Maury County.* The name is biblical, being the ancient name of Palestine. One source gives the literal meaning as "belonging to the land of red-purple," perhaps a reference to a colorant traded in the biblical Canaan.

Canadaville *Fayette County.* The place has been known as Canadaville since at least 1871. That year, the Reverend John Byron Canada listed his address as Canadaville in the meeting minutes of the Baptist Big Hatchie Association. Three Canada brothers had come here earlier—including John in 1851. Wilkes had arrived in 1850 and Daniel W. in 1847. In 1874, Thomas S. Canada was listed as postmaster at Canada-ville.

Cane Creek *Hickman County.* Some of the first frontiersmen to locate in this area observed that the creek bottom was dense with canebrakes and thus named the waterway Cane Creek. The community that arose also assumed that name.

Caney Spring *Marshall County.* This hamlet takes its name from nearby Caney Creek, adjacent to which an early settler planted a crop.

Capleville *Shelby County.* Several Caples were associated with this region. Sallie A. Caple and J. R. Caples were two. E. B. Caple was the husband of Sarah Abigal (Abigale? Abigail?).

Capp's Gap *Sumner County.* When the 1850 state census was taken, Nancy Capp was a nearby resident. This place-name undoubtedly has some connection with her or with members of the Capp clan.

Carlisle *Stewart County.* Although some believe the village took the name from Carlisle, England, others subscribe to the theory that it was named for Carlisle, Pennsylvania, because the latter town produced the same kind of pig iron that was manufactured here. A furnace went on-line here in 1828.

Carlock *McMinn County.* When the state's 1870 census was recorded, four persons with the Carlock surname were citizens of the county. They included Daniel, Ewing, Isaac, and Benjamin. The place-name and the family/families were probably intertwined.

Carnegie *Washington County.* This locality takes its name from Andrew Carnegie, famed in part for being a benefactor of libraries. The Carnegie Furnace Company was identified with this place, as was the Carnegie Land and Development Company, which was organized in 1890. Both were the concerns of General John T. Wilder.

Carpenter Campground *Blount County.* Sometimes called Montvale Station or Carpenter, this community owes its name to Thomas Carpenter. He was proprietor of the land where a church was erected. The site became a popular venue for Methodist camp meetings. In 1862, Thomas Carpenter was the first person buried in the church graveyard. "Uncle Abe" Carpenter was another individual associated with this neighborhood.

Carson Spring *Cocke County.* A family named Carson received a land grant in this locale in 1816. It was once a popular resort with a hotel; visitors used it as a retreat where they could escape the summer's heat and partake of the cool springwater.

Carter *Carter County.* This hamlet may have taken its name from the county, but it is possible that the label refers to an early resident or residents having the Carter surname. In *County Wills to 1850,* references are found to A. M. Carter and his daughter, Elizabeth.

Carter's Creek *Maury County.* The North Carolina government made a land grant here to General Daniel Carter, to whom the place owes its name. He was an officer in the Revolutionary War. Another source states that the place-name also refers to Daniel's brother, Benjamin. The first settler here may have been James Black. Other early settlers here, by surname, included Polk, Gordon, Campbell, and Witherspoon. Surveyed as early as 1780, it was dubbed Hardin's Creek by surveyors.

Carthage *Smith County (seat).* This label was inspired by the famed North African city of antiquity. Exotic place-names were in vogue in the United States for a period, and this site was probably named during that time. It was founded in 1804 and incorporated in 1817.

Cartwright *Sequatchie County.* The name was probably chosen by the operator of a small store here, G. P. Cartwright. He was also the first postmaster for the community.

Cartwright *Smith County.* In 1850, local citizens included Adison, Harry, Richerson C., and Thomas Cartwright. The place probably traces its name to this family or these families.

Caryville *Campbell County.* This place-name may relate in some manner to William Carey, who served as a delegate to the Knoxville Convention in mid-1861, or to William Carey, a county clerk of 1834–1838. Settlement began very early, probably before 1800. The site had previous names, including Walnut Cove and Wheeler's Station. The latter designation referred to a prominent merchant and landowner, H. D. Wheeler. The Caryville label dates from 1866 to the present.

Cash Point *Lincoln County.* Several men were said to have been sitting at the store, and one remarked, "Why not call this place Cash Point?" His observation was prompted by the facts that you had to have cash to buy a pint of whiskey, and two roads came to a point here.

Castalian Springs *Sumner County.* Apparently, there were one or more springs here. The "Castalian" portion of the name refers to the legendary spring of Castalia that issued from the foot of Mount Parnassus in Greece.

Castle Heights *Cocke County.* This place-name is of a more recent vintage. It was originally assigned to a subdivision in the 1950s by a developer named M. M. Bullard, probably due to the favorable image the name conjured up.

Cater *Bedford County.* A local family named Cater gave this designation to the site.

Cates *Lake County.* In the state's 1870 census records, the only Cates listed for the county was Susan, age 43. This geographical designation may be in some way related to her or her family.

Catlettsburg *Sevier County.* All the Tennessee Catletts recorded at the time of the 1850 census resided here, in Sevier County. Included at that time were George W., Henry, James, two Johns, Lofty, Samuel, and William.

Cato *Trousdale County.* The 1850 state census records disclose that Robert W. Cato was a Smith County resident at that time. Later, a portion of Smith County helped constitute Trousdale County. It is likely that the place known as Cato was once part of Smith County and probably related in some manner to Robert or other family members. In the early 1900s, Joe Cato was a Trousdale County farmer; Clarence and Ola Cato were local residents. A county history also mentions C. L. Cato as being a local citizen in 1934, while during the World War II era, Rosalie Cato is listed as having been a Trousdale resident—probably at this location.

Caton's Chapel *Sevier County.* The community takes its name from a place of worship, Caton's Chapel, a Methodist church organized in 1865 by the Reverend G. M. Caton.

Caton's Grove *Cocke County.* An early Methodist minister serving this area was Thomas Caton (1819–1911). He resided locally, and the site may have been named for him. As an additional point of interest, several county residents listed on the rolls of the 1870 census have the Caton surname, including Giles, James F., and Stephen Caton, aged 22, 51, and 24, respectively.

Catoosa *Morgan County.* There is a county in Georgia of the same name. The origin is thought to be Cherokee. It may designate a hill or elevation, or may have been the name of a Cherokee chief, or both.

Cedar Grove *Carroll County.* (See following explanation.)

Cedar Grove *Carter County.* The Eastern red cedar grows throughout Tennessee, accounting for application of the name here.

Cedar Grove *Henderson County.* See preceding entry.

Cedar Grove *Knox County.* See explanation for Cedar Grove, Carter County.

Cedar Grove *Pickett County.* See explanation for Cedar Grove, Carter County.

Cedar Grove *Rutherford County.* A dense concentration of virgin cedar marked this locality.

Cedar Grove *Sullivan County.* See preceding entry.

Cedar Grove *Sumner County.* See explanation for Cedar Grove, Carter County.

Cedar Hill *Robertson County.* Incorporation took place in 1963. There were numerous cedars growing in this vicinity, with the town taking its name from them. Jefferson W. Gooch was the proprietor of most of the townsite before divesting himself of it. The first commercial enterprise, a store, was erected not far away in 1855, on a hill covered with cedar timber.

Cedar Springs *Knox County.* The existence of natural springs at this site, as well as a profusion of Eastern red cedar, accounted for this place-name.

Cedar Springs *McMinn County.* (See preceding explanation.)

Celina *Clay County (seat).* A prominent early educator, Moses Fisk, had a daughter named Celina. It was for her that this place was named. Incorporation took place in 1909.

Center *Cumberland County.* The site proprietors were Robert Burke and Dr. Haley. Some farmland here was purchased in 1855 by Thomas Center. Hugh Center is another individual mentioned in early county records.

Center *Lawrence County.* This site assumed its designation due to its situation on the "turnpike," near the intersection of Red Hill, Napier, and Self Roads.

Center Hill *Warren County.* Located in upland terrain, the place was likely dubbed Center Hill in reference to a local topographical feature.

Center Point *Lawrence County.* Being virtually equidistant from Bluewater and Idaho, this location took on the name Center Point. A school existed here as early as 1886, but the town failed to flourish until about 1909.

Centertown *Warren County.* Incorporation took place in 1951. The initial label on the site may have been Glascock, a reference to a George Glascock, who left for Texas following the Civil War. This locality later became known as Centertown, due to its position approximately equidistant from Woodbury and McMinnville. There was a store here, kept in the early 1900s by John Ayers, which served as a landmark and stopping point.

Centerville *Hickman County (seat).* At one time, this place-name may have been styled Centreville. It was so labeled due to the town's central orientation in the county. In 1823 it became the seat of county government, but it was not until 1911 that it was incorporated. Charles Stewart and J. C. McLemore donated land for the townsite.

Cerro Gordo *Hardin County.* Early on, the place was known as White's Ferry, until John White's demise in the 1840s. Thereafter, it became known as Cerro Gordo, after a battle of that name that occurred during the Mexican War. (*Cerro* is Spanish for "hill," *gordo* for "big.") It was also known at one time as Hardin's Ferry, until the death of James Hardin in 1826. James was the son of Colonel Joseph Hardin, for whom the county was named.

Chambers *McNairy County.* When the 1830 census of West Tennessee was recorded, Elijah P. and Henry R. Chambers were citizens of Dyer County, while Green B. Chambers was a Gibson County resident. Later, portions of both their counties contributed to the makeup of McNairy County; so it is likely the place-name relates in some manner to one of these families.

Champ *Lincoln County.* The first postmaster at the site, Bert Jennings, was a great admirer of James Beauchamp Clark, at the time a popular congressman who became Speaker of the House. Jennings chose the name in 1899 when the post office opened, using a portion of Clark's middle name.

Chapel Hill *Marshall County.* After graduating from college in the early 1800s, John Laws headed west and settled at this place, starting a school. He named the hamlet for his hometown, Chapel Hill, North Carolina.

Chapel Hill *Maury County.* The site was probably populated by pioneers moving westward from North Carolina. There is a well-known Chapel Hill in the Tarheel State.

Chapman Grove *Roane County.* In 1880, two Chapmans are shown on rolls of the census for this county—Francis, age 68, and Frances, age 16. The former may have been the father or grandfather of the latter. The place-name probably came about as a result of these individuals, or their ancestors, residing here, coupled with the presence of a grove of trees.

Chapman's *Giles County.* A number of Chapmans were present in this area in 1830, according to census rolls. Included were Asa, Ben, Elja, John, William, James, and several named Thomas.

Charleston *Bradley County.* This site is believed to be named after Charleston, South Carolina.

Charley's Branch *Anderson County*. A portion of the name stems from an early resident, Charley Phillips.

Charlotte *Dickson County (seat)*. The name traces back to Charlotte Reeves Robertson (Mrs. James Robertson). An early pioneer, James opened up much of the central portion of the state. The town was established in 1804. In a separate source, Charlotte Robertson is described as "the wife of Richard Napier."

Chaska *Campbell County*. According to *American Place-Names*, in Minnesota this Siouan term was a name given to a first-born child. It is not known why it was applied to this Tennessee site.

Chattanooga *Hamilton County (seat)*. According to *American Place-Names*, this name is thought to translate as "rock rising to a point." It is believed to be a reference to Lookout Mountain. The Creek word is thought to be *Chatanuga*.

Cherokee *Washington County*. The Cherokee Indians once resided in this area. The hamlet is on the edge of the Cherokee National Forest.

Cherry *Lauderdale County*. Sometime before 1850, Amanda Clay Cherry and her husband, Norman T., settled at this locale. The immediate area became known as Cherryville. By 1870, local citizens included Robert Cherry, 39, and Edmond Cherry, 60.

Cherry Chapel *Hardin County*. In 1840, the county was home to David, Eli, Benjamin, and Jesse Cherry, one of whom may have been a clergyman, accounting for the designation on this site.

Cherry Hill *DeKalb County*. This name was conferred upon the school in this hamlet, probably after 1910, and no doubt due to the wild cherry trees growing on nearby hills.

Chesney *Union County*. Gordon, Daniel, Margarette, Tilmon, and William Chesney are known to have been local residents in 1880. Family ancestors may have lived here before them, as well. The place-name probably borrows from the family surname. All of the above-named individuals were between the ages of 23 and 34 in 1880.

Chestnut Glade *Weakley County*. In early years, this place was characterized by its many stately, old chestnut trees.

Chestnut Grove *Grainger County*. The American chestnut thrives in this area of the state. The site took its name from a nearby grove of the trees.

Chestnut Grove *Grundy County*. See preceding entry.

Chestnut Grove *Jefferson County*. See entry for Chestnut Grove, Grainger County.

Chestnut Grove *Perry County.* See entry for Chestnut Grove, Grainger County.

Chestnut Grove *Stewart County.* This site owes its name to the fact that a community school and church were established among a grove of chestnut trees.

Chestnut Grove *Sumner County.* See entry for Chestnut Grove, Grainger County.

Chestnut Grove *Union County.* A grove of chestnut trees characterized this location.

Chestnut Grove *Warren County.* See entry for Chestnut Grove, Grainger County.

Chestnut Hill *Cumberland County.* This promontory was dotted with American chestnut trees, common to the eastern five-sixths of the state.

Chestnut Hill *Jefferson County.* Like a nearby place called Chestnut Grove, this place probably assumed the label because of chestnut trees growing locally.

Chestnut Hill *Sumner County.* See entry for Chestnut Hill, Cumberland County.

Chestnut Ridge *Greene County.* A ridge lined with American chestnut trees inspired this place's name.

Chewalla *McNairy County.* According to *American Place-Names,* the Choctaws used this term to refer to cedar. It may be Muskogean in origin. Pronounced the same, a slightly variant spelling of a possibly Spokane term referred to a snake. A second source claims that when the first settlers arrived, an Indian named Chewalla (some historians say Walla Walla) ran a trading post on the Cherokee Trail. The arising local community was called Chief Walla, according to this version.

Chickamauga *Hamilton County.* The village is situated on the shore of Lake Chickamauga. A scholar in Native American languages believes the translation from the Cherokee to be "much muddy or red waters," or "much big waters, red" (*tsi-gwa-amo-gi*). Earlier, he had thought Chickamauga to be a Creek word, *cukko-micco,* believed to mean "dwelling place of the war chief." In a television documentary covering the Civil War battle, the name was translated as "river of blood." The town incorporated in 1972. Some maps designate it as Lakesite.

Childress *Sullivan County.* The 1870 census rolls verify that a number of persons with this surname resided locally. Counted among them were Moses, Noah, William, William B., Thomas, Sarah E., George W., Finley C., Jessee, John, J. M., and Thomas. This place-name is probably traceable to one or more of them.

Chilhowee *Blount County.* This was the name of an early Cherokee village at the site. The name is Cherokee, but its meaning remains uncertain.

China Grove *Gibson County.* The designation here may have been "imported" from China Grove in Rowan County, North Carolina. Many Tennessee towns were settled by individuals moving west from that state. The "Grove" part of a name usually suggests a shady setting. The term China traces all the way back to Qin (pronounced "chin"), after whom China was named.

Chinquapin Grove *Sullivan County.* This name may have been "imported" to the county from a hamlet in Duplin County, North Carolina. In either venue, it could indicate the local existence of a species of oak or chestnut that occurs in the southeastern United States. Northeast Tennessee, where Sullivan County is located, is known to feature a type of oak known as the Allegheny chinkapin.

Chinubee *Lawrence County.* The Native American term is believed to translate as "land of the mighty wind."

Chota *Blount County.* A Cherokee "city of refuge" was located along the Little Tennessee River and was called Echota. This site adopts a shortened version of that name.

Christianburg *Monroe County.* William C. and Mary Christian were listed as local citizens at the time of the 1830 East Tennessee census. The surname was probably coupled with *burg* to label the settlement that arose.

Christy Hill *Blount County.* The name is thought to derive from an individual named Christian ("Christy") Best. (One source gives Best's given name as Christopher.) At one time, a church and school stood at this elevation. A farmer, Best had donated the land for the school, which also took his name. He died in 1915.

Chuckey *Greene County.* Chuckey probably derives its name from the nearby Nolachuckey River. *Nolachuckey* is believed to be a Cherokee word, but the translation is unclear. A variant spelling of the river's name is Nolichuckey.

Church Hill *Hawkins County.* Church Hill was previously known as Spencer's Mill and Patterson Mill. It took its current name from a prominent local landmark: a Methodist church that stood on an elevation above the town's main thoroughfare. It is uncertain whether this edifice was the hilltop log church constructed in 1840, found in historical references. The community was incorporated in 1958.

Citico Beach *Monroe County.* The "Beach" part of the name comes from its location near the shore of Tellico Lake. The "Citico" part derives from an early Cherokee settlement, but the meaning of the term has never been ascertained.

Clarkrange *Fentress County.* Apparently, this name could be construed as "Clark's range," from either a landowner's given name or surname, and his farm. Clark Peters lived in the area from 1819 to 1903. Cattle were driven to an unfenced, free-range pasture at a high elevation where the grasses were lush. When Cyrus Clark arrived, he purchased an inn known as Bledsoe Stand and began farming on the side. When a post office was approved for the location, it was in the name Clark Range. Eventually, the style became Clarkrange.

Clarksburg *Carroll County.* An early landholder here, surnamed Clark, gave his name to this community. Scant detail could be located on Clark or the town's founding.

Clarksville *Montgomery County (seat).* This future city is said to have been laid out at an extremely early year, 1784, by Martin Armstrong. Its namesake was General George Rogers Clark, best remembered for the Lewis and Clark expedition that helped open up the West. The namesake of the county, Colonel John Montgomery, is credited with founding Clarksville.

Claylick *Dickson County.* This designation appeared on deeds as early as 1802—before the county was formed. The full name was Big Clay Lick. This probably was inspired by the presence of clay soil at the site. Inclusion of the term *lick* in place-names usually suggests the presence of a creek or stream, and/or a location where wild animals came to "lick" minerals from surfaces.

Clear Creek Landing *Perry County.* This site comes by its name naturally, being situated where Clear Creek meets the Tennessee River.

Clearmont *Warren County.* The site has been known by many names in its history, including Barren Fork, New, Big Spring, Oak Grove, and Davenport. Located on Youngblood Creek, it had a gristmill and dam that later were washed away by floodwaters. The name was probably inspired by the spring-fed creek, which was pure and clear; "mont" in the name is usually attributed to the French term for "mountain."

Clementsville *Clay County.* Peter White and his family were perhaps the first whites to put down roots here, in 1812. George W. Clements, Clarence Clements, Andrew Jackson Clements, and Henderson M. Clements were other family members whose names were associated with this locale. Jackson County contributed some area to the formation of Clay County. Living in Jackson County at about that time were Christopher and Montgomery Clements, as reflected in the 1850 census figures. In fact, at one time, Christopher Clements served as postmaster here for twelve years, when the site was still known as McLeansville. The Clementsville place-name does not seem to have been applied until 1857. The origin of this name probably relates to one of these persons, or one or more of the family members.

Cleveland *Bradley County (seat).* Three differing explanations for the name can be found in the annals. One states that an early settler who emigrated from North Carolina, John Cleveland, founded the city, and that it is named for him. A second, taken from a city brochure, claims that "the name honors Benjamin Cleveland, a veteran of the Revolutionary War who had seen action at Kings Mountain." Still another source states unequivocally that the place took its name from Cleveland, Ohio. Possibly lending credence to this last explanation is the fact that the name was spelled Cleaveland numerous times in early records, until gradually Cleveland became the accepted spelling. (Cleveland, Ohio, was named for early surveyor Moses Cleaveland.) The Tennessee Cleveland occupies a site previously known as Taylor's Place, and was incorporated in 1842.

Clevenger *Cocke County*. This locale has also gone by the names Clevenger Town and Clevenger's Crossroads. The name traces back to Zeb Clevenger, who resided nearby, and his father, John M. Clevenger. From a separate source—the 1830 East Tennessee census rolls—we find in Cocke County mentions of John, Nancy, and Elias Clevinger, possibly a variant spelling of the same family's surname.

Click Mill *Cocke County*. In the 1800s, numerous individuals with the Click surname populated this area. Some spelled the name with an *e* on the end. Lewis, D. P., Jane, Mary A., William, and T. J. Click were among them. There were also three named William. One or more of the family members undoubtedly operated this mill.

Clifton *Wayne County*. Incorporation took place in 1946. As with an identically named community in Ohio, this Clifton traces its name to local cliffs bordering the river. It was settled prior to 1840.

Clifton Junction *Wayne County*. This intersection of thoroughfares is located three or four miles south of Clifton. (See preceding entry.)

Clinton *Anderson County (seat)*. At an earlier time, the city bore the name Burrville, for Aaron Burr. Later, by a legislative act, this was changed (1809) to Clinton, to pay tribute to New York Governor DeWitt Clinton. But others feel the name honors DeWitt's uncle, George Clinton, who served as vice president under two presidents and was six times mayor of New York City. Incorporation took place in 1835.

Clopton *Tipton County*. When grounds for a Methodist campsite at this locality were sought, an individual named Anthony Clopton signed over the required parcel. In gratitude, the place took on his surname.

Cloud Creek *Claiborne County*. In 1840, several Clouds resided near the banks of this stream. Abner, Benjamin, Greenberry, Benjamin F., Jane, Jacob, and Stanwix Cloud all called the neighborhood home.

Coalfield *Morgan County*. This name was influenced by the operators of coal mining enterprises conducted here. At first, the operators dubbed the site Rio, Spanish for "river," because the roads were so bad in wintertime that they "ran like a river"— probably with a mixture of water, mud, and soot. When they moved the post office off the mountain and into the valley, they renamed it Coalfield.

Coaling *Dickson County.* Before the Civil War, charcoal was made here to supply the Tennessee Iron Works. The "coal" part of the name probably derives from the iron industry's truncated term for charcoal.

Coalmont *Grundy County.* As the name implies, this was a coal mining community. Earlier, however, the name was Coal Dale. When a post office was secured, the wife of the president of the coal company disliked the Coal Dale label and changed it to Coalmont. The year was 1903. Four years later, the community incorporated.

Coble *Hickman County.* One of the pioneer families in this vicinity bore the surname Coble. The community succeeded a once-thriving nearby town of Whitfield. The principle industry was lumber. It is said that the first rail shipment of cobalt departed from near this town in 1906, when Thomas Edison arrived in search of deposits and found them near Cow Hollow, on Wolf Creek. A wagonload was pulled to Grinder's Switch and sent to Edison's lab in Orange, New Jersey.

Coffman Camp *Grainger County.* A number of Coffmans resided locally in 1850, mostly in the Thirteenth District. They included John, Elizabeth, Sally, John, and George. The reason for appending "Camp" to the Coffman surname is uncertain. Perhaps at the outset, the settlement resembled an encampment more than a town or homestead.

Cokercreek *Monroe County.* Sometimes styled Coker Creek, this label was inspired by the Cherokee term for squash, *kuku.*

Cold Spring *Blount County.* The water source here was, quite literally, a cold spring, fed by the higher elevations.

Coldwater *Lincoln County.* The aptly named Coldwater Creek runs through this community, giving it its name.

Colesburg *Dickson County.* According to local lore, a coal chute was erected here, resulting in the name Colesburgh being affixed to the site. This was later shortened to Colesburg. Earlier, it bore the names Bon Air and Guntersville, the latter having a variant of Gunkleville.

Coletown *Polk County.* The site adopted its name from early Cole families who resided here, "behind the acid plant and Smelter's Hill," according to the county historian. Windom Cole and Ader Cole Brown were among the Coles still remembered by local residents.

College *Bledsoe County.* One local source states that the name of the site is due to the establishment of Sequatchie College, which he says operated here from 1866 to 1881. Previously, it was referred to as Roberson's Crossroads. A second correspondent agrees, saying that the institution may have been a school of medicine. She adds that often the site is called College Station, the "Station" part of the name being the result of the site's function as a train station.

Collegedale *Hamilton County.* In 1916, Seventh Day Adventists purchased the Thatcher property at this locality, and moved their school here from Graysville, Tennessee. It is recorded that a church elder, Carlyle B. Haynes, was inspired by the setting and suggested Collegedale as the new name. The institution soon grew from an academy into a four-year college, the Southern College of Seventh Day Adventists. In the pre-Collegedale days, the site was owned by Jim Thatcher, who shipped limestone and lime from a nearby siding known as Thatcher's Switch. An alternative source states simply that the place took its name from Southern Missionary College.

Collier's Corner *Jefferson County.* William Collier resided in this vicinity in 1850, probably inspiring this place-label.

Collierville *Shelby County. Collier* being a term applied to a coal miner, it was a natural to apply to this site, since there were coal mining operations conducted nearby. However, a dissenting source claims that the "Collier" portion of the label was taken from a family of pioneers.

Collins *Grundy County.* Information on this community is vague, but the name is believed to have been the surname of a local family.

Collins Mill *McMinn County.* Apparently, a mill was operated at this site for a period of time. In 1850, Anne, Alfred, LeRoy, Eliza, Elizabeth, and G. W. Collins lived nearby. The family, or one or more of these individuals, may have run the mill.

Collinwood *Wayne County.* A town was laid out here in 1912 and was incorporated three years later. In 1913, a firm to which the place-name traces, Collinwood & Company, began business at the site, obtaining land from J. E. Wilburn. It is unclear whether the company was involved in one of the several local manufacturing enterprises making wood products such as staves and wagon spokes.

Columbia *Maury County (seat).* Using the variant or Anglicized spelling, this label was inspired by the South American nation of Colombia.

Comfort *Marion County.* A correspondent in the area writes, "Comfort . . . was a post office named for my maternal grandmother, Comfort Tate Raulston. Her son (my uncle), John Tate Raulston of Monkey Trial fame, applied for this post office and established it (in 1888). He ran (it) for a month and then my grandmother took over."

Commerce *Wilson County.* Joshua Taylor was the proprietor. He is believed to have suggested the name for the community, which arose about 1822, because of the busy trade that promptly sprang up.

Como *Henry County.* This designation was applied in the United States quite a few times by those laying railroad lines. It may have been favored for its brevity, and may have come from the city and lake of the same name in Italy.

Compton *Rutherford County.* John Compton, age 86 at the time, was a local resident in 1870. He is probably connected in a direct way to this place-name. Elisha Compton, then 42, also resided in the county.

Conasauga *Polk County.* According to *American Place-Names,* this designation has been applied to certain ancient Cherokee settlements, but its meaning remains obscure.

Condra *Marion County.* The 1880 census rolls of East Tennessee disclose the residency of a number of Condras. The individuals and their ages at the time are as follows: James, 74; Sarah, 54; Benjamin, 25; Elijah, 34; William, 29; Wilson, 57; and John, 55. One passage states that James arrived by raft from Kentucky. James Condra was born sometime between 1760 and 1765 and died in 1830 or 1831. Audley W. Condra was born in 1875. The place-name likely traces back to one or more of these families.

Conyersville *Henry County.* On the occasion of the 1850 census, a number of persons with the Conyers surname were county citizens. Variant spellings were found in both given and surnames, possibly resulting from transcription errors. Those residing here included Mordicai M. Conyer, W. H. Conyers, W. J. Conyers, Paschal Conyers, and Mordecai Conyers.

Cookeville *Putnam County* (*seat*). The city derives its name from a Virginia native, Richard Fielding Cooke, born in 1787. He served as a senator from Jackson County, and introduced the measure to reestablish Putnam County. He was also a veteran of the Mexican War.

Cooper's *Fentress County.* At the time of the 1870 census, numerous Coopers resided in the area. Among them were John, age 44; Joe, 56; Jane, 50; Jacob, 28; Alip, 45; Jepthia, 45; Mary, 27; Charly, 50; and three named William.

Cooper's *Gibson County.* Sometimes known as Cooper's Mill, this enclave was once referred to as Shaw's Mill, for Solomon Shaw. Shaw was a plantation owner in pre–Civil War times. After the war, Captain Wise A. Cooper married Shaw's daughter and assumed operation of the milling business. Thus, the post office was renamed. One source calls the stream here the Middle Fork of the Forked Deer River. Current maps may designate it as the Rutherford Fork.

Coopertown *Montgomery County.* Living in this general locality during its formative years were Hiram, Edmund, Nathaniel, C. R., Amelia, Vincent, and Vison Cooper. Probably one of them—or the clan in general—was responsible for this site taking on the Coopertown name.

Coopertown *Robertson County.* In earlier times, this site was called Naive's Crossroads, after a David Naive who settled here about 1825. Later, it acquired the Coopertown name because of the large number of local men engaged in making barrels for the Red River Mills. (*Cooper* is another term for a barrelmaker.)

Copperhill *Polk County.* A copper mining enterprise once flourished here.

Cordell *Scott County.* In 1870, several Cordells lived nearby, probably giving their surname to this site. John Cordell, 59, was the eldest of those listed. Also present were William J., 32; Jesse K., 33; and John M., 26.

Corder's Crossroads *Lincoln County.* In one source, this place is styled as Corder Cross Roads. Thomas Corder and two John Corders are found in records of the 1850 census, suggesting that the family or families may have been associated with this locale. Lending credence to these findings, another chronicle states that one of the earliest settlers was Jacob Corder, along with several siblings. A number of Corder families are said to have settled along both intersecting thoroughfares.

Cordova *Shelby County.* This label, referring to a prominent city in Spain, was probably used because it had a romantic ring to it.

Corinth *Knox County.* See following entry.

Corinth *Sumner County.* Most of the many U.S. places bearing this name trace it back ultimately to the classical Greek city also mentioned in the New Testament. The Greek Corinth is still an important city and port situated on the northeastern Peloponnesus.

Cornersville *Marshall County.* The location was previously known as Marathon. Before the creation of Marshall County, corners of Maury, Bedford, Lincoln, and Giles counties met there, resulting in the current name. Cornersville was settled by or before 1815.

Cornpone *Sevier County.* The dictionary defines *cornpone* as a plain or simple cornbread, common in the southern United States. Most early local laborers were probably engaged in agriculture, and the dish was probably a staple of their diets.

Corryton *Knox County.* Colonel John Sawyers settled here in 1785. In the following century, the station at the site was called Floyd. When Corryton M. Woodbury arrived in 1887, he secured several hundred acres of land near the tracks, laid out lots for a town, and named the station for himself.

Cortner *Bedford County.* A man named Cortner operated Cortner's Mill at this location.

Cosby *Cocke County.* Several versions attempt to explain this place-name. One holds that the site is named for the first government distiller in Cocke County, Jonathan Cosby. *Ramsey's Annals,* however, states that it was named for General Cosby. In her book *Over the Misty Blue Hills,* Ruth Webb O'Dell says that it was named for a Dr. James Cozby of Knox County, a close friend of John Sevier. There were no settlers here until after 1807.

Cottage Grove *Henry County.* Logically enough, this label survived due to the fact that, in the site's formative days, a cottage was situated in a grove of nearby trees, possibly constituting the sole landmark. The earliest settlers may have been Jim Killebrew and Sampson Kennedy, in 1820. Moses Todd operated a general store from the year 1852; so for a time the location was known as Todd Town. Postal service came to the site a year later, and from then on it was designated Cottage Grove.

Cotton Grove *Madison County.* In 1819 this place became the first white settlement in the county. Two years later, the first cotton in the county was grown here by an individual named Maddin. The town's initial settlers included John and Thomas Brown, John Hargrove, Elijah Jones, William Woolfolk, and Roderick and Duncan McIver.

Cottontown *Sumner County.* This place-name apparently traces back to a prominent local family bearing the surname of Cotton. The patriarch's given name was Thomas.

Cottonwood Grove *Lake County.* The swamp cottonwood was indigenous to this area, thus justifying the name of the site.

Coulterville *Hamilton County.* An elderly and respected resident, T. J. Coulter, was honored in the naming of the railroad depot here. He had formerly headed the county militia.

Counce *Hardin County.* The community derives its name from families with the Counce surname that emigrated from North Carolina and populated this location.

County Line *Grainger County.* This hamlet comes by its name quite naturally, situated as it is near the boundary with Hawkins County and County Line Road.

Cove Creek *Carter County.* Located at a cove on the stream here, this hamlet takes its name from that waterway. Until 1922, it is said, the site was referred to as Lost Cove, for a child who was lost there, "Little Charles" Hughes.

Covington *Tipton County (seat).* Where it occurs, this place-name can usually be attributed to a hero of the War of 1812, General Leonard Wales Covington (1768–1813). The year 1826 marked incorporation.

Cowan *Franklin County.* An earlier name of this locality was Hawkins. The current name recognizes a Dr. J. B. Cowan. Dr. Cowan served under General Nathan Bedford Forrest as a medical staffer.

Coxville *Crockett County.* Enos Cox and F. S. Coxe were Haywood County citizens in 1830, while Moses Cox resided in Gibson County and Gabriel Cox in Madison County. Haywood, Gibson, Madison, and Dyer Counties all gave up land to help constitute Crockett County. Thus, one or more of these Coxes may have influenced the place-name now found on the Crockett County map.

Cozette *Decatur County.* A contributor from Parsons, Tennessee, provides the following account, which has been abridged: "My father was the owner of the general merchandise store where the name was decided on, and I witnessed it. My parents were Barney Lee ("Bunc") Miller and Lucy Baker Miller. We lived in the Norford Community, about one and a half miles from Cozette. Daddy also ran the Norford post office. In 1931, they decided to move to the main road, so we boys could go to Parsons School and receive a better education. So Daddy found land, purchased 111 acres, and moved his business to the new location. A salesman named Aaron Houston came weekly and made out a merchandise order. The first week he asked 'Mr. Bunc,' as Dad was called, what address should be written on the shipping order. Mr. Bunc said he hadn't decided yet. The following week, he still hadn't decided what he wanted it named, so Mr. Houston said, 'Why don't you call it Cozette, after my daughter?' After thinking a moment, Mr. Miller said that sounded fine to him; 'we will just call it the Cozette Community.' And it has been so called from that day forward. The only thing that exists there is the old home place and it has about seen its last days. I gave the place to my son in 1997. He plans to move back to Cozette from Arlington, Texas, and build a new home. . . . My story can also be verified by a niece of Aaron Houston."

Crab Orchard *Cumberland County.* One area correspondent explains that the whole side of the mountain here was once covered with wild crabapple trees. Agreeing, another states that the site acquired its name from the fragrance of the wild crabapple blooms.

Craigfield *Williamson County.* Listings for Alexander, Andrew, James, and William Craig are found for this county in the 1830 Middle Tennessee census records. It is possible they were farmers, their "fields" were at this site, and over time the neighborhood became known as Craigfield.

Cranmore Cove *Rhea County.* An early area settler, Josiah Cranmore, gave his surname to this location.

Crawfish Valley *Lawrence County.* This hamlet is located on Crawfish Creek, from which it derives its name. The creek was undoubtedly named for the crawfish it harbored.

Crawford *Overton County.* Once a small mining community, Crawford takes its current name from a wealthy ironmaster, Alexander L. Crawford, who arrived from New Castle, Pennsylvania, with his four sons. The Crawfords purchased timber and coal lands in the vicinity and were influential in persuading a railroad line from Knoxville to Nashville to build through the area.

Crewstown *Lawrence County.* Among the early families settling this location was at least one having the Crews surname, for whom the site was named. When the 1840 census was taken, those having the Crews surname and residing locally included Hardy Jr.; Ben Jr. and Ben Sr.; Thomas; Jonathan; and William.

Crippen Gap *Knox County.* This label traces back to the numerous Crippens residing at or near this passage among the foothills. In 1870 they included A. J., George, Henry, J. F., J. L., Martha, James, Mat, Pompy, and William Crippen. Martha was the eldest of them at the time, at 70 years of age, while A. J. was the youngest, at 25.

Crockett Mills *Crockett County.* Like the county, this site derives its name from frontiersman Davy Crockett, who died at the Alamo in 1836. (At one time, it was labeled Robertsonville, after a family with the Robertson surname.) Crockett represented the state in Congress during the periods 1827–1831 and 1833–1835. There may have been a mill on Tucker Creek here, or on another nearby stream. Settlement here began circa 1850.

Crockettsville *Sevier County.* This community took the name from the Crockettsville School, which was said to be named for David Crockett, the frontiersman.

Cromwell Crossroads *Wayne County.* According to the 1850 census rolls, William F. Cromwell resided in the vicinity. It is likely he, or a family member, lived near this intersection.

Cronanville *Lake County.* In 1870, James Cronin lived here. He was 39 at the time. The location probably derives its label from him or his family.

Crosby *Grainger County.* Calup Crosby, age 62, is identified by the 1870 census records as a resident of this area. It is likely this place-name refers to him or a relative.

Cross Plains *Robertson County.* Since north-south and east-west roads intersected here, the Cross Plains name seemed logical. (One account claims the label stemmed from an offhand comment made by James Yates that people were constantly "coming and going across the plains.") A town was founded in 1828, although settlers resided at the site much earlier. At a very early year, 1778, Thomas Kilgore (1715–1823) emigrated to this locality on foot from North Carolina, taking refuge in a cave on what was later referred to as the Carr Farm. So, before 1812, the place took on the designation Kilgore's Station. Cross Plains was incorporated in 1970.

Cross Road *Scott County.* East-west and north-south roads intersect at this junction.

Crossroads *DeKalb County.* This place-name traces back to the Crossroads School, begun sometime prior to 1904 near the point where the road from Dry Creek and New Home Road intersect. A Baptist church was also erected at that point at about the same time.

Cross Roads *Dyer County.* Slab Road, Wyrick Road, and Twin Rivers Road cross at this site.

Crossroads *Hardin County.* Intersecting roads characterize this location, accounting for the name.

Crossroads *Lawrence County.* Ethridge-Red Hill Road and Buffalo Road intersect here, resulting in this name.

Crossroads *Shelby County.* Crossroads comes by its name logically, being at the intersection of Monterey and Arlington Roads.

Crossville *Cumberland County (seat).* The site takes its name from the simple fact that two roads intersected here. Livestock were driven through the town over the Chattanooga-Kentucky Road, and at this site it intersected the Nashville-Knoxville route. At an earlier date, it was known as Scott's Cross Roads. The current name is said to have been conferred about 1856 by a woman named Amanda Scott, probably the person for whom the "Cross Roads" were designated. Another designation in the sequence, Lambeth Crossroads, traces back to an early citizen, Samuel Lambeth.

Crouch Crossroad *Washington County.* Numerous Crouches resided in this area where roads intersect. In 1850, they included Ann, W. H., T. H., Thomas, two Nancys, Landon, Martin, George, Elijah, two Jesses, three Johns, William, Joseph, James, and James H.

Crowley's Store *Weakley County.* The location assumed its name due to a store owner surnamed Crowley, about whom little else could be located.

Crucifer *Henderson County.* The likelihood exists that this designation derives from crossing roads in the vicinity. A less likely possibility is that plants of the cruciferous variety abounded in the area.

Crunk *Robertson County.* Richard and Walter D. Crunk resided near here when the 1850 census was taken. There is probably a connection between the name of the hamlet and these persons. By 1870, Walter, age 56, and H. C. Crunk, age 26, were residing in this vicinity.

Crystal Ridge *Lincoln County.* The ridge community here owes its name to clearwater springs and wells existing at the site.

Cub Creek *Stewart County.* Cub Creek is said to have taken its name from the experience of some early explorers, who encountered a bear cub wading in the creek. A very old community, its first settlers arrived as early as 1780.

Culleoka *Maury County.* The exact meaning of this Native American name is unclear, but it is said to have been conferred by the noted chieftain Tecumseh. In 1860, the Reverend W. H. Wilkes founded the settlement. A native of the town claims *Culleoka* was evoked by a spring at the front of the business district that was developing. The water was described as "sweet," and the Indian term for "sweet" was *culle,* while the term for "water" was *oka.* One source claims that this is the last place in Tennessee retaining its original Indian name. The same source states that the village was platted in 1857. The local post office was known as Pleasant Grove until 1860.

Cumberland City *Stewart County.* Cumberland County, England, is believed to have inspired the place-name at this site, although it is located on the Cumberland River. This community dates back to 1814. At an early time, it was known as New Lisbon, and at another time as Bowling Green. The Bowling Green name was discarded because of the existence of too many Bowling Greens elsewhere. Nathan Thomas is credited with laying out the town. The land was owned by Thomas, William Gift, or Major Irwin, depending upon which source is to be believed.

Cumberland Furnace *Dickson County.* The "Cumberland" part of the name traces eventually to Cumberland County, England, or to the second son of George II, William Augustus Cumberland (1721–1765), who was a duke. The "Furnace" segment is credited to "the father of Middle Tennessee," General James Robertson. Robertson in 1793 established the first furnace west of the Allegheny. Co-owners of the operation were Anthony Vanleer, J. P. Drouillard, Montgomery Bell, the Southern Iron Company, Joe Warner, the Buffalo Iron Company, and Warner Brothers Iron Company. The furnace's last owner, in 1942, was Roger Calwell. A thriving community existed here.

Cumberland Gap *Claiborne County.* Reference is to the Cumberland Mountains and the nearby gap through which thousands of pioneers traveled to the West and South. The Cumberland Gap National Park is partially located in this sector of the county.

Cumberland Heights *Grundy County.* The hamlet is situated on the Cumberland Plateau.

Cumberland Springs *Rhea County.* Local springs discovered here by early settlers account for part of the name. For the "Cumberland" part, refer to the preceding entry.

Cumberland View *Campbell County.* One of the higher elevations in the county is called Cumberland Mountain. The Cumberland range cuts across this (northeast) region of Tennessee. (Also see Cumberland references in preceding entries.)

Cummings *White County.* According to the *History of Tennessee Illustrated: White, Warren, DeKalb, Coffee, and Cannon Counties,* a merchant named J. J. Cummings did business in the area in the 1800s. There is likely a link between him and this hamlet.

Cummings Crossroads *Sumner County.* Numerous Cummingses resided near this junction in 1870. Some of them, and their ages at that time, were Jessee, 22; V. M., 27; Hahley, 37; Enoch, 51; Mordecar (Mordecai?), 58; Peggy, 70; F., 25; and Richerson, 52. Another source mentions seven Cummingses, including S. E., a farmer born in 1830 who arrived here in 1841. Children of S. E. and Sarah included John E., Thomas E., and Mabel.

Cummingsville *Van Buren County.* In 1850, Joseph, G. P., and W. B. Cummings resided in Van Buren County. Likely, one or more of them lived at this very locality, giving it its name. From another source comes the information that Gabe Cummings, an African American of this town, enlisted for military service in 1918.

Cupp Mill *Claiborne County.* Charles L., Isaac, and Jacob Cupp apparently lived nearby at the time of the 1850 census. There is a good chance that they, or someone in their family, ran a mill at this location.

Curlee *Cannon County.* There is little information pointing to how this location took on the Curlee name. There was a Calvin Curlee known to reside in Cannon County at the time of the 1840 census.

Curve *Lauderdale County.* The town arose in 1882 at a site where the railroad track has a large bend in it. The highway bisecting the community also possesses a very noticeable curve at this juncture.

Cusick *Sevier County.* In April of 1861, a post office opened here, with Andrew Cusick as postmaster. It was sometimes referred to as the Cusick Cross Roads Post Office. That is how the place-name came about. Much earlier—in 1830—David and Samuel Cusick were local citizens.

Cypress *McNairy County.* Cypress Creek ran alongside this place, where, in 1857, the Memphis & Charleston Railroad came through. A site called Cypress Tank held water for the trains, pumped from Cypress Creek. In time, the location became known as simply Cypress.

Cypress Inn *Wayne County.* Located on Big Cypress Creek, this place takes its name from the creek and an inn (or "stand") along the Natchez Trace. Later (1836), it became a post office village.

Dale Hollow *Clay County.* William Dale resided in bordering Overton County in 1850. Twenty years later, a portion of Overton went to help constitute Clay County. Elizabeth Dale is also listed as a local resident. The map designation may owe to one or both of these individuals, although some believe attribution of the place-name goes to an 1808 settler named William Dale (possibly an ancestor of the one named above?), who was engaged in determining the Tennessee-Kentucky boundary.

Dallas Hills *Hamilton County.* This location in rolling countryside derives its name from a U.S. secretary of the treasury under Madison, Alexander James Dallas. Dallas, who passed away in 1817, at various times was a financier, educator, attorney, and political figure.

Dancyville *Haywood County.* The first merchants here were John Sutherland and Fennell T. Carpenter, who, more or less, established the community in 1837. The story is found in Haywood County lore that when Sutherland and Carpenter ordered their merchandise in St. Louis, they were asked where it should be shipped. At the time, the site was without a name or post office. The vendor inquired as to whether there were any businesses in the town. The merchants replied, "Nothing but Isaac Dancy's blacksmith shop." Thus, the sellers suggested, "We will refer to it as Dancyville and ship the goods there." Down the Mississippi and up the Hatchie to Lowery's Landing the goods went, then on to Dancyville by ox cart. The first "official" mention of Dancyville appeared in court minutes early in 1838. Isaac Dancy had arrived at the locality in 1831, but families that had preceded him included those with the Emry, Koonce, Neal, Kerr, McFarland, Jones, and Johnson surnames.

Dandridge *Jefferson County (seat).* In its name, this community honors the wife of George Washington, Martha Dandridge Custis Washington. One source claims the community was laid out in 1793.

Darden *Henderson County.* The place-name is attributed to a local resident, Mills (or Miles) Darden, born in Virginia in 1799. Darden passed away in 1857, possibly from complications brought on by his great size. He is said to have been eight feet, five inches tall.

Dark's Mill *Maury County.* A water mill here was operated by Stephen (one source spells the name Stephan) Dark at an early time, where Rutherford Creek and Carter's

Creek merge. The depot was called Dark's Station. The surnames of his local contemporaries included Green, Voorhies, and Gordon.

Darnall *Lake County.* The label stems from a person named Henry M. Darnall, probably an ancestor of the first (1882) postmaster at the site, Richard Darnall. The location had formerly been known as Marr's Landing, in honor of George Washington Marr of Obion County, who became a landholder in this area.

Daus *Sequatchie County.* This community arose in the early 1800s. The area was first settled by William Stone (or Stones), who dubbed it Delphi. Stone sold large parcels of family property to Daus Rogers, but later, dissension arose between the two. Eventually, a railroad wished to built a depot on Rogers's property. Rogers gave his permission, with the stipulation that it could not be called Delphi, Stonesville, or anything similar. The railroad agreed and decided to christen it Daus.

Davenport *Warren County.* One family of settlers in this vicinity had the Davenport surname. The community traces its name to them.

Davidson *Fentress County.* A person who owned mines here is said to be the source of the place-name.

Davis Chapel *Campbell County.* Land for the community's church and school was donated by the Davis family.

Daylight *Warren County.* An account in an early Warren County history includes more than one version of the possible name selection process. The most entertaining one holds that Harvey Dodd, Oliver Towles, and U. S. Knight were conferring on what to name the hamlet. It is said that Knight preferred "Knight," but the others dissented, with Dodd opining that he would prefer "daylight" to "Knight." Some, however, subscribe to the belief that Daylight was one of three names submitted, the others being Yager (for local storekeeper Edward Yager) and Hickory Grove. Obviously, Daylight won out.

Day's Crossroads *Macon County.* At the time of the 1850 census, Thomas B. Day was a local citizen. It is likely he resided near the intersecting roads here. Another source discloses the presence of the Day surname in area businesses. Turner, Day, & Woolworth Manufacturing produced ax handles in nearby Lafayette, while Day & Allen operated a stage line, with service between Lafayette and nearby county seats.

Daysville *Cumberland County.* Although little detail could be found, the place is said to have been named for a pioneer with the surname of Days (or Day). A family having this last name is said to have settled on Mammy's Creek. In 1901, George W. Day was appointed postmaster.

Dayton *Rhea County (seat).* Dayton, Ohio, is the namesake of this community, which in turn was named for the Honorable Jonathan Dayton (1760–1824), a soldier in the Revolution, member of Congress, and delegate to the Constitutional Convention. In 1925, Dayton, Tennessee, was the site of the famous Scopes "Monkey Trial," which showcased the oratorical skills of William Jennings Bryan.

Deanburg *Chester County.* Located a mile from the Hardeman County line, this site was once probably part of Hardeman County, which contributed land toward the composition of Chester County. Hardeman County residents in 1850 included John A., Ansley, Wiley, William R., and Charles Dean. It is likely this community was home to one or more of these Dean families.

DeArmond *Roane County.* Two DeArmonds lived in this vicinity at the time of the 1880 census. They were S. J. (a male), age 64, and Joseph, 27. It is likely their family name had become attached to this place.

Deason *Bedford County.* This designation probably comes from the family name of Enoch Deason.

DeBusk *Greene County.* Sealy and Elijah DeBusk are named on the rolls of the 1840 census as residing in this county. It is likely the place-name is associated in some way with them.

Decatur *Meigs County (seat).* U.S. Navy Commodore Stephen F. Decatur (1779–1820) fought in the War of 1812 as well as in struggles against the Barbary pirates. He inspired the naming of a number of U.S. places, including this one. In 1820, he was mortally wounded in a duel with another officer. He is credited with having uttered the often-quoted line, "May she always be in the right; but our country, right or wrong."

Decaturville *Decatur County (seat).* The explanation of this place-name is the same as for Decatur. (See Decatur entry.)

Decherd *Franklin County.* Four Decherds—Peter S., David, Benjamin, and Jon—are mentioned in the county census rolls of 1840. This site's name probably relates in some way to their family or families. By 1870, fourteen Decherds were listed in the index of the county census.

Deen's *Hickman County.* This community name is sometimes seen styled as Deen's Switch, or even as Dean's. The railroad switching site that was once located here handled mostly logs and phosphate. The town is the namesake of Ransom Deen, who managed the phosphate mines and had a general store at the locality. He also was proprietor of a good deal of the surrounding real estate. According to *A Patchwork History of Hickman County,* Deen's mines and store closed about 1908. Born in Centerville in 1810, Deen is said to have lived to the age of 96.

Deerfield *Lawrence County.* So many deer were attracted to a salt lick here that the site became known as Deerfield. Earlier, it was known as Abner, in honor of an early citizen. The post office was known as Abner at least as far back as 1881, until it was closed in 1913.

Deer Lodge *Morgan County.* Deer were plentiful here in settlement times. One native believes the place took its name from the "fights" or jousting between bucks, when their horns would lock or "lodge" together. From the *Deer Lodge Centennial, 1894–1994* publication, this statement is taken: "I came to the deer lodge." This may have been a platform erected in a tree, or merely the place where bucks locked antlers during mating season. An earlier name of the locale was Dead Level. In 1884, Abner Ross bought six hundred acres here and platted the town. The earliest permanent resident at the place may have been James Davidson, who purchased three hundred acres in about 1813.

Del Rio *Cocke County.* The Spanish translation of this term is "of the river." A person named Swan L. Burnett decided the place should bear this name instead of Big Creek.

Delano *Polk County.* An earlier name for the location was Prendergast, after a family that operated the local cotton mill. The mill closed and was taken over by new management in 1931; so the name was changed to Delano, after Franklin Delano Roosevelt.

Dellrose *Lincoln County.* Dellrose arose about 1867; "Hog" Bruce is considered the founder. One *l* was omitted from the name, making it Delrose, when the railroad influence was asserted later on. D. C. Sherrell (Sherrill?) became one of its best-known residents and businessmen. There are a number of versions of how this place was so named. Some of them are somewhat similar. One has it that Sherrell conferred the name, construed as being in a "dell of roses," a reference to the many wild rosebushes growing locally. An earlier name was Maryville, but since there was another town by that name in Tennessee, this one assumed its second name, Roosterville, prior to the current label. (There were numerous buzzards roosting in area trees.) Some historians state that an early settler had daughters named Dell and Rose, who were honored in the town's naming.

Denmark *Madison County.* The site owes its name to the Scandinavian country.

Denny *Putnam County.* One map lists a community called Denny Seminary in Putnam County, an institution that was probably located at this site. In 1870, three Dennys resided nearby: James, age 52; John S., 44; and Johnathan, 50.

Denson's Landing *Perry County.* Two Densons named William and one named Mary resided near here when the 1850 census was recorded. The family probably had close ties to this hamlet.

Denton *Cocke County.* In about 1785, Captain John Denton settled at this place and established a mill on the Big Pigeon River. Numerous Dentons dotted the rolls by 1870. Abraham, age 38, was one of them. Others included John B., 52; Nancy, 65; Thomas, 30; William, 31; Isaac, 47; William, 57; John, 47; and Jefferson, 60.

Desha *Sumner County.* Either from the way it was pronounced or due to a transcription error, this designation differs slightly in spelling from the surname of the individual to whom it traces: Robert Deshay, in 1830, a merchant in Gallatin.

Detroit *Tipton County.* Probably inspired by the prominence of Detroit, Michigan, this designation traces back to the French term for "strait."

Diana *Giles County.* Contemporary county archivists can only speculate that this designation honored a woman residing in the area at the time of naming.

Dibrell *Warren County.* There were many Dibrells in this region, some in Warren County and some in White County, just to the northeast. A General Dibrell served in the Civil War. Among the Dibrells who populated this general area were Anthony, Mary E., Mildred, G. G., M., C., W. C., W. L., and George G.

Dickson *Dickson County.* Like the county, this community traces its name to a Nashville physician, Dr. William Dickson. For a time, he served in the state House of Representatives, and later was elected to Congress. An earlier name of the location was Smeadville (or Sneadville, or Sneedsville), after a civil engineer, E. C. Smead, responsible for locating a rail siding here. The Sneadville spelling apparently was the result of the application being misread and processed incorrectly by the Post Office Department. Later, when it was discovered that a Sneedville existed in Hancock County, the Dickson name was adopted. When the Union army was constructing a railroad here during the Civil War, the place was designated Mile Post 42.

Difficult *Smith County.* Either the establishment of a post office at this site, or a name suggested for such an office, was rejected by the Post Office Department as being too difficult; whereupon the designation Difficult itself was adopted.

Dill *Bledsoe County.* This name may trace back to a local mail carrier named Eli Dill. Another local person, John Dill, served as sheriff of Bledsoe County for a time. The cemetery is referred to variously as the Dill or Rainey Cemetery, because of the number of persons buried there who had one of these two common area surnames. In the mid-twentieth century, local land was purchased from a Mr. Dill for the purpose of erecting a new school building that would eliminate several localized school buildings. After that, the Dill name became more widely applied—such as to the school and the voting precinct.

Dilton *Rutherford County.* According to an article by Gene Sloan, quoting the investigations of Rebecca Smith, the label memorializes a beloved, one-time local physician, Dr. James M. Dill. One source styles the name Dillton.

Disney *Campbell County.* John, Elisha, and Elisha A. Disney lived at or near this juncture in 1880. Their ages at the time were 55, 23, and 45. The site likely took on the family name as a result of these persons, or related predecessors, living close by. A Lillian Disney was associated with the Vasper Baptist Church. From 1899 to 1900, Andrew Disney was the Vasper postmaster, followed by John H. Disney (1901–1902) and Andrew Disney (1903–1904).

Ditty *Putnam County.* Abraham and John Ditty were local citizens in 1830. Andy, Derry, A. H., and Sarah Ditty lived in the county when the 1870 census was taken. The place-name probably traces back to these families.

Dixon Springs *Smith County.* In 1799, the first county court convened for a three-day meeting at the home of Major Tillman Dixon. The locality was labeled Dixon Springs, for a freshwater spring on the west side of Major Dixon's home. The creek feeding the area is Dixon Creek, and the historical home, which still stands, is known as Dixonia. An obscure reference is also found in old county records to a Don C. Dixon, circa 1837. Any connection between the two is not readily evident.

Doak's Crossroads *Wilson County.* Residing nearby in 1850 were Robert, Martha, and Elizabeth Doak. In 1840, John F. Doak was a local citizen. This place-name probably traces back to one or more of these individuals.

Dodd's Mill *Wayne County.* Upon recording of the state's 1850 census, Elijah Dodd was a local citizen. It is likely he was somehow associated with the mill.

Dodson *Roane County.* A number of persons with the Dodson surname were local residents in 1880. Among them were Henry, age 33; Willilalm (possibly misspelled in recording the census), 70; a female with the initials M. J., 52; Hariet, 15; and William, 23. The surname of these folks, or their ancestors, probably became attached to the place.

Dodson Branch *Jackson County.* Although the site designated as Dodson Branch is on the opposite side of the county from Smith County, there may be a relationship to the Dodsons of Smith County. (A portion of Smith County contributed to the makeup of Jackson County.) James Dodson was a Smith County resident in 1840. "Branch" refers to a branch of Spring Creek.

Dogtown *Polk County.* Dogtown, located between Ducktown and Turtletown, was previously known as Carrolltown. It is located near the junction of three states. Two of them—North Carolina and Georgia—taxed both chickens and dogs. As a result, many of the out-of-staters would haul their unwanted dogs over the Tennessee line and dump them here, in the area that became known as Dogtown.

Dogwood Mudhole *Wayne County.* A local historian writes, "A mudhole on the Natchez Trace . . . was full of dogwood trees. In Summer, it was a dust bowl, but rain turned it into a huge mudhole."

Donelson *Davidson County.* Andrew Jackson's father-in-law was John Donelson. The community takes its name from him.

Donnel Chapel *Rutherford County.* Quite a few Donnell-surnamed individuals resided nearby in 1870. Among them were Chesley, age 55; Elvira, 25; A. B., 62; Newton, 25; John, 42; Jack, 33; C. S., 41; and George, 30.

Donoho *Smith County.* E. C. and F. W. Donoho are known to have lived in Smith County when the 1830 census of Middle Tennessee was recorded. One of them, or one of their ancestors or descendants, probably inspired this site to be so designated.

Dorton *Cumberland County.* According to *Cumberland County's First Hundred Years,* this location was named for James W. Dorton. The name was assigned about 1900 by railroad officials out of respect for Dorton, who served as their local attorney. When the 1870 census was taken, Azariah, Joseph, and Nancy Dorton also called this county home.

Dossett *Anderson County.* In the 1800s, Jacob and Cynthia Dossett resided at this site, according to one of their grandchildren. They are buried in a family cemetery near the site where they resided. Also buried at Dossett are their son—Robert Fletcher Dossett—and his wife, Mary Edna. Both a nearby Southern Railway station and the Louisville & Nashville (L&N) station used the Dossett name for identification.

Dotsontown *Greene County.* Although it is not known specifically to which Dotson the town name traces, the community in the late 1990s still was populated by many persons having this surname.

Doty's Chapel *Greene County.* Ephraim and Jesse Doty were local residents in 1840. One of them may have donated land or materials for a church, and/or pastored a congregation here.

Double Springs *Putnam County.* There are said to be five mineral springs at this locality. Perhaps only two of them were discovered at first, inspiring the Double Springs name.

Douglas *Williamson County.* When the 1870 census was taken, twelve county persons with the Douglass surname were counted. (The concluding s may have been dropped from the place-name over time.) Included were Elizabeth, Ella, Tabitha, Martha J., Hugh, and Samuel Douglass. Earlier still, for the 1830 Middle Tennessee census, Thomas L. Douglass and John Douglass were listed as residing nearby.

Dover *Hamblen County.* Reference is probably to the port city on the English Channel. However, *American Place-Names* suggests that many applications of this label in the South were inspired by the Dover Association Report (1832), "which caused many churches of the Baptist and Christian denominations to take that name."

Dover *Stewart County (seat).* Incorporation took place in 1820, although the location was settled late in the previous century and initially known as Monroe. Many of the citizens were English, and the pale, whitish bluffs along the nearby Cumberland River conjured up images of the "white cliffs of Dover," in England; so the designation Dover replaced Monroe. The town's most recent rechartering was in 1954.

Dowelltown *DeKalb County.* The settlement was developed beginning in about 1867 by W. Frank Dowell, after whom the post office was named. Later, the town itself became known by his surname. One source gives 1876 as the year of founding. Incorporation took place in 1949.

Doyle *White County.* This surname occurred locally. Early records mention John Doyle Jr. and Adelphia Doyle White. One historical source states, "An early resident of Irish descent with the Doyle surname" inspired this place-name.

Draper's Crossroads *Macon County.* Isaac and Joshua Draper lived nearby in 1850. By 1870, Andrew J. Draper, age 48, was a resident of the neighborhood. The intersection was probably named for them, or some member(s) of the Draper clan. One map calls the community simply Draper.

Dresden *Weakley County (seat).* Mears Warner (1799–1863) is credited with naming the place in honor of Dresden, Germany, his father's birthplace. Mears arrived at the site as a commissioner, authorized to lay out a town. A second source states simply that the site was settled by German immigrants.

Drummonds *Tipton County.* The Tennessee 1850 census rolls disclose that two men having a surname pronounced like this place-name called Tipton County home in that year. Their given names were James and Mack, but the census listing spells their surnames as Drummons. (In recording, the names may have been misspelled.)

Dry Creek *Washington County.* Located at the foot of Buffalo Mountain, this "sometime stream" often had no water in it. Thus, the hamlet that arose here came to be known as Dry Creek.

Ducktown *Polk County.* At one time, this site was known as Hiwassee Town. Edward Mueller, a mine captain in the 1870s, did the surveying. Copper mining was the principal industry. The current name honors the memory of Chief Duck, a Cherokee who befriended the white settlers. According to legend, he is buried in the hills nearby. Incorporation took place in 1951.

Ducktown *Washington County.* This site was probably settled in the mid-1800s. Numerous ducks were a common sight, sitting on a large pond located here, thus suggesting the name.

Dudney Hill *Jackson County.* In 1850, Patrick N. and Shelby Dudney resided in this vicinity. However, as early as 1820, records show the local residency of Anne Dudney. It is likely their surname was applied to the community at this elevation.

Duff *Campbell County.* Captain Frank Duff was one of those who settled here in 1868.

Dukedom *Weakley County.* The first merchant and postmaster, Duke A. Beadler, is the town's namesake. The community was founded in 1830.

Dumplin *Jefferson County.* The appearance of Dumplin Valley is believed to have given this community its name. One source states, "On both sides of the valley, there are rows of hills that remind the viewer of rows of dumplings."

Dunbar *Decatur County.* It is said that a man named Dunn owned and operated a tavern here. Gradually, the site began to be known as Dunbar, or "The Dunbar Community."

Duncantown *Franklin County.* Several families surnamed Duncan settled this site in an early year. At one time, it consisted of a tanning yard and several small industries. His great-great-great-grandson writes that the name traces back to John Hawkins Duncan, who came to the state in 1834. Reportedly, Duncan in 1840 purchased two hundred acres of land and a house for $8,125. Eventually, he owned some two thousand acres, and after the Civil War the area became known as Duncantown. At this writing (1997), much of the land still belongs to members of the Duncan family. The name is also seen styled as Duncan Town. It is interesting to note that thirty-eight persons surnamed Duncan are found on the rolls of the 1870 county census. Among those Duncans are Walter, Telitha, Emily, Joseph, Robert, Missouri, and Alfred.

Dunlap *Sequatchie County (seat).* Dunlap was incorporated in 1909. In 1858, it was still known as Coop's Creek, but yet that year the name was changed to Dunlap, for one of the community's leading residents, James Dunlap.

Dunn *Lawrence County.* Not long after the conclusion of the Civil War, a businessman named Thomas Dunn came to this site and settled down. When the railroad was extended south from Lawrenceburg, Dunn donated a great many crossties; so the depot was dubbed Dunn Station. Sometimes the place is referred to as New Carbon (or Nucarbon) because of a National Carbon plant that operated here.

Dupont *Sevier County.* This name is sometimes seen styled as DuPont, although some historians feel the designation does not come from a family name, but rather is an adaptation of the words "dew point." The community is located in the "knobs" area, and the name may have been inspired by springs originating on Chilhowee Mountain "above the dew point."

Durhamville *Lauderdale County.* The founder of this town was Thomas Durham, a militia colonel.

Dutch Valley *Anderson County.* Dutch settlers originally settled this location. At least one of them had the surname Shinliver, reports a descendant.

Dycus *Bradley County.* Local residents in 1840 included James and John Dycus, probably members of a family that settled here in an early year and who gave their surname to the site.

Dyer *Gibson County.* Dyer was incorporated in 1899. Like Dyersburg, seat of adjoining Dyer County, Dyer traces its name ultimately to Colonel Robert Henry Dyer (see following entry), a well-known combatant during the Indian wars. Originally known as Dyer Station, this site may have been so named in an attempt to siphon off business headed for Dyer County or Dyersburg.

Dyersburg *Dyer County (seat).* Incorporation took place in 1836. The city derives its name from Dyer County, which was designated for a prominent Indian fighter, Colonel Robert Henry Dyer. Some sources contend that Joel H. Dyer, another Indian fighter, shares credit for the place-name. McIver's Bluff was the label once accorded this site.

Eagan *Claiborne County.* Two possibilities for the naming of Eagan are set forth in *Clearfork and More,* by Bonnie Page. One suggests that the town takes its name from an Atlanta financier, A. M. Eagan, who was also an official of a mining company operating locally. The other version states that the Campbell brothers opened a coal mine here in 1903, with a post office following in 1908. The brothers had a good friend, an Atlanta minister named Eagan, and requested that the post office be christened Eagan.

Eagleton Village *Blount County.* The development takes its name from Eagleton School, which in turn was named after an early local settler, David Eagleton. Its nucleus was housing built starting in 1941 for workers at a nearby Alcoa plant, staffing up for World War II production.

Eagleville *Rutherford County.* Nancy and Absalom Scales may have been the first settlers here, in 1790. According to local lore, Chesley Williams killed a large eagle in the wilderness near the settlement, resulting in the place becoming known as Eagleville. At one time, Manchester was the designation for the place, but apparently there was another Manchester in the state, so a change was agreed upon. Incorporation took place in 1949.

East Cleveland *Bradley County.* This community is just east of Cleveland. (See Cleveland entry.)

East Etowah *McMinn County.* This community is just east (actually, *southe*ast) of Etowah. (See Etowah entry.)

East Fork *Sevier County.* East Fork takes its name from the east fork of the Little Pigeon River. The community is located on this tributary. It was settled as early as the end of the 1780s.

East Jamestown *Fentress County.* East Jamestown is located about two miles east of Jamestown, the county seat. (See entry for Jamestown.)

East Kingsport *Sullivan County.* East Kingsport is located east of Kingsport. (See Kingsport entry.)

Eastland *White County.* Local records disclose the marriages of several Eastlands: George and Charles, both in 1855, and Robert M. in 1843. Thomas Eastland held a large parcel of land here; the place is probably named after him. Were it not for the existence of persons with this surname, one might assume the designation was due to the hamlet's location, in the extreme eastern portion of the county.

East Miller's Cove *Blount County.* The Miller's Cove communities take their name from an early settler having the Miller surname, who eventually relocated from this area. East Miller's Cove may have been known as Waters Town. The "Cove" part of the designation refers to where the Little River has cut a cove into the shoreline. Logically, it is east of West Miller's Cove.

Eastport *Pickett County.* Eastport is located on the Obey River, and no doubt goods were shipped on the river from this location, accounting for the "port." The "East" part of the name is somewhat mystifying; the town is in one of the southernmost sections of the county.

East Ridge *Hamilton County.* This name may be interpreted as "east of the ridge," the reference being to Missionary Ridge. It is also slightly east of Chattanooga. *What's in a Name?* states that previous names here included Penny Row, Smokey Row, and Nickel Row. Incorporation took place in the 1920s.

Eastside *Dickson County.* This place-name may be seen styled as two words. It was so named for its location within the county.

Eastview *McNairy County.* A family with the Littlejohn surname established a three-room dwelling and a filling station here in 1927. These first buildings faced east, and consequently it took on the name Eastview. Incorporation dates to 1969 or 1967, depending upon which source is correct.

Eaton *Gibson County.* The community was founded in 1824 by J. W. Buckner and dubbed Buckner's Bluff. Three years later the name was changed to honor President Andrew Jackson's secretary of war, John Eaton.

Eaton Crossroads *Loudon County.* This name probably leads back to one of the early residents of the area having this surname. James, John, and Elijah Eaton were listed as taxpayers as early as 1808. Others mentioned in early records include Marv, Julia, and Mrs. R. P. Eaton.

Ebenezer *Knox County.* A cabin was erected here in about 1786 by an individual named Ebenezer Byram (or Biram), whose given name clung to the site.

Ebenezer *Marion County.* Applied as a place-name, this label is usually biblically inspired. One source states that it means "stone of help."

Eden Corner *Robertson County.* This intersection was named for an Eden family who resided in the area many decades ago.

Edgemont *Cocke County.* Land for a school in this neighborhood was donated by Governor Ben W. Hooper and his wife. An early school building was situated at the edge of English Mountain; thus the site became known as Edgemont.

Edison *Gibson County.* At one time, there was a school here called the Edison Institute, in honor of Thomas A. Edison, the inventor. The institution was known previously as Atkins School.

Edwina *Cocke County.* For some unknown reason, John F. Stanbery dubbed this site Edwina. At earlier times, it bore the names Taylorsburg and Sweetwater. It was still Sweetwater when the time came to open a post office. Then, it was discovered there was another Sweetwater in Tennessee, and Stanbery came up with the accepted new name.

Eidson *Hawkins County.* Only two Eidsons could be found mentioned in early local records, and both of those individuals lived in the twentieth century—George A. Eidson, born in 1920, and Gladys Goins Eidson, who lived from 1925 until 1972. It is possible that their forebears are responsible for the name.

Elbethel *Bedford County.* The usual style for such a name is El Bethel. A Baptist church here used the name. (See explanation for towns named Bethel.)

Elbridge *Obion County.* The town utilizes the given name of a physician who at one time resided here and was well respected, Elbridge Richardson. At an earlier time, due to a large stand of stately beech trees at the site, it was known as Beech Point.

Elizabethton *Carter County (seat).* This venerable community was first established by legislative act in 1799. The name traces to Landon Carter's wife, Elizabeth MacLin Carter. A separate source states that the community has existed since 1797.

Elkins Switch *Hickman County.* Information on the place-name is sketchy. An Elkins family lived in the vicinity, and the railroad switch here assumed their name.

Elkmont *Sevier County.* According to *Tennessee: A Guide to the State,* an excursion of Knoxville Elks members to the site caused it to be referred to as Elks' Mountain. This later was shortened to Elkmont.

Elkton *Giles County.* Herds of elk once roamed this locality in considerable numbers. The suffix *ton* is usually construed as "town"—thus, Elk Town. The Elk River flows nearby. James and William Price laid out a town, possibly between 1807 and 1810, and began selling lots. The settlement was known as Elkton. Later, three miles upstream, Dr. William Purnell and others laid out another community. To avoid confusion, one became referred to as Lower Elkton and the other Upper Elkton. "Lower" eventually waned and the remaining one became simply Elkton.

Elk Valley *Campbell County.* A well-known hunter, Colonel James Dysart, is believed to have referred to this area as Elk Valley in 1765, due to numerous elk in the region.

Ellejoy *Blount County.* This name is said to derive from the Native American words *Eilah Jay,* which refer to Owl Creek.

Ellendale *Shelby County.* This label falls in the category of railroad-inspired placenames. The Louisville & Nashville (L&N) line ran through here. The descriptive suffix *dale* is believed to have been appended to "L 'n' N" (Ellen).

Ellistown *Knox County.* In 1830, Abner Ellis claimed local residence, as reflected in the East Tennessee census for that year. It is likely that the community was named for him.

Elm Grove *Tipton County.* American elms and slippery elms grew throughout Tennessee. This site was named for a prominent stand of one variety or the other.

Elm Springs *Grainger County.* This natural water source was encircled by the elms that once flourished across the region.

Elmwood *Smith County.* See explanation for preceding entry.

Embreeville *Washington County.* A pair of anti-slavery Quakers, Eluhu and Thomas Embree, are the persons to whom this place-name leads. In a 1797 edition of the *Knoxville Gazette,* Embree is quoted as urging the formation of an abolition society.

Emery Gap *Roane County.* Variant spellings of Emery include Emory, Emeries, Embry, and Embree. The name is commonly applied in this vicinity, with other venues including Emery Heights and the Emery River. It apparently traces back to a Revolutionary War soldier, William Emery. In the course of an expedition during the Indian wars (ca. 1779), Emery attempted to swim the river while laden down with too much gear and drowned. Subsequently, the stream was dubbed the Emery River.

Emmett *Sullivan County.* Several persons whose surnames were pronounced the same as this place-name resided in the county when the 1850 census was taken. William Emmet, Peter Emmit, and John Emmitt were three. The spelling variations may be those actually used by the individuals, or they may have resulted from copying or reading errors when the census was recorded. In any event, the label on this site likely is connected to one or more of these individuals. Thirty years later, the names of George Emmett and Ruth Emmett were listed in local census records. George was 30 at the time, and Ruth was 59.

Emory Heights *Roane County.* Emory Heights arose above the banks of the Emory (or Emery) River.

Englewood *McMinn County.* To Nannie Chesnutt, an avid reader as a child, the name Englewood conjured up visions of Robin Hood's forested fictional home. So she nominated it as the name for this community, and her recommendation was accepted.

English *Cocke County.* A church was organized near this spot, and held services in James English's house. The place probably assumed his surname as a site name. The place of worship was termed the Big Pigeon Primitive Baptist Church, being near the Pigeon River.

Eno *Dickson County.* A 1975 edition of the *Dickson Free Press* carried an article that discussed the origin of this place-name. A family having the Walker surname arrived by covered wagon from Virginia in the early 1800s, settling here. The wife's given name was Piney. Other families soon joined them, forming a close-knit community of mostly farmers. In 1844, after a good crop year, Mr. Walker suggested to his neighbors that they should "build a church house." The men set to work cutting logs, snaking them to the chosen location using horses and oxen. The round logs were squared with broadaxes, notched and saddled with saws and axes. It is recounted that Walker climbed atop a high stack of logs and shouted, "We have enough logs now." Upon completion of the building the workers felt the need for an appropriate name for the church. Someone suggested the name Eno, said to be contracted from the word "enough."

Enon *Macon County.* In the New Testament, a site called Aenon is mentioned. This designation is probably a shortened version of it, and was probably favored because it was terse and euphonious.

Ensor *Putnam County.* The only Ensor who can be placed in this general area was Ruth, a Jackson County resident in 1830. Jackson County is immediately north of Putnam and portions of it were taken to help make up Putnam. Probably in the portion taken from Jackson was this community of Ensor.

Enterprise *Maury County.* After a mill and store arose at this location, the hamlet seemed to give early indications that it would become an "enterprising" community.

Enville *Chester County.* Nineteen forty-three is the year of incorporation. Early on, this locality was known as Wild Goose, for the many geese attracted to the millpond formed on White Oak Creek by a gristmill established by W. R. Hardin. The hamlet had a busy commercial and social life, and in time residents came to consider the Wild Goose label as undignified. The change to Enville honored B. A. Enroe, their congressman.

Ephesus *Carroll County.* According to *Harper's Bible Dictionary,* Ephesus was a port city of western Asia Minor, between Smyrna and Miletus. It is mentioned numerous times in the Acts of the Apostles and in 1 Corinthians.

Erie *Loudon County.* The name comes from the Erie Indians. It is thought to translate as "cat," or "the nation of the cats." In the Huron tongue, *eriche* or *erige* is thought to signify "lake of the cats." The name is believed to refer to a species of wildcat that frequented the region occupied by the Erie Indians.

Erin *Houston County (seat).* Three of the earliest settlers at this site were natives of Ireland. According to oral history, they were aboard a train journeying through this region and were taken with the beauty of the spot, which reminded them of Ireland. They decided to settle here, so Erin (a poetic name for Ireland) served as a reference to their homeland. The locale was, indeed, green and fertile and reminiscent of Ireland. One account claims the Erin label was bestowed by Irish immigrants working on local railroads in 1859 or 1860. According to the story, some alcoholic libations led to a fistfight, and onlookers shouted, "Erin Go Bragh!" Surnames of some of the earliest Irish and Scotch-Irish families to settle this vicinity included McDonald, McMillan, McAuley, McKinsey, and McLeod. They arrived between 1810 and 1825, but they were not the first settlers in the area.

Erwin *Unicoi County (seat).* The person who deeded the real estate for the townsite—Dr. J. N. Erwin—was honored with the naming of the community. Previous labels for the site included Unika, Greasy Cove, and Longmire.

Estanaula *Haywood County.* A ferry on the Hatchie was located at this site. The designation is said to be Cherokee for "here we cross."

Estill Springs *Franklin County.* A widely acclaimed Indian fighter in the early days was James Estill. The community uses his surname as a portion of its name. Early records also refer to Dr. William Estill, mentioned in the 1840 county census records, and Dr. Wallis Estill. As with so many Tennessee hamlets, springs undoubtedly bubbled nearby.

Ethridge *Lawrence County.* Nineteen seventy-three marked the year of incorporation. The place-name is a misspelled version of the surname of a state legislator and congressman, Emerson Etheridge. A local storekeeper is said to have been a strong booster of Etheridge for governor, and was successful in influencing the railroad to adopt the name. Etheridge sought the state's highest office in 1867 but was unsuccessful. Earlier names of this juncture were Hudson's Spring or simply, the "Kerpleinker place." Two versions of the Ethridge spelling occur in this vicinity, the other being Etheridge. Thomas Etheridge resided in Lawrence County in 1820, while Luis, Thomas, Rhody, and John Ethridge were Hickman County residents. The last three named were listed in the 1820 census rolls, while Luis was on the rolls in 1870. A portion of Hickman County became part of Lawrence County.

Etowah *McMinn County.* The meaning of this Native American term is unclear. Some speculate that it may mean "town," while others claim that it translates as "muddy water" or "muddy waters," and was so named by workers building the railroad. The Cherokees termed two of their encampments *Etowah.* A separate source speculates that this term of vague meaning is Creek or Cherokee in origin, and may translate as "tribe," "high tower," or "village."

Eureka *Hardin County.* Meaning "I have found it" in Greek, this designation was popular with settlers feeling that they had located "just the right spot" to send down roots, according to the *Illustrated Dictionary of Place Names.*

Eureka *Roane County.* See preceding entry.

Eurekaton *Haywood County.* This community was first called Eureka, from the exclamation by Greek mathematician Archimedes (see entry for Eureka, Hardin County); however, when the existence of another Eureka in Tennessee was discovered, the *ton* was appended in order to make the name distinctive.

Eva *Benton County.* This community arose about 1868. The accepted account is that the postmaster in 1882, Thomas Lowery, gave the village its name. Eva was Eva Steele, a childhood friend of his daughter, Lola. A previous name of the location was Bartlett's Switch.

Evensville *Rhea County.* Residing in the county in 1821 was an individual named Andrew Evens. It is likely that this community owes its name to him, or a member of his family.

Evins Mill *DeKalb County.* In 1870, John Evins, then age 51, resided in this county. It is likely he, or some member of his family, ran a mill at this location and gave the family name to the site.

Ewingville *Williamson County.* At the time the 1850 census was taken, Felix, Martha, and H. S. Ewing resided nearby, in all probability lending their surname to the community.

F

Factory *Wayne County.* A local authority states that this name has been badly corrupted from the original label. Factor's Stand was an inn and trading post along the Natchez Trace. The first "factor" (or trader) became known as Old Factor. Later, a younger man became the factor, and the place was known as Young Factor's Stand, on a branch of Sycamore Shoals River. The branch became known as Factor's Branch of Shoals Creek, which was then corrupted into Factory Creek. Finally, some maps carried only the Factory label.

Fairfield *Bedford County.* This town resulted from the consolidation of three small local settlements: Davisville, Garrison Fork, and Petersburg. The union took place about 1840. The name was probably pulled out of the air as being descriptive and appealing for the new entity.

Fairview *Clay County.* "From Fairview, the scene was beautiful and fair, with a clear and scenic view for many miles, over hills and vales," writes a local resident.

Fairview *Williamson County.* This vantage point afforded early residents a "fair view" of the surroundings.

Falcon *McNairy County.* According to oral history, the community adopted its name from a man named Falcon. It sprang up in the early 1870s along the Mobile & Ohio Railroad.

Fall Branch *Washington County.* According to one source, there is a forty-foot waterfall near this hamlet, which inspired the name of both the community and the stream. A flour mill was once situated near the head of the falls. A second source offers the opinion that a schoolteacher provided the Fall Branch name, citing a nearby seventy-five-foot-high waterfall dropping over a bluff near the village. This local source also pointed to several springs of ice-cold water that fed the creek running through the community and over the bluff. The springs created many "branches" of water. She adds that the site was once known as Crouchtown, for one or more local families having the Crouch surname. The current name is sometimes seen styled as Falls Branch.

Falling Water *Hamilton County.* This site is near an area of swiftly moving streams (one of them called Falling Water Creek) that cascade over rocks, creating a sound that can be heard for some distance. The cascades are known as Falling Water Falls.

Fall River *Lawrence County.* This site has seen a number of names over the years. Before the Civil War, it was known as Garner Falls. When the Hagen family relocated to the site (about 1862) and donated land for a school, church, and cemetery, it became known as Hagen's Chapel. A stream running through the site features three small waterfalls, resulting in the eventual name.

Farmer's Exchange *Hickman County.* This town is said to have been named by the prominent merchant-postmaster J. R. Sutton, who observed (in about 1850) that a great many farmers flocked to the site to trade in produce and other agricultural products, including cotton, corn, and peanuts. The locality was generic "Indian territory" until early in the nineteenth century, when Irish and Scottish settlers began to send down roots here. After the lumber industry and agrarian pursuits ran their course, other types of industry replaced them at this location.

Farmington *Marshall County.* Located in an ideal farming region, this community was so named because it was a "town of farmers." The *History of Tennessee* also describes the area as "a splendid farming region." Settled by or before 1809, the community was incorporated in 1830 but later surrendered its charter.

Farner *Polk County.* A local source could advise only that the place-name traces back to a member of the Farner family.

Farragut *Knox County.* During the Franco-Mexican War, the ship *Erie* was under the command (1838) of a Navy officer named David Glasgow Farragut (1801–1870). Farragut later became the first U.S. Navy admiral. He is famous for uttering the words, "Damn the torpedoes! Full speed ahead!" This community traces its name back to Admiral Farragut. Farragut was incorporated in 1981. It had once been known as Campbell's Station.

Farris Chapel *Franklin County.* Quite a few Farrises made their homes in Franklin County in 1870, probably at or near this site. Among them were Henry, age 30; Littleton, 61; Mack, 50; Saunders, 67; Susan, 49; James, 76; Thomases, ages 32, 35, and 26; William D., 59; Washington, 35; Fletcher, 57; Cheney, 30; A., 43; Henry, 30; and W. C., 55. Often, a surname was placed before a "Chapel" designation when someone of that family donated land or materials for a place of worship, ministered to a congregation there, or both.

Faulkner Springs *Warren County.* In the *Tennessee 1850 Census Index,* several Faulkners are recorded as having resided in this vicinity, where some springs undoubtedly served as a drawing card. Included were Archibald, Asa, James C., Elizabeth A., and William. *History of Tennessee Illustrated* refers to twenty persons named Faulkner in Warren County. Thomas H., a manufacturer, was born in 1842. Clay F., born in 1845, owned the Mountain City Woolen Mills.

Faxon *Benton County.* George B. Faxon was the first postmaster at the community's post office. He and his family resided here for several years. The information is found in *Historic Benton.* In other sources is found the information that Charles Faxon (b. 1799) was the patriarch of Tennessee Faxon families. He was a bookseller, printer, and journalist. In America, the Faxon name hearkens back to a Thomas Faxon, born in England in 1601, who immigrated to Braintree, Massachusetts, in 1647. By 1870, the only Faxon listed on local census rolls was Lavinia, age 30, from Humphreys County, a section of which went to help form Benton County.

Fayette Corners *Fayette County.* Like the name of the county, this designation refers to the Marquis de Lafayette, and to the fact that thoroughfares intersect here. It is also in the northeast corner of the county.

Fayetteville *Lincoln County (seat).* Like Fayette County, Tennessee, this community probably commemorates the French nobleman Marquis de Lafayette. Lafayette struggled on the side of America during its revolution and inspired sympathy for the colonies among Europeans.

Feathers' Chapel *Fayette County.* The site is named for William F. Feathers, whose family in 1917 donated land for the relocated Reeder's Grove Baptist Church. (In 1911, the church was located on the Layton Reeder farm.)

Felker *Bradley County.* Peter Felker resided in the county in 1840. He—or a relative—probably gave the surname to the location.

Few Chapel *Humphreys County.* In the *1880 Humphreys County Census,* several persons with this surname are shown to have been living locally—nine, to be precise. Included were William, 68, a farmer; Jonathan W., 18, a laborer; and Wash, 23, also a farmer. A place of worship probably characterized this site; perhaps one of the men served it part-time as minister.

Fincastle *Campbell County.* This town adopted the name of the place from which its early settlers came—Fincastle, Virginia, in the Shenandoah Valley. (Another source states that both towns are in the Powell Valley, which extends 125 miles from Caryville, Tennessee, into the state of Virginia.) Early settlers here felt the place resembled their former home in topography and general appearance. In earlier times, the site was labeled Glade Springs, for a local spring surrounded by a glade.

Finger *McNairy County.* This site was probably named for an 1860 county citizen named A. J. Finger, for reasons not clear. However, a dubious account holds that when officials would not approve the existing name, McIntyre Switch, as the name for a new post office, postal authorities submitted a list of name possibilities. Local residents were peering over the postmaster's shoulder as he pointed to each name with his finger, which covered all the names below as he did so. A jokester in the group suggested that they simply name the place Finger, and as the story goes, the label became reality. However, in the book *Reflections: A History of McNairy County, Tennessee, 1823–1996,* compilers side with the surname attribution: "The town . . . was named by Joseph Henry (Sam) Finger for his deceased father, Andrew Jackson

Finger (1815–1888)." Sam Finger was a blacksmith and veterinarian, and passed away in 1912. A third, probably fanciful, name explanation is recounted in a work by B. J. Naylor, Ed.D., and John E. Talbott: "The origin of the name centers around a heated discussion in which fingers were pointed at one another." Supposedly, someone remarked, "Well, with all this shaking of fingers, why don't we just go ahead and name it Finger?" Just as suspect is the theory that the name was adopted when an early settler moistened a finger and raised it in the air to gauge the direction of the wind. Incorporation took place in 1970.

Finley *Dyer County.* John and Thomas Finley resided locally in 1850. The site was probably named for them, ancestors, or descendants.

Fisherville *Shelby County.* In 1847, John Fisher acquired eighty-nine acres in this vicinity, accounting for the name the site retains. However, many still refer to it as Granberry, the surname of another early proprietor of large land parcels nearby.

Five Point *Lawrence County.* From this junction, thoroughfares branch out in five different directions.

Five Points *Giles County.* Pisgah Road, Green Valley Road, Britton Hollow Road, Buchanan Road, and Pisgah Pike converge here.

Five Points *Rhea County.* Five roads intersected here, resulting in the name.

Flat Creek *Bedford County.* Flat Creek takes its name from that stream, which was wide and shallow and in many places had a rock bottom. Originally, the place was known as Newsom's, from a small store located at the site. But when the post office required a name, in the 1850s, it became Flat Creek.

Flewellyn *Robertson County.* William Flewellen is listed on the 1820 census rolls as having resided nearby, probably accounting for this place-name. It is not known for certain which spelling is correct.

Flintville *Lincoln County.* Earlier names for this locality included Counts and Cunningham Station. "Cunningham" probably referred to an early merchant, co-operator of the Cunningham and Myrick enterprise, or his family. The current name honors a prominent resident, Bill Flint.

Flippin *Lauderdale County.* The town was probably named in honor of John Flippin or his sons. The elder Flippin settled here in 1822, coming from Knox County. One son, Benjamin M., became quite prominent.

Florence *Rutherford County.* An earlier name of the hamlet may have been McClure. Its current name is believed to honor Mrs. Florence Inness Anderson, and is thought to have been conferred by her father, who was agent at the railway station.

Flourville *Washington County.* One long-time resident of the locality believes this label to be the result of an early flour mill having operated at the site. Another source elaborates, stating that "there were six mills on Boone's Creek, from which Flourville probably got its name in the early 1800s."

Fly *Maury County.* Several Fly family descendants took up residency in this neighborhood. When a rail line passed through, the stop was dubbed Fly's Station, and a local store was called Fly's Store. It is believed that Maurice Fly was the store owner.

Flynn's Lick *Jackson County.* When the 1850 census was recorded, William, Andrew, Hiram, and George Flynn called the county home. It is likely they resided at this point, which assumed their surname and was probably near a spot where a natural salt lick attracted deer and other animals. Andrew, George, and William resided in the Eighth Civil District.

Forbus *Fentress County.* Fentress County was formed in part from Overton County lands. In 1820, there was a Mary *Forbes* residing in Overton County. In all probability, the styling of this place-name resulted from a misspelling of the Forbes surname.

Fordtown *Campbell County.* Since this community arose on the banks of a stream where the river could be forded, it assumed the name Fordtown.

Fordtown *Sullivan County.* This label adhered to the site because of the many persons with the Ford surname residing nearby. By the time of the 1880 census of East Tennessee, local Fords included Andrew, two named Benjamin, Ann, Britton, Charles, two named William, Harry, three named Henry, three named John, three named James, Daniel P., David J., Ezekiel, and George.

Forest Hills *Davidson County.* The designation is believed to have been assigned by developers, inspired by the rolling, forested land and because it had a nice "ring" to it.

Fork Mountain *Anderson County.* This was a mining community situated in the mountains. The reasoning behind the "Fork" portion of the label is unclear.

Forty-Five *Fayette County.* Located on the Norfolk & Southern Railroad, the community's name was inspired by its distance from Memphis, forty-five miles. Many years ago, the name was changed briefly to Rather, but apparently local citizens preferred Forty-Five, so it was changed back to that.

Fosterville *Rutherford County.* The first railroad station agent to serve here, Samuel Foster, was honored in the naming of the village. At an earlier time, the town center was east of the current business district.

Fountain Head *Sumner County.* According to a column authored by Pat Meguiar, the hamlet was settled by the Gwin family in 1792. The availability of freshwater was vital, and the Gwins had observed that a number of bubbling springs existed nearby, forming a tributary to the west fork of Drake's Creek. One spring in particular was dubbed Fountain Head, and overflowed to form what was referred to as the Fountain Head Fork of Drake's Creek.

Fourmile Board Hill *Wayne County.* According to a local historian, the name derives from the fact that the old Ashland Road intersected the Columbia Central Turnpike four miles east of Waynesboro, at the four-mile post. He adds that the actual name is Fourmile *Post* Hill. At least one contemporary county maps reference book, however, uses the designation of Fourmile Board Hill.

Fowlkes *Dyer County.* There were families using several variations of this spelling residing in Dyer County in 1870, including George Fowlkes and John Fowlk. In addition, Allen, Alf, Asa, Alx., George, James, Jinnie, William, Ranie, Nat, Jo, Lucie, and Martha Fowlks are listed in records.

Fox Bluff *Cheatham County.* Few references to this community could be found. In the words of an area correspondent, "There was a Fox family who lived between Pleasant View and Thomasville, but I don't know if that was Fox Bluff or not."

Frankewing *Giles County.* A more direct rail line between Decatur (Alabama) and Nashville was constructed by the Louisville & Nashville (L&N) Railroad starting in 1911. They built a depot east of Bradshaw, naming it Frankewing for Frank Ewing, who used his influence with state representatives to secure appropriations for the line's construction. Citizens relocated closer to the site, creating a thriving community. The Frankewing of today has moved closer to the intersection of Interstate 65 and U.S. Route 64.

Franklin *Williamson County (seat).* Benjamin Franklin (1706–1790) is the town's namesake. He was renowned as inventor, statesman, and author. Henry Rutherford surveyed and laid out the site in 1800.

Frayser *Shelby County.* Sometime prior to 1873, a Dr. J. W. Frayser erected a home here. When the railroad came through and an adjacent post office was opened, the place became known as Frayser Station.

Fredonia *Coffee County.* See entry for Fredonia, Montgomery County.

Fredonia *Haywood County.* See entry for Fredonia, Montgomery County.

Fredonia *Montgomery County.* The label is said to have been taken from *freedom* and given a Latin ending, to be construed as a "place of freedom." *American Place-Names* states that it was coined by Dr. Samuel Latham shortly after 1800 and advanced as a name for the nation. Although it failed to gain favor for that application, a number of smaller habitations adopted it.

Fredonia *Sequatchie County.* See entry for Fredonia, Montgomery County.

Free Hills *Clay County.* Some sources give the name as Free Hill. As the story is told, prior to the Civil War, four slaves were freed at this site, given four hundred acres of land, and took on the surname Hill, which was that of the family that had owned them. A predominantly black community grew up here, descended, for the most part, from the original four settlers.

French Broad *Cocke County.* This label is taken from the French Broad River, the waterway on which the hamlet is situated. Some believe the river was so named due to early exploration by French explorers, and the breadth of the river in some stretches. (Also see entry for French Broad, Macon County.)

French Broad *Jefferson County.* See next entry.

French Broad *Macon County.* The community's name is a reference to the French Broad River. In her book *Over the Misty Blue Hills,* Ruth Webb O'Dell cites an instance in which William French told a noted historian he had seen deeds in which the waterway was called John French's Broad River. The Cherokees referred to the stream as *Tah-kee-os-kee,* for "racing waters," or *Agiqua,* for "broad." There is some disagreement over how the name became French Broad. Some point out that the label French Broad River appears on certain maps that pre-date John French. Others believe waters flowing east of the mountains were thought to be in the possession of the English, while waters flowing westward from the Blue Ridge Mountains were conceded to the French. Still others feel the "French" name was the name of a noted hunter.

Friends Station *Jefferson County.* The Lost Creek Friends Church, a Quaker (Society of Friends) congregation, was established here in the late 1700s. Trains later stopped here, accounting for the "Station" portion of the name.

Friendsville *Blount County.* The spirit of friendship is basic to the beliefs of the Society of Friends, or American Quakers, who settled here, inspiring the name. Their emigration from North Carolina to this point began in the late 1700s.

Frog Jump *Crockett County.* The community was so small that local jesters observed that a frog could probably go from one end of town to the other in a single bound.

Frog Jump *Gibson County.* An individual named Everett Hall is said to have termed this site "the frog jump and lightning bug center," because its lowlands constituted a hospitable environment for a great number of these creatures. This was in the early 1900s, prior to which the place was better known as Davis Springs. This earlier label traced back to a pioneer, Isham F. Davis, who died in 1846.

Frost Bottom *Anderson County.* This low-lying area was settled by a family with the Frost surname.

Fruitland *Gibson County.* A railroad switch, or siding, was needed at this locality in 1885, approximately halfway between Trenton and Humboldt. Its purpose was to give trains the time and clearance required to load fruits and vegetables, which were grown in abundance in the neighborhood. The activity here gave the site its Fruitland name. The railroad was the Mobile & Ohio.

Fullen's *Greene County.* This designation probably traces back to James Fullen, a local citizen in 1850.

Fulton *Lauderdale County.* The situation of this place, overlooking the Mississippi River and its passing steamboats, may have inspired the name. An individual by the name of Vincent is thought to have founded the settlement in 1819.

Gabtown *Washington County.* The community arose in the early 1800s. One historian speculated that those who moved here constructed their cabins close together for fellowship and met frequently to exchange news and gossip. Someone conferred upon the town the name Gabtown, which is recognized to this day.

Gadsden *Crockett County.* The community takes its name from a diplomat and military figure hailing from South Carolina, James Gadsden. At one time, he served as the country's minister to Mexico. Gadsden lived from 1788 to 1858. He is also the namesake of the Alabama city of the same name.

Gainesboro *Jackson County (seat).* The community was incorporated in 1817. The place-name commemorates an officer in the War of 1812, Edmund Pendleton Gaines (1777–1849).

Gainesville *Tipton County.* Andrew Gaines, age 60, and Munro Gaines, 25 at the time, lived locally in 1870. They or their ancestors are probably responsible for this place-name.

Galbraith Springs *Hawkins County.* When the 1840 census was recorded, several Galbraiths resided nearby: Joseph, Arthur, Joseph B., Jacob, and two named Andrew. The springs, and the hamlet that arose around them, were probably named for this family.

Gallatin *Sumner County (seat).* The site is thought to have appropriated the surname of Albert Gallatin, Jefferson's secretary of the treasury. Gallatin had emigrated from Switzerland. Among other posts he held were minister to England and minister to France.

Gallaway *Fayette County.* A well-known mill operator, J. M. Gallaway, was the person for whom the community was named. It was incorporated in 1966. Before a single place-name was settled upon, the general area was dubbed Concordia, within which were two entities, Gallaway and Braden. The Gallaway designation was eventually (in 1855) chosen.

Galloway Mill *Sullivan County.* Adam Galloway, a local resident in 1850, may have been the individual who operated a mill at the site. A mention is also found in records of the same period of a Mary Gallaway, whose surname was spelled (correctly or incorrectly) differently from Adam's.

Gandy *Lawrence County.* Davy Crockett once lobbied for the county seat to be located at this very small hamlet. Although it is not known why it was so named, it may be connected to railroad jargon, since track-laying workers were often referred to as "gandy dancers."

Gann *Gibson County.* At first this locality was known as Belew's. When Rufus Gann operated a store at the site, it became known by his surname.

Garber's *Washington County.* Garber's dates to the 1820s, when a gristmill was established here. Isaac Garber was the town's namesake. In 1891, the railroad came to Garber's with great attendant fanfare.

Gardner *Weakley County.* Colonel James Almus Gardner gave his surname to the town, which was founded in 1856 on land that he owned. Prominent in local and state affairs, Colonel Gardner was the first president of what was then the Nashville & North Western Railroad.

Garland *Tipton County.* The name of this place honors a man who served as a U.S. senator from Arkansas, Augustus Hill Garland. Garland served from 1877 until 1885 and was apparently so well respected locally that this site adopted his surname.

Gassaway *Cannon County.* Benjamin Gassaway, the father of the community's first merchant, Charles Gassaway, was the individual for whom the town was named. Benjamin put down roots here in an early—but uncertain—year. He was also the father of Hiram Gassaway, a farmer, and James R. Gassaway, who was a soldier in the Mexican War.

Gates *Lauderdale County.* The community was founded about 1850 and incorporated in 1886. Its name honors General Horatio Gates, a Revolutionary War officer who commanded the Army of the South. Those who gave the place its name were the first farmers at the site, Frank Robison, Joseph Crockett, and John Johnson. Incorporation took place in 1901.

Gath *Warren County.* An earlier name for the locality is said to have been Fuston. When a Baptist church went up here in 1902, it assumed the name of a city in the Bible, Gath.

Gatlinburg *Sevier County.* The initial designation for the place was White Oak Flats, when the first post office was established in 1860. The office was in the store of Radford Gatlin, a locally influential and prosperous pro-slavery individual. At some point, White Oak Flats was dropped as the name and Gatlinburg was implemented.

Gattistown *Lincoln County.* Numerous Gattises resided here in 1870. Among them were Berry W., Charles, Green C., Mary, Robert, Isaac N., William, Willis, and Nathaniel Gattis. "Town" was probably affixed to the end of their surname to compose a proper community name.

Gause *Robertson County.* A family having the Gause surname resided here, giving the site its name.

Gennett *Scott County.* Andrew Gennett became the first postmaster here, in 1927, accounting for the place-name.

Gentry *Putnam County.* Charles and William Gentry are found listed in rolls of the 1820 census as residing in Overton County. Later, Overton County gave up some territory to help form Putnam County; so this site may have been in that sector and is now listed as being in Putnam County.

Georgetown *Hamilton County.* In 1870, William R. George, age 58, and Elizabeth George, age 31, were nearby citizens, possibly accounting for this label. However, there are three Georgetowns in North Carolina, which sent many pioneers westward into Tennessee. It is possible one of these emigrants imported the name to this locality.

Germantown *Shelby County.* Like most other U.S. communities having this name, the site was settled largely by those of German heritage. The site proprietor was Nancy Shephard. A store opened in 1830, and the hamlet began to thrive. Incorporation took place in 1848, although the charter was surrendered in the early 1860s. In 1880, Germantown was rechartered and is now a city.

Gibbs *Obion County.* George Gibbs resided at or near this locality in 1870. In all probability, he or his ancestors are in some direct way related to this place-name. A check of the 1850 census also reveals the Second District residency of a George Gibbs, probably the same individual.

Gibbs Crossroads *Macon County.* This intersection may have gotten its name because Alfred and Gilbert Gibbs were identified with the site in 1850.

Gibson *Gibson County.* One of the military leaders in General Andrew Jackson's Natchez Expedition, during the War of 1812, was Major (one source says Colonel) John Gibson. Like the county in which it is situated, this community takes his name. At an earlier time, the site was known as Pickettville, but it has been Gibson since 1870.

Gibson Wells *Gibson County.* One of the earliest settlers in the area was Colonel Thomas Gibson, sometime after 1819. (Also see preceding entry.) At one time, this site was known as Bland's Wells, for a John Bland, who discovered the many mineral springs here; later, they were the central attraction for a popular health spa.

Gift *Tipton County.* Probably between 1895 and 1905, a store was opened at this site by a man from nearby Covington, William Robert Gift.

Gilchrist *McNairy County.* The Gilchrist family and William Sanders were early settlers here. The place takes its name from the Gilchrists. There was a school here, and a church organized in 1866.

Gilestown *Shelby County.* A source on county history refers to William Hodge Giles (1802–1869) as "a blacksmith of Gilestown."

Gilt Edge *Tipton County.* This designation is said, by one account, to have been inspired by a brand of shoe polish having this name. Another source, however, suggests that it embodied citizens' idea of the town's worth or value—perhaps meaning that they saw the potential for it to become a very prosperous community.

Gladesville *Wilson County.* This site was observed to be a "rocky glade," and from that fact took its name. It arose in 1852. The proprietor was Benjamin Hooker Jr.

Glass *Obion County.* This town was originally called Palestine. Later, it was changed to Glass out of respect for a senator, according to the *Obion County History.* According to this source, the name was "changed by the government" in the second half of the nineteenth century. David Miller erected the first house.

Gleason *Weakley County.* Gleason was originally known as Oakwood, owing to a prominent oak tree that stood near W. W. Gleason's general store. (An alternative source states that the noted oak tree grew up through a crack in the post office floor.) At a later date, the community adopted Gleason as its name. The town arose in 1850. One source gives the year of incorporation as 1871, while another puts it at 1903. The nickname of the town is Tatertown, due to the abundance and quality of sweet potatoes grown there.

Glendale *Maury County.* At an earlier time, the site was known by the label Hurricane Switch. However, postal authorities cited the existence of another Hurricane Switch in the state and asked a local postal clerk, W. H. Puryear, to select something else. He looked for a name not often duplicated, or far away, and the only Glendale he could readily identify was in California. So in 1899, Glendale was assigned as the name.

Glenwylde *Dickson County.* Early settlers are believed to have viewed the site as a "wild glen."

Glimp *Lauderdale County.* Blackfoot, for the Indian tribe, was the initial name, either at this site, or very close by. The Glimp post office was established in 1880, and apparently a different one in the county was known as Glimpville, which may have opened in 1871. In 1874, John A. Glimp was appointed postmaster. Eight Glimps were listed in the 1877 Tenth District poll tax book.

Glover *Robertson County.* The Glovers residing in this vicinity at the time of the 1850 census included Selia, W. W., Henry, Joseph, Julia, Richard, and Riley Glover. The census of 1870 disclosed Glovers named R. A., Nathan, Edwin E., John, K. G., and Franklin. A local authority verifies that the site was "named for the Glover family," without pinpointing which Glover family.

Goad *Fentress County.* In 1870, William Goad, age 31, resided locally. The probable result is that the location assumed his, or his family's, surname.

Goat City *Gibson County.* At one time, this community was referred to as Centerville. It is said to have acquired its current colorful label when a frustrated resident called it Goat City because folks were constantly "butting into other people's business." Apparently, the remark was overheard and repeated, the result being that the name stuck.

Godwin *Maury County.* For some time, up until 1890, this site was referred to as Duck River. However, it was discovered that there was another community called Duck River in another Tennessee county. So to avoid further confusion, this location took on the name Godwin, for longtime agent Colonel Aaron S. Godwin. It is also thought that Godwin was dubbed Trough Spring at one time. Either this spot—or one very near—went through a succession of names. "The Tank" was one of them, and may have evolved from "The Trough." Later it was known as Winsett, later still, Bristow, followed by Timmons. The latter label became Timmonsville for a time, but was shortened back to Timmons, which itself was changed to Athendale. J. K. P. Timmons became postmaster at the site in 1878. In an essay in 1936, Dr. Ernest A. Timmons recorded his recollections regarding the procession of names. An ancestor, Squire H. Timmons, settled here in about 1845. When the 1840 census was taken, Godwins living locally included Seth, James, and Samuel.

Goin *Claiborne County.* Several individuals with the Goin surname are found in the annals of local history, including John L. Goin, J. P. Goin, and Iona Holt Goin. In addition, there was Uriah Goins, whose name was spelled with an *s* on the end. Uriah purchased land in the vicinity in 1810. Iona served locally as a teacher in about 1907; she was the wife of John L. J. P. was a member of the county court in 1905, and in 1910 was serving as a justice.

Goodbars *Warren County.* This hamlet arose around a water-powered gristmill on Rocky River that was run by William Goodbar. In 1876, the local postmaster was William T. Goodbar.

Goodlettsville *Davidson and Sumner Counties.* A previous name of this place was Mansker's Station. The current name was chosen out of respect for an area man, Dr. Adam Goodlett.

Goodrich *Hickman County.* This name eventually leads back to Levin Goodrich, an early railroad builder in this locale, who also became an ironworker. In 1882, an operation called Goodrich Iron Furnace went on-stream near Nunnelly, a short distance away.

Goodspring *Giles County.* Six thousand Confederate cavalrymen under the command of General Nathan Bedford Forrest waited atop Anthony Hill on Christmas Day, 1864, for a Federal army contingent estimated at two thousand. The Union army, under Colonel Harrison, stopped to allow other Federals to catch up. They waited at a site known as Good Spring. Both Confederate and Union troops used the spring for drinking water, prompting both camps to comment on the excellent quality and taste of the water and resulting in the name of the community. It is variously styled as Good Spring or Goodspring.

Gooseneck *Anderson County.* Two versions of the name explanation exist. One concerns a resident in the distant past—whose surname may have been Pyle—who raised a number of geese here. The second refers to wild geese who made this a favorite stopover in the spring, to eat the lush green grass growing in the lowland in the center of the hollow. At various times, three small stores operated here, run by E. E. Elliott, Stell Bell, and Mamie Wallace. "There was no town," our informant states, but for a place with no town, it had an "official boundary": three hundred yards north of Luther Clear's spring to the foot of Belmont Hill. The name is seen styled as Goose Neck, as well as Gooseneck Hollow.

Gooseneck *Blount County.* According to accounts, a peddler named Granville Morton used to travel this area. One day, he remarked that women craning their necks out their windows to see his products resembled geese with their necks extended. This observation is said to have resulted in the place-name.

Gordonville *Smith County.* The place-name is sometimes styled Gordonsville. Sixteen Gordons are listed in a biographical index of the area. In 1836, a Dr. F. H. Gordon was teaching at Clinton College and raising cattle near here. John Harrison Gordon, born 1852, a merchant, is identified with a place a mile north of Gordonville. His parents were Matthew A. L. Gordon and Lucy Lee (Ward) Gordon. John Gordan [*sic*] is identified as having resided in the county in 1837.

Gorman *Humphreys County.* The name traces back to a family with the Gorman surname who settled at this place. Specifically, it is thought to have been named for Frank Gorman, who arrived here from New York. Frank married Lucy McKelvey of Humphreys County; they built a large house and farmed many acres. The Porters and the Hollarans were other early residents of the site.

Goshen *Hawkins County.* This name was probably biblically inspired. It refers to the district in ancient Egypt where Jacob's descendants lived until the exodus. The word may imply "rich soil."

Gossburg *Coffee County.* No one with the Goss surname could be placed in this locality in the 1830–1870 period. However, Johnson Gossett resided in the county when it was organized. It's reasonable to surmise that someone borrowed the "Goss" from his surname and coupled it with *burg* to create this label.

Gower *Davidson County.* A great many Gowers were associated with this area as early as 1850. Included were two named William, four named John, Albert, Elisha, Felix, Lorenzo, Margaret, Gideon N., Mary, Martha, George F., Joseph, and L. F.

Graball *Sumner County.* According to a story passed down locally, a group of residents were partaking in an illegal activity—possibly a cockfight or card game—when the sheriff arrived. One of the shocked participants was heard to shout, "Grab all you can get and run." The name is said to have adhered since that incident.

Graham *Hickman County.* A northerner, Samuel Graham, is the person for whom this locality was named. Graham arrived in the 1820s and obtained an existing sawmill operation as well as six thousand acres for farming. He also expanded into other types of milling and various other enterprises, becoming one of the wealthiest persons around. Upon learning that a branch line of the Nashville, Chattanooga & St. Louis (NC&StL) Railway was projected to go through nearby Pinewood, Graham offered the rail company $5,000 if they would reroute the line to come through Graham, instead. His offer was accepted, and Graham for a period became an important shipping point.

Grand Junction *Hardeman County.* The first settler at Grand Junction is believed to have been D. R. Bryant. The year was 1854. The label is thought to be the result of the meeting of the Illinois Central and Memphis & Charleston Railways at this location. (One source says the Illinois Central and Southern Railways.)

Grandview *Rhea County.* A correspondent advises us that Grandview is situated atop Walden's Ridge, with a commanding view of the surrounding mountains and valley.

Grant *Smith County.* An individual referred to as Squire Grant was a member of a survey party ordered to penetrate this area in 1786. The place-name may refer to him, or to his children or descendants. In 1850, Nancy and Rachel L. Grant resided nearby, in Wilson County, while Edward and Elizabeth Grant lived in Smith County. A portion of Wilson County contributed to the makeup of Smith County; so all these persons could have been living at, or in close proximity to, the place on maps designated as Grant.

Grantsboro *Campbell County.* At the time of the 1850 census, a number of Grants resided locally. Included were Helen, Harvey, Abigail, two named Mary, Cynthia, James H., Jonathan, Rufus, and John. It is likely some of them lived at this location, imparting the Grantsboro name.

Grant's Chapel *Jefferson County.* A correspondent advises us that, in 1897, lumber and land for a Methodist church were donated by Isaac Grant.

Granville *Jackson County.* Although possible that the label stems from an early family with the Granville surname, usually this label is inspired by the earl of Granville (John Carteret, 1690–1763).

Grassy Cove *Cumberland County.* According to *Tennessee: A Guide to the Volunteer State,* this locale produces grains, grasses, clovers, and other crops from alluvial deposits of sandy loam and soil washed down from surrounding hillsides. It describes the cove as a large sink in the plateau, about three hundred feet below the land that encircles it.

Grassy Creek *Polk County.* William Humphreys, one of the first whites to settle in this area after the forced removal of the Indians in 1838, selected a site where large oak trees and grassy banks bordered a stream. These characteristics gave the site its name.

Grassy Fork *Cocke County.* The prevalence of grassy areas suggested this town's name.

Gravel Hill *McNairy County.* This is one of several clustered communities with "Hill" in their names—Sand Hill, Pebble Hill, Spring Hill, and Rocky Hill are also nearby. One source states that "Gravel Hill had only a few pebbles, and Pebble Hill had gravel pits." However, one authority does state that the center of the town was on a graveled hill. White settlers arrived as early as 1832 or before.

Gravelly Hill *Blount County.* Residents took note of the large amount of gravel and larger rock present in the soil. An early resident of the area recalls that fields were full of small rocks and gravel mixed with the dirt; you could begin plowing with a very rusty plow, he said, and soon have a bright, shiny one, the rust having been polished off by the gravel.

Graveston *Knox County.* Some of the early settlers nearby had the Graves surname. G. C. Graves is known to have resided in the vicinity in 1834. At the time of the 1830 East Tennessee census, Boston, Daniel, David, George, and Henry Graves were listed as local citizens. During the Civil War years, J. R. Graves is known to have sided with the Confederates. Eighteen-fifty residents included Hannah, Adelin, and Arminda Graves.

Gray *Washington County.* Local tax records in 1814 list Robert, James, and John Gray, while Robert, Nathan, and James Gray are listed for the year 1819. Eighteen-fifty census rolls reveal the residency of two Joshua Grays, plus James, John W., Robert H., and Lanegu Gray. The place-name may relate to one or more of these families having the Gray surname. However, an area source claims that an Anderson Gray received a land grant in this vicinity from North Carolina. Later, a train station was built on the property, which was dubbed Gray for Anderson's family. This may have been relatively late; the Carolina, Clinchfield & Ohio (CC&O) Railroad came through in 1907–1908, and the town is said to have come into existence at that time.

Graysville *Rhea County.* Incorporation took place in 1917. Billy Gray allowed the Cincinnati & Chattanooga Railroad a variance through his property, and his name remained attached to the site. Gray also served as the first (one source says second) postmaster for the town. The place began to take on its own identity early in the 1870s. The community was laid out by surveyor John Wesley Clouse, who named the town after his friend Gray.

Graytown *Hickman County.* About 1810, an individual named Alexander Gray settled near a bend in the Duck River. In time, the location took on the name Graytown. Initially, it was known as Gray's Bend.

Greenback *Loudon County.* Although one source claims that the community probably took its name from the luxuriant flora of the site, it seems possible that it may refer to the Greenback Party, which had a short political life.

Greenbrier *Robertson County.* According to legend, when the railroad was constructed in the 1850s, workers complained about the green briers that grew here in profusion.

Green Hill *Wilson County.* The John Williamson and John Cloyd families settled this locale. Although the appearance of the fertile, rolling hills in the area might well have contributed to the place-name, one source states that the designation was inspired by a "former state treasurer of North Carolina whose Seawell and Mabry kin lived not far away." The name of that former state treasurer has not yet been determined. . . . In support of the first explanation is a passage from an essay by G. Frank Burns, which states in part that the place "took its name from the green grove by which it was then surrounded." The same source claims that the town was founded in about 1837 on lands belonging to Hugh Robinson.

Greeneville *Greene County (seat).* General Nathaniel Greene, who gained fame during the Revolutionary War, is the town's namesake. Of the many places in the United States named for him, Greeneville is thought to be the only one using this spelling—retaining the *e* in the middle. (Most others are spelled Greenville.)

Greenfield *Weakley County.* After the Mississippi Central Railroad (a second source terms it the Illinois Central Gulf Railroad) entered the site in 1873, area residents began moving closer to the line, creating a town. It is said by some that the engineer or conductor on the first train to come through observed the spacious fields of still-green wheat nearby and suggested the Greenfield name. The year of incorporation is given as 1880.

Green's Crossroad *Warren County.* In 1850, the following Greens resided at or near this locality: William G., Marvel, Sanford V., two named Shadrick, Solomon, Susan, Abner, David, Elias H., Hambal, two named John, Samuel, Lewis, and Joseph. One or more of these families probably resided where roads intersect, giving this place its designation on maps.

Greenwood *Washington County.* The name was undoubtedly inspired by the dense timberland of the area. The name was changed to Greenwood from Big Cherokee in 1858.

Greystone *Greene County.* Near the "Tennessee end" of North Carolina, a town named Greystone exists. The Greene County Greystone is not far from the North Carolina border. It is likely some emigrants from Greystone, North Carolina, made a modest move westward, settling here and naming the site after their former abode.

Griffen *Fayette County.* The spelling is probably a corruption of Griffin. Ira, Owen, James E., Jehoiacun, and Wilson Griffin were local residents in 1830.

Griffintown *Cheatham County.* In 1850, in Davidson County, which provided part of its area to help form Cheatham County, several Griffins resided. Among them were Dawson, Sarah, two Johns, Joseph N., Thomas, W. C., William, J., and H. Griffin. Their surname likely influenced the designation of this place.

Griffith *Bledsoe County.* When the 1870 census was taken, local citizens included G. Griffith, age 18; Jefferson Griffith, 36; and D. M. Griffith, 64.

Griffith *Blount County.* David M. Griffith resided here in 1840, according to that year's census.

Griffith Creek *Marion County.* The stream and the hamlet that grew up around it are probably named for the many Griffiths who resided here as early as 1830. The census taker recorded their surname as Griffeth in each case, which may or may not have been their spelling preference. Those listed were James, Arden E., Thomas G., Samuel, and Matthew.

Grimsley *Fentress County.* Although it was settled well before the Grimsley name was attached, it was not until 1901 that John Hogue so named the place. He dubbed it in honor of his friend, Bart Grimsley, who operated a way station near Celina, Tennessee, according to a 1986 newspaper article. One section is referred to as Old Grimsley. The surnames of the earliest settlers here included Richards, Beaty, Young, Flannigan, Morgan, Hogue, Stephens, and Scroggins.

Grinder's Switch *Hickman County.* A railroad was probably built through this area, with a switching area or siding that gave the place part of its name. Robert and Matilda Grinder were local residents at the time of the 1850 census, probably accounting for the other segment of the name.

Grizzard *Gibson County.* This place-name probably traces back to an 1870 resident, Robert Grizzard, age 32 at the time, or his ancestors.

Gruetli *Grundy County.* Swiss people settled here in 1869. Many of them were from Zurich and Glarus, the latter containing the commune of Gruetli, which in turn gave its name to this settlement.

Gudger *Monroe County.* Gudger is very near the boundary with McMinn County. In 1870, Gudgers still residing in McMinn included Harriet, W. A., M. F., and William. A portion of McMinn County was taken to help constitute Monroe County.

Guild *Marion County.* The label on this site probably traces back to an engineer named Josephus C. Guild, or his family.

Gum Branch *Dickson County.* An elderly correspondent provides this account: "Gum Branch—This was a road that ran out from Burns. When I was a young girl, if you got any chewing gum, you kept it and chewed it for days. The girls all kept their gum and chewed it for more than one day. My dad, Walter Wyburn, named the road Gum Branch. There was a creek near the road, so it was also called Gum Branch."

Gum Creek *Franklin County.* One might assume this waterway was lined with gum trees, but according to one local source, that is not how the place got its name. Instead, it is said that the lowland on either side of the stream was so "gummy" that horses had a very difficult time crossing it. Another local source writes that Gum Swamp was the name of an area near here on a Civil War map, and that the designation Gum Swamp Branch is found on deeds and maps dating well back into the 1800s. A school, church, and store are believed to have marked the site.

Gum Springs *Lawrence County.* A spring was discovered here, surrounded by a number of sweet gum trees, resulting in the name.

Gum Springs *Van Buren County.* In an early year, a hollowed-out black gum tree was discovered growing out of a spring at this location, furnishing the place with its name.

Guy's *McNairy County.* A lumberman having the surname Guy had a siding constructed from the Mobile & Ohio Railroad (later, the Gulf, Mobile, & Ohio). This enabled him the easier shipment of timber and wood products. The site was known at the time as Guy's Switch. In time, the word "switch" was dropped. When a post office was opened, it dropped the possessive form of the name and was located in a store owned by early settler and Confederate veteran T. B. Hooker. The town became quite a busy center of activity.

Habersham *Campbell County.* From 1901 until 1925, this place was known as Cupp. The Habersham label derived from a prominent railroad family living in the vicinity.

Hackberry *Montgomery County.* According to *Webster's Third New International Dictionary,* this term refers to North American trees or shrubs of the *Celtis* genus. One such tree has a rounded top and edible berries that have a dark purple appearance and may also be referred to as sugarberries. It is likely they occurred commonly here, and suggested this name to settlers or those passing through.

Hale *Washington County.* Individuals having the Hale surname dotted the local landscape in 1850, according to census records. Included were two named Landon, two named William, two named Mary, and two named John, as well as William K., David, Dorcas A., Charles, James, Joseph, Manera, Mark, Samuel, Robert G., Merah, Messick, and Louisa.

Haletown *Marion County.* Willis, Albert G., and William Hale were among individuals residing near this site in 1840. The likelihood exists that the community assumed the Hale name. A later census counted at least fourteen Hales residing in the vicinity, seven of whom were African Americans.

Haley *Bedford County.* It is said that a man named Haley sold wood at this location for the wood-burning locomotives on the Louisville & Nashville Railroad in about 1852. It was often referred to as Haley's Station.

Hall's *Lauderdale County.* The proprietor of real estate here was General Benjamen (Benjamin?) Smith, although he never came to this site. A family of settlers possessed the Hall surname. A postal worker was named Hansford Hall; some credit him with being the place's namesake. An individual named Tolbert Hall served as recorder, and became mayor. Incorporation took place in 1884, but in 1901 the community was rechartered.

Hall's Creek *Humphreys County.* The waterway and community probably trace their name to one of the Halls residing locally in 1840. Numbered among them were William A., Abraham, D., Curtis, Henry, James A., two Johns, and John T. Hall.

Hall's Crossroads *Knox County.* A number of Halls had ties to this locality, including Alf, M. L., William, and Thomas. Thomas was a clergyman, and in 1865 William was killed in a fight between returning soldiers of both sides.

Hall's Hill *Rutherford County.* Numerous Halls called the county home in 1870. A sampling of them includes Narcissa, age 48; Nathan, 66; Johue, 25; Alfred, 49; Gordon, 50; Munroe, 27; two Thomases, 80 and 85; several named John; G. S., 43; Jacob, 37; and Angeline, 24. The hamlet apparently is situated at an elevation.

Hall's Mill *Bedford County.* A great many Halls resided in this locale in 1870. Some of them were Elvira, Ceasar (Caesar?), Harrison, Susan, J. M., and Henry Sr. One or more family members probably conducted milling operations at this site, giving it its name.

Hall's Mill *Sullivan County.* In 1880, the following Halls were nearby residents: James, age 58; John H., 13; A. J., 49; Amos, 39; Alexander, 42; Edward F., 11; Fulton, 44; David N., 47; and Hiram, 52. In all probability, one or more of them operated a local mill.

Hamilton Mill *Lincoln County.* Numerous Hamiltons resided in the vicinity when the 1850 census was taken. Included were Mary, Martha, three named William, Peter J., Peter M., Anna, Daniel, David, Jasper, John, Jacob, Eunoch, and Hugh. One or several of them probably operated the mill at the site. One source says, however, that a mill was constructed long prior to the Civil War, and was operated by John Hamilton. There, corn was ground into flour and meal. A wood-carving operation also was carried on within the mill.

Hammon Chapel *Johnson County.* John Hammon was a local resident in 1880, according to census records. There also were three other individuals who spelled the name with an s on the end: Mat, Thomas, and Sarah Hammons. At the time, the respective ages of the four were 19, 25, 23, and 64. Possibly an ancestor or relative of one of these individuals was a clergyman, or donated the land or materials for a church.

Hampshire *Maury County.* This place-name usually refers to the state of New Hampshire, or to its antecedent, County Hampshire, in England.

Hampton *Carter County.* This community was founded by Elijah Simerly, who laid out the site. His ancestor John Simerly had claimed a grant parcel of three hundred acres at this locale in 1792. Elijah, who served as president of the East Tennessee & Western North Carolina (ET&WNC) Railroad, named the location for his wife, Mary Hampton. The place-name was briefly changed to Allentown, but some citizens didn't care for the name and it was changed back to Hampton. The community was incorporated in 1890, 1894, or somewhere in that time frame. In 1850, Hamptons residing in the vicinity were Johnson, Johnson Sr., Lawson W., and Margaret.

Hampton's Crossroads *White County.* The label on this intersection traces back to Zachariah Hampton, who lived here in 1830 and perhaps even earlier.

Hampton Station *Montgomery County.* Wade and John Hampton were county citizens in 1850. John is also listed in the 1830 census rolls. Their surname was probably adopted as a means of identifying this location. Apparently, it was a stop on the R. J. Corman/Memphis Line of the railroad, accounting for the "Station" portion of the name. By 1870, the Hamptons listed as residing here included Overton, age 42; Leah, 35; Mariah, 53; John, 26; Isabella, 43; and George, 37.

Handleyton *Robertson County.* In 1884, Benjamin T. Handley was named first postmaster at this locality, resulting in the place-name that survives to this day.

Hanging Limb *Overton County.* In early days, farmers would herd their cattle to a grazing site high in the Cumberland Mountains, establishing camp there. A large nearby tree had a huge trunk and many sturdy limbs. The workers would hang their saddlebags and bridles on the limbs to keep wild hogs and rats from gnawing on them. Thus, the place became known as Hanging Limb.

Happy Valley *Blount County.* Originally, this place was recognized as Rhea's Valley, for the county's first coroner, Robert Rhea. A Revolutionary War veteran, Rhea had received a land grant in 1823. But emigrants from Carter County called it Happy Valley because it reminded them of a site known as Happy Valley that they had left behind.

Harbuck *Polk County.* One explanation for this place-name is that it represents the mountain dialect pronunciation of "Arbuckle." Proponents say a man with the Arbuckle surname resided in the community at an early time. Another possible—but perhaps less likely—explanation held by many has been passed down through generations. Apparently, a railroad tie yard was located locally, to supply ties for the track being laid between Copperhill and Etowah. Many laborers with strength and stamina were required for the project, and one day some young Indian "bucks" appeared before the foreman, hoping to be hired. In their imperfect English, the request came out, "Har a buck?" Another name of this site was Hunter's Switch.

Hardy *Overton County.* William Hardy deeded property for a community school and church, which became known as Hardy's Chapel. The William B. Hardy residing nearby at the time of the 1850 census was probably the same individual.

Harmony *Washington County.* In 1850, a handful of local residents met at Keeblers' Meeting House, the intent being to organize a church. Being of "one accord," they christened the church Harmony Baptist. Land was obtained at no cost from Enon Kincheloe, William B. Chase, and E. Chase. A small hamlet grew up around the place of worship.

Harmony Grove *Cocke County.* It is said that local citizen Sol Rollins conferred this label upon the community because all its families were so friendly to one another.

Harms *Lincoln County.* The community's namesake is John C. Harms (1821–1886), a native of Germany with engineering expertise who constructed a dam and water-powered gristmill on the Elk River that served the surrounding area.

Harpeth Valley *Dickson County.* The valley takes its name from the Harpeth River, Harpeth having been the surname of an early settler in the region.

Harriman *Morgan and Roane Counties.* The namesake of the town is a former governor of New Hampshire, General Walter Harriman. Incorporation took place in 1891.

Harriman Junction *Roane County.* A railroad junction existed here. (See preceding entry.)

Harrison *Hamilton County.* Like a number of U.S. places, this site bears the name of General William Henry Harrison, who became president. Approximately the same site was known earlier as Vannville and Vann Town, for a wealthy Cherokee, Chief Joseph Vann, who left the region in 1838.

Harris Station *Obion County.* Also known simply as Harris, this hamlet was known during earlier times as Mink. The Harris Station name came into vogue when the Memphis & Paducah Railroad was extended through the community. According to the *Obion County History,* the name traces to John F. Harris, surveyor of the railway.

Hartford *Cocke County.* This name, applied in 1905, derives from a combination of two surnames, Hart and Ford. A Ford family resided locally, as did John Hart, who dealt in timber. The site went through a procession of names prior to Hartford: Dryce, Pigeon Valley, Helterbrand Station, and Camp Hercules.

Hartmantown *Washington County.* Possibly in the 1850s, several Hartman families were local residents, and inspired the name of this hamlet.

Hartsville *Trousdale County (seat).* An early settler, James Hart, conferred his surname upon this place. Prior to that it was called Damascuss, or Damascus, no doubt inspired by the city mentioned in the Bible. Incorporation came in 1833.

Haskins' Chapel *Bedford County.* A local family's name and the existence of a church here resulted in this designation on maps.

Hatchie *Madison County.* It is believed that *hatchie* was a Chickasaw word for "river." If so, that would make the name of the major nearby waterway, the Hatchie River, a redundancy ("river river"). This site was also known as Hatchie Station, not to be confused with Hatchie Town, which became Bolivar, in next-door Hardeman County.

Hathaway *Lake County.* An individual named W. Hathaway resided in Dyer County in 1870. He or his family may be linked to this hamlet, as Lake County was not formed until 1870, using some area from Dyer County. The 1870 census records would probably still have shown W. Hathaway as a resident of Dyer County, even though the *place* may now be in Lake County.

Hawkinsville *Dyer County.* P. W. Hawkins was a local citizen in 1850. The place-name undoubtedly relates in some way to him (her?) or members of his/her family.

Haws' Crossroads *Washington County.* A family having the Haws surname resided at this juncture in the early nineteenth century, when this place was named. The thoroughfares involved are now known as Highway 93 and Fordtown Road.

Haysville *Macon County.* The exact derivation of this name is vague. Between the years 1779 and 1786, a James Hays resided in nearby Sumner County; so it is likely that he, one of his children, or another relative crossed the county line at a later time and founded this site, or it became known by his or her surname.

Heard *Pickett County.* Heard probably arose about 1890 and may have been named by the postmaster for either W. E. Heard or Jessie Heard, who owned much of the property in the vicinity. A local geographical feature was known as Heard Ridge.

Heath *Johnson County.* The name Levi Heath is located on the roster of Johnson County citizens in the *Tennessee 1850 Census Index.* It cannot be shown with certainty that he resided at—or gave his name to—this place, but it is probable that he was in some way related to the place-name.

Hebbertsburg *Cumberland County.* It is said that the community took its name from an early postmaster, Hebbert Hamby.

Hebron *Fayette County.* The name is of biblical origin. Founded about 1700 B.C., the original Hebron was a city in the hill country of Judah.

Hebron *Hardeman County.* See preceding entry.

Heiskell *Knox County.* The designation probably traces back to T. S. Heiskell. Other prominent area persons with the surname included Carrick White Heiskell, Frederic Heiskell, William Heiskell, Fred Heiskell, Frederick Steidinger Heiskell, J. N. Heiskell, Samuel Gordon Heiskell, and Joseph Brown Heiskell. Heiskell's Station was recognized as a fruit-growing center.

Helenwood *Scott County.* Then called Homestead, this town was laid out in 1859. Ninety-five lots were sold. The current name was styled Hellenwood briefly. There are conflicting versions of how it came to have the Helenwood name. Some say it was referred to as "Hell-in-the-Woods" because of rough and rowdy escapades during its saloon days. Others hold that it was named for a Captain Wood's daughter, Helen. Ike Shoemaker owned the town's first store.

Helton Creek *DeKalb County.* The name of the creek and community probably trace back to a Mr. Helton, or Hylton, who cannot be positively identified. Records prior to 1820 sometimes spell this surname Hylton.

Heltonville *Grainger County.* Five Heltons were county citizens in 1870—John, James, David, and two named Alexander. It is likely their family name was joined to the commonly used *ville* to indicate a settlement.

Hematite *Montgomery County.* It is likely some iron mining was undertaken here; if not, this common iron ore was probably present in large quantities. The reddish-brown (when powdered) mineral is widely distributed and is sometimes referred to as bloodstone.

Hembree *Scott County.* James and Martha Hembree were citizens of Morgan County in about 1849, when a portion of their county was appropriated to help form Scott County. In all probability, they resided at this site, which may at one time have been located in Morgan County. It is located about three miles from the current boundary of Morgan County.

Henardtown *Hawkins County.* At the time of the 1870 census, a number of Henards were residing in this vicinity. Among them were Elijah, age 74 at the time; Elijah J., 53; Mary, 47; William, 39; and John, 24. The site probably took on its designation from being associated with this family.

Henderson *Chester County (seat).* The *Illustrated Dictionary of Place Names* reveals that the city owes its name to an officer under the command of Andrew Jackson in the War of 1812, James Henderson. The site proprietors had been James Simmons and Dr. J. D. Smith. Earlier labels for the place included Dayton, Henderson City, and Henderson Station.

Hendersonville *Sumner County.* The town's namesake is William Henderson (b. 1752), who became the community's first postmaster. Born in Virginia, Henderson ascended to the rank of captain during the American Revolution.

Henning *Lauderdale County.* Dr. D. M. Henning is thought to be the person to whom the place-name traces. In 1837, Dr. Henning graduated from Philadelphia's Jefferson Medical College and subsequently practiced in Tennessee, where he acquired large land parcels. He also became an executive with the local railroad line, to which he contributed five acres for the depot/stationhouse. In 1873, he retired from the railroad and founded the community, which his former employer named in the doctor's honor.

Henry *Henry County.* Like the county, the site uses the name of the patriot Patrick Henry. The name began here as Henry Station, in 1861, a stop on the Memphis & Ohio Railroad. It was first incorporated in 1874, but apparently the charter was surrendered or lapsed, and in 1907 the community reincorporated as Henry.

Henry Crossroads *Sevier County.* This designation probably traces back to Major Hugh Henry, who establishd a small community in 1782. Major Henry signed the Treaty of Dumplin with the Cherokee Indians at his home three years later. Henry's Crossroads United Methodist Church—at the time, Henry's Chapel—was founded in 1782. Henry's Crossroads and the Oak Grove Methodist Church were unified in 1994.

Henryville *Lawrence County.* As the first permanent settlement in the county, Henryville was occupied as early as 1815. Jacob Pennington and his five sons were among the earliest settlers; so the site took on the Pennington label. The Henry name was adopted in 1847, it being either the surname or given name of the first postmaster. Later, the Henryville name was accepted. Old Town, a Chickasaw Indian village, had been very close by.

Hermitage *Davidson County.* This label refers to the name of Andrew Jackson's Nashville-area estate.

Hermitage Springs *Clay County.* The "Hermitage" part of the name may be a reference to Andrew Jackson's estate, some miles to the south. Sulfur- and mineral-water wells existed here, and an effort was made to turn the locality into a resort area. Hotels were constructed here between 1900 and 1920. In earlier times, the site was known simply as Trace Creek and Spivey. There were several Spiveys in the neighborhood, including Hamilton H. Spivey, a merchant, and Lynn Spivey. Settlement began early in the 1800s.

Hiawassee *Warren County.* This is a variant of *hiwassee,* which is thought to mean "meadow" in Cherokee.

Hickerson Station *Coffee County.* Numerous Hickersons resided in the county in 1850. A railroad depot probably gave the site the "Station" part of its name. Some of those having the Hickerson surname were two named Charles, two named David, Litle, Nancy, two named Joseph, William A., and William P.

Hickey *Putnam County.* Fifty-four-year-old Elijah Hickey resided in Putnam County in 1870, as did Sandy Hickey, 27, and W. M. Hickey, 32. It is likely they were related, and collectively or individually gave their surname to this location.

Hickman *Smith County.* Wyatt Hickman, age 55; A. Hickman, 90; G. W. Hickman, 25; and H. Hickman, 32, resided locally in 1870. A strong likelihood exists that they and this place-name are related. One source refers to a location in the county by saying "at Hickman Mills"; so one or more of the family members may have operated a milling business here.

Hickory Flat *Carroll County.* Several varieties of hickory trees dotted this level area, including mockernut, pignut, bitternut, and shagbark, accounting for the name assigned to it.

Hickory Grove *Sumner County.* The sand hickory grows in this region and likely accounts for this designation being applied here.

Hickory Point *Cocke County.* This site takes its name from sand hickory trees that dot this section of the county.

Hickory Point *Montgomery County.* Pignut, butternut, mockernut, and shagbark hickory thrive throughout the state and undoubtedly grew here, giving the site its name.

Hickory Tree *Sullivan County.* The butternut, shagbark, pignut, and mockernut hickories all grow throughout Tennessee. A prominent hickory tree set this place apart from its surroundings.

Hickory Valley *Hardeman County.* A valley encircling this site was teeming with hickory trees.

Hickory Valley *Union County.* Hickory Valley is part of Big Valley, lying south of Norris Lake. Significant numbers of hickory trees characterize the site.

Hickory Withe *Shelby County.* A withe is a twig or slender branch. There were probably hickory trees growing at this locality. It is uncertain why this name was styled in this manner.

Hicks Chapel *Marion County.* Elijah and Isaac Hicks were identified with this locale in 1840. One of them may have been a minister at a church here, or donated land or materials for the building of a church.

Highcliff *Campbell County.* This site assumed its name as a result of high mountain cliffs in the vicinity.

Highland *Overton County.* This site took on its label owing to its location on "high land."

High Point *Morgan County.* A correspondent born and reared at High Point (or Highpoint) opines that the site inspired this name due to its elevation and the fact that, after the leaves had fallen, you could stand in High Point Cemetery and see places and people at a great distance.

Hilham *Overton County.* The village was founded by Moses Fisk, who laid it out prior to 1805. A Harvard graduate from Massachusetts, Fisk welcomed the first post office into his home and assumed the duties of postmaster. He referred to the town as his "hamlet in the hills," and from that phrase "Hilham" was derived. In 1806, Fisk established an academy for females at the site.

Hillard *Carroll County.* In 1850, Adison Hillard was a citizen of this locality, probably leaving it with his surname. However, in 1830, John Hilliard was a county resident as well. It was not uncommon for census takers to transcribe names incorrectly; so Adison's name may actually have been Hilliard, or perhaps Hillard was a variant of Hilliard.

Hillsboro *Coffee County.* Located on the Great Stage Road, Hillsboro was settled at an early year and narrowly missed becoming the county seat. At first, it was referred to as Pond Springs. When it was renamed, it was given the name of the county seat of Chatham County, North Carolina (Hillsboro). A great many Tennessee settlers arrived from North Carolina.

Hill Top *Bedford County.* This site was first known as Pleasant Hill. In 1890, blacksmith, photographer, and store owner James S. Smith was designated to submit a name for a post office to Washington, and submitted Pleasant Hill. The name was rejected because of the existence of another Pleasant Hill in the state. A second, unknown name was submitted, but that, too, was rejected. Hill Top was the third choice, and was accepted. The first settler at the site may have been a Baptist minister, Hezikiah Ray, who arrived with his son from South Carolina in 1811.

Hill Town *Maury County.* In 1870, at least twenty-three persons with the Hill surname resided in the county, probably accounting for this place-name. Included among them were Andrew, Abram, Booker, Jennett, Elizabeth, and two named Henry.

Hillville *Haywood County.* A native of the town who has done extensive genealogical research on the Hill surname suggests that the community gained the name by virtue of the many Hill families that resided here. The town was never formally laid out. Although it does not relate specifically to the town's name, an anecdote regarding the town's Methodist church proved amusing. Apparently, the church is widely referred to as Do-Me-Good. Supposedly, a worshiper once stated, "It do me good to go to church."

Hinkle *Hardin County.* Johnathan and Asbury Hinkle were local citizens in 1850, according to census rolls, probably accounting for this designation.

Hixson *Hamilton County.* An early local justice, Ephraim Hixson, is probably the individual for whom this hamlet was named, according to one source. A second source, the *Illustrated Dictionary of Place Names,* states that the community owes its name to E. F. Hixson (1862–1932), but identifies him as the station agent, postmaster, and proprietor of the local general store. It adds that the name was conferred by the Southern Railway Company. In mid-1861, a Wilson Hixson served as a delegate to the Knoxville Convention.

Hodges *Jefferson County.* As a common family name in the area, the place-name Hodges probably traces back to a local family. At one time, the site was referred to as Hodges' Switch. An Edmond Hodges, a Charles Hodges, and a Captain Hodges apparently had ties to this town.

Hoggtown *Smith County.* Hogg is not a particularly uncommon surname, and at the time the 1830 census was recorded for Middle Tennessee, David and Harvey Hogg resided in the county. They may have resided at this specific juncture, or later, one or more descendants may have lived here and inspired the place designation. In fact, by the time of the 1850 census, Hoggs listed as residing nearby included Griffin, Kanneday M., Leonaders D., Starky, and Sarah J.

Hohenwald *Lewis County* (*seat*). The *Illustrated Dictionary of Place Names* discloses that this name comes from the German for "high woods." The explorer Meriwether Lewis died nearby under mysterious circumstances in 1809.

Holladay *Benton County.* It is said that Congressman John M. Taylor was friends with John M. Holladay, and caused this site to be named for him.

Holladay *Putnam County.* The name of the site probably traces to the Holladay family, which came to Tennessee in an early year. Thomas and Martha (Whitehorn) Holladay were early settlers of the state. John Holladay came to the state in 1833, settling in this county. William A. Holladay, John's son, was born in 1850. William became the father of Oscar Holladay, who became prominent and served as a legislator.

Holland *Greene County.* At the time of the 1880 West Tennessee census, a number of Hollands resided locally. Included were John, age 39; N., 51; Sarah, 68; Nancy, 36; Jane, 3; and Eliza J., 50. The place-name was probably inspired by the family name.

Holloway *Wilson County.* Listed in the 1850 census rolls were Levi, Richard, Noah, and Ezekiel Holloway. They resided in Wilson County, and were probably identified with this locality.

Hollow Rock *Carroll County.* One source states that Hollow Rock takes its name from a nearby landmark, a huge (possibly glacial) rock described as being about the size of a boxcar, and partially hollowed out. Two rail lines crossed near here, with a village growing up around the intersection. Some referred to the place as Hollow Rock Junction. A second correspondent from the area describes the landmark boulder as being 45 feet long, 12 feet high, and 13 feet through, with a 13-foot chamber inside.

Holly Springs *Monroe County.* The place-name refers to Mitchell Holly, a local citizen in 1830, and the existence of one of Tennessee's many natural springs.

Hollywood *Maury County.* According to a source close to the scene, George Grissom opened a store here, on U.S. Route 31, in the 1930s. He built a couple small houses and moved his family here. About two hundred yards behind the store stood a solitary holly tree, on Millen Matthews's property. From its presence, the name Hollywood was adopted. The tree stood in the middle of a fifteen-acre field, and was the largest holly tree in the area. It was toppled by winds in the 1980s.

Holston *Sullivan County.* Widely applied and recognized in this region, the Holston name leads back to Stephen Holston, a river traveler and explorer who maintained a cabin locally as early as 1746. The Holston River also owes its name to him. This hamlet is about a mile from the river's south fork.

Holston Valley *Sullivan County.* This community lies in the valley of the Holston River. (See Holston entry.)

Holt *Cocke County.* A number of Holts were citizens of the nearby area when the 1840 census was enrolled, probably lending their name to this location. Among them were Sandy, Zebedee, Paskel, Edward, John, Agness, William, and Asa.

Holt *Wayne County.* The Holt label on Wayne County maps probably traces back to Keaton Holt, Elizabeth Holt, William T. Holt, or Joseph Holt. All were residents of the local area in 1830.

Holt's Corner *Marshall County.* Holt's Corner was formerly dubbed Holtland. The Post Office Department probably named it for John Hardeman Holt or a member of his family. Mr. Holt and his sons operated a general store here, at the northwest corner of his property.

Hoover's Gap *Rutherford County.* At the time of the 1870 census, there were quite a few Hoovers claiming local residency. Among them were Thomas, age 47; several Williams in their twenties and thirties; Joal D., 14; Calvin, 30; Mathius, 33; Bell, 22; John W., 33; and two with the given name Benjamin. The "Gap" part of this label no doubt refers to a passage between hills, or where a stream flows through, at this site.

Hopson *Carter County.* At least one family of early land proprietors at this locality had the Hopson surname.

Hornbeak *Obion County.* While some historians feel this label originated as a local person's surname, which seems unlikely, others feel it was inspired by a nearby geological/topographical feature.

Horner *Perry County.* When the 1850 county census was completed, its rolls revealed the names of Unus, John, and James J. Horner. In all probability, one or more had ties to this site.

Hornertown *Hickman County.* One source is quoted as saying, "Around the turn of the century," members of a Horner family purchased real estate in this vicinity and proceeded to clear some of the land and build homes. Exactly which century is referred to is unclear, but it was probably at the end of the 1800s. When a store opened and the site began to appear more like a community, it was given the name Hornertown.

Hornsby *Hardeman County.* Kimbrough Hornsby is the individual to whom this place-name traces back.

Horn Springs *Wilson County.* William, Richard, W., and Mathias Horn were local residents in 1840. One source speculates that their surname probably coupled with the existence of a natural spring here to constitute the place-name. A second source is more specific, claiming that the beneficial mineral content of the springwaters here was discovered in 1870 by James Baker Horn.

Horseshoe *Carter County.* A waterway off the Watauga River, leading to Wilbur Dam, features a large horseshoe bend in the shoreline. The community of Horseshoe is located along this bend.

Houston *Wayne County.* By 1870 only one Houston was located on the county's census rolls of that year—Mary. It is likely that the place took its name either from her or her ancestors.

Houston Station *Blount County.* This name goes back as far as 1785, when an uncle of the noted Sam Houston, Major James Houston, stationed troops at a fort erected here.

Houston Valley *Greene County.* Howell Houston and William Houston Jr. were 1840 residents of this between-mountains area. The name found on today's maps probably relates in some manner to these individuals, or other members of their family.

Howard *Monroe County.* Franklin, Briant, Antoni, and Harrison Howard were county residents in 1870. They ranged in age from 25 to 50. Some of the local Howards carried a designation in census records of the day that indicates they were African Americans.

Howard Hill *Sullivan County.* This elevation probably traces its name to Edward and/or John Howard, local citizens in 1870, or their ancestors. Edward was 36 at the time, while John was 21.

Howell *Lincoln County.* Howell Harris, an early storekeeper, is believed to be the namesake of the village, which at an earlier time was known as Cane Creek. At one time, it may have been referred to as Renfro Station, when Lawson Renfro was postmaster. The Howell name may have come into usage in 1881.

Howell Hill *Lincoln County.* David Howell and Reese Howell arrived in this vicinity in the early part of the 1800s, coming from the Bowling Green, Kentucky, area. They had received government land grants to property here, but Reese eventually moved on, to Howell's Cove, in Alabama, while David remained here, residing at the bottom of the hill. Many Howells eventually populated this area. Marion Howell was a grandson of David, while Charles Reese Howell Sr. was a great-grandson. A son of David had the given name Charlie (probably Charles). On the rolls of the county's 1850 census were Moses, Charles S., James, Elizabeth, Jefferson, and William Howell. C. R. Howell Jr. still resided in the hamlet in the late 1980s.

Hubbard *Blount County.* When the 1850 state census was recorded, it revealed a number of Hubbards residing in Blount County. Among them were Absalom, Charles, Elijah, and Sally Hubbard, as well as James J. and Nell Hubbart. One or more of these families was probably recognized with this place-name on maps. The surname ending in a *t* could have been a variant spelling or misrecorded. Even earlier, in 1840, John Hubbard was in the area. By 1880, census rolls were showing Elisabeth Hubbard, age 78, as a local resident.

Hudson *Lawrence County.* In the late 1800s this locality was settled by several families, among whom was one with the Hudson surname.

Hughett *Scott County.* This name undoubtedly traces back to the first postmaster at the site, Jasper Hughett, whose appointment became effective in June 1887.

Hughey *Lincoln County.* In 1890, Alonzo Hughey was appointed postmaster here, maintaining the facilities in his home until they were later moved into a store in the village. His wife's name was Nora. The area in general was settled in the early 1800s. A nearby site was at first known as Needmore. The post office was called Hughey; so in time the community, too, was dubbed Hughey.

Humboldt *Gibson County.* A German naturalist, Baron von Humboldt, is commemorated in the name of this city.

Hunter *Carter County.* The place-name is probably attributable to one of the families surnamed Hunter who populated this vicinity. Some of those included Dr. Edward Eugene Hunter (1845–1918), or his father, Joseph, who was born in 1808. The archives also mention a Maranda Hunter and a Joseph Hunter residing in this general vicinity at an early year.

Huntersville *Madison County.* A store and physician's office were operated here by Dr. John Hunter, who passed away in 1876.

Huntersville *Rutherford County.* An early postmaster here, Robert L. Hunt, gives his name to the village. Mr. Hunt was also a storekeeper for a period during the community's early days.

Huntingdon *Carroll County (seat).* This city was founded in 1822 on a parcel donated by Mimican Hunt for the purpose of establishing a county seat. Hunt held deed to some five thousand acres in the vicinity. Huntington was named in his honor. The town may have been platted by James H. Gee, and was incorporated the year after its founding. Its previous name was Huntsville. It was renamed by Robert E. C. Daugherty. An additional contributor on Huntingdon holds the opinion that Huntingdon, Tennessee; Huntingdon, Pennsylvania; and Huntingdon, England are the only places tracing their name back to an original English county with the same name. That entity, he states, was the Anglo-Saxon kingdom of Mercia, which became Huntingdon-Godmanchester and is today Huntingdon-Peterborough. The Tennessee city was once the home of Davy Crockett, and two of the state's governors came from here.

Huntland *Franklin County.* State census records for 1870 reveal the local residency of several Hunts: Benjamin P., Clinton, David, Nancy, George, Henry, and two with the given name Spencer. The family—or families—were probably related to this hamlet's naming.

Huntsville *Scott County (seat).* Incorporation took place in 1965. Huntsville may have been so named for a local family with the Hunt surname, or for what was considered to be "good hunting" in the vicinity. One source actually includes both explanations, claiming that a hunter having the Hunt surname first settled this place. Previously, the site was dubbed Hunter's Spring (there were several springs in the area).

Hurdlow *Moore County.* This name became ensconced in the early 1890s when a post office was opened and citizens were asked to submit name suggestions. Miss Ella Hurdlow was a popular teacher at nearby Liberty Hill School, and her surname was accepted as the name for the post office. The surrounding community also took on that designation. Ella later married a Lincoln County farmer and landowner, Edward Baldwin.

Hurley *Hardin County.* When the 1840 census was taken, Thomas and Josiah Hurley lived nearby. They probably gave this place its name.

Huron *Henderson County.* The reason this hamlet was given its name is uncertain, but the term is French-Canadian in origin. It is said to translate loosely as "rough person," and Canada's French applied the term to members of a Native American nation, who became known as Hurons. When they moved into the northern United States, they changed their name to Wyandot.

Hurricane Mills *Humphreys County.* One or more mills were located here. Farmers brought their corn here to be ground for cornmeal, and their wheat to be returned to them in the form of flour. A resident states that a hurricane came through, and thereafter the place was known as Hurricane Mills. The "hurricane" was probably what would today be termed a tornado.

Hustburg *Humphreys County.* Local marriage records reveal that William Hust and William H. Hust took brides in 1891 and 1892, respectively. One of the Williams was married to a woman named Harriet; they had children named John and Sarah J. Several Husts resided in the county during these times. Thus there is probably a relationship between the place-name and the surname.

Hyndsver *Weakley County.* All that could be learned about this place-name is that it refers to a pioneer family named Hynds, who donated land for a church and school.

I

Iconium *Cannon County.* This is another biblically inspired place-name. The ancient city mentioned in Acts of the Apostles 14 was at one time known for its beauty and prosperity and was located in south-central Asia Minor.

Idaville *Tipton County.* This community was founded by the first postmaster, John Gettys McCain, who in naming the site did so in honor of Ida McCain, his daughter.

Idlewild *Gibson County.* The locality had two earlier names—Thedford and then Sprawling—tracing back to the surnames of early settlers (John R. Thetford and a man named Sprawling, who either influenced the establishment of a depot or was himself associated with the railroad). The community began to arise in about 1877. Later, it adopted the Idlewild name. Although somewhat suspect, the local explanation is that, at the time (according to Gus Baker, a grocer), the men of the town were "idle" and "wild."

Indian Mound *DeKalb County.* A local historian speculates that the site derived its name from a prehistoric Native American mound in the vicinity, most likely located in nearby bottomland and since covered by the waters of Center Hill Lake.

Indian Mound *Stewart County.* This name caught on with early area settlers, who discovered a large Indian mound at the site. Early deeds used it as a reference point. An iron production facility arose here.

Indian Springs *Sullivan County.* A correspondent from this town advises that there are two natural springs on her property, and probably others in the immediate vicinity. She states, "We have found a large number of Indian stone artifacts that wash out of the soil every time it rains . . . including stone flakes and arrowheads . . . leading us to believe Indians were manufacturing stone tools in this area. . . . Our back yard would have formed an ideal campsite, being sheltered from the winds and located near the springs and creek. . . . It would seem the encampment was here over a long period of time."

Iron City *Lawrence County.* The locality featured an iron foundry in its formative years; so the Iron City name was conferred upon it. Mining began here as early as 1832. A branch railroad line to service the mines was built in 1886; so the town was actually established that year. The following year it was incorporated. The community lost its charter in 1901 but was reincorporated in 1962.

Iron Hill *Dickson County.* Iron Hill received its name by virtue of the many tons of iron ore that were removed from the hills here, and shipped by train to other states.

Ironsburg *Monroe County.* James Irons, age 55, and Alvin J. Irons, age 36, were local residents in 1880. The site at which they lived probably came to be referred to as Ironsburg.

Irving College *Warren County.* A prestigious educational institute was located here, having been founded in 1838. Its originators named it for Washington Irving. It flourished between 1840 and 1890, attracting students from the entire South, many of whom went on to become noted leaders in high-profile fields. The place was once called Morrison's Crossroads.

Isbell *Maury County.* In 1840 James Isbell lived in the county. This site probably refers to him or one of his descendants.

Isom *Maury County.* In 1870, A., J. A., J. L., and S. H. Isom called this area home. The Isom designation on maps probably harks back to one or more of these individuals.

Ivydell *Campbell County.* David, William, Sarah, Robert, and Absalom Ivy were county residents when the 1850 census was recorded. It is likely the family name was joined with the descriptive term *dell* to form the place-name.

Jacksboro *Campbell County (seat).* A local hero, Captain James W. Jack, is the referent of this place-name.

Jacksboro *Warren County.* In the early 1800s, this site was given its name in honor of General Andrew Jackson, although its first post office took the name Trousdale, for early Tennessee settler and governor William Trousdale.

Jackson *Madison County (seat).* The city is named for the hero of the Battle of New Orleans and the nation's seventh president, Andrew Jackson. It is said to have been named by its founder, William Edward Butler, because his wife was Andrew Jackson's wife's niece. The community was established on lands belonging to Joseph Lynn, James Trousdale, and B. G. Stewart. William H. Doak is believed to have first settled the locality. The incorporation of Jackson took place in 1845.

Jackson Chapel *Dickson County.* The place-name refers to a place of worship identified closely with the Reverend Judge Jackson (his given name was Judge). A Methodist congregation assembled here, starting prior to the Civil War. A number of Jacksons lived in the vicinity as early as 1850, including Willis, Peter, James, Jane, and two with the given name of Green.

Jackson Ridge *Rutherford County.* The 1830 Middle Tennessee census records identify Coleman and Nancy J. Jackson as residing in the county at the time. It is possible, or probable, that these persons or their ancestors were closely identified with this topographical feature and community.

Jalapa *Monroe County.* During the Mexican War, Americans occupied a city by this name in Mexico. One Jalapa is south of Villahermosa, and a larger one northwest of the coastal city of Veracruz. This place-name was probably appropriated from one of those in Mexico.

Jameson *Maury County.* The name of the site was inspired by early settler John Jameson, who came here by or before 1820.

Jamestown *Fentress County (seat).* The city takes its name from the older, larger, better-known community of Jamestown, Virginia.

Jarrell *Carroll County.* The community was once known as Gwin Station. A sawmill operating here was named B. C. Jarrell & Co., of Humboldt. A request was made, perhaps in the 1920s, to change the name from Gwin Station to Jarrell Switch. Mr. Jarrell reportedly resided here. It was a place where trains on the Louisville & Nashville (L&N) could "switch" off the main line to let another train pass. Most now refer to the site simply as Jarrell.

Jasper *Marion County (seat).* The hero of the Battle of Fort Sullivan, Sergeant William Jasper (1750–1779), is the community's namesake. Hailing from South Carolina, Jasper served with distinction during the American Revolution, losing his life at Savannah.

Jeannette *Decatur County.* Once a fairly busy community, Jeannette was previously known as Howesville. It is not known why the name was changed to Jeannette. A map uses the Jeannette spelling, but local sources spell it Jeanette.

Jefferson City *Jefferson County.* The country's third president, Thomas Jefferson (1743–1826), inspired the name of both this town and the county. Among his many accomplishments and claims to fame, Jefferson was a skilled architect.

Jefferson Estates *Jefferson County.* As an offshoot of Jefferson City, Jefferson Estates also owes its name to Thomas Jefferson.

Jellico *Campbell County.* According to one source, oddly enough the name derives from a plant, the root of which was used to brew a beverage called jelka. The main ingredient was angelica root. This name was applied in 1883, but previously the site was known as Smithburg. Starting as early as 1795, several families of Smiths had settled at the location. A second source claims that the place-name was Jerrico, but was misspelled as Jellico, and became accepted in that style. If so, the intended Jerrico name may have been a misspelling itself, if inspired by the biblical Jericho. Jellico's initial incorporation took place in 1885, but reincorporations occurred in 1903 and 1907.

Jernigan Town *Robertson County.* A local source states only that the place was "named for the numerous Jernigan families living there." The state's 1870 census records disclose a large number of Jernigans, most of them identified only by their initials. Included were T. W., age 41; Mary, 60; William, 55; L. B., 43; E. G., 32; J. A., 56; J. S., 30; E. T., 23; W. F., 33; and J. P., 22.

Jessie *Warren County.* For a period, the locality was known as Mountain Creek. In 1881, it was changed to Jessie, for Jessie Coffee, sister of Major P. H. Coffee of McMinnville, who worked in the postmaster general's office in the nation's capital during the 1880s.

Jewel *Weakley County.* A Mr. Fowler served as postmaster at this locality. According to archival material, his son was named Jewel Fowler, and since the office needed a name, the postmaster named it by using his son's given name. Some maps style the name as Jewell.

Jewel Cave *Dickson County.* Jewel Cave was discovered in 1886 on land belonging to a merchant farmer from Cave Mills, Thomas Rogers. In a book by William Nesbitt, it is said that Rogers and his young daughter, Fannie, were exploring the opening of a stream that flowed from the ridge. They crawled through a small, narrow opening to find a cave about 350 square feet in size, featuring a number of exquisite formations. The cave had numerous rooms. Not knowing the extent of the labyrinth they'd discovered, Rogers took along a pine board and along their route, he whittled wood shavings onto the path so they could find their way back. Rogers is said to have initially mistaken the stalactites and stalagmites for tombstones marking Indian graves. Upon emerging from the recess, they told the entire neighborhood of their discovery. Eventually, the entrance was enlarged, and many people came to see this natural marvel. A cavern in back of Jewel Cave was found in 1930. There, explorers found more stalactites, flowstone, quartz crystal formations, and the ancient bones of a cave bear. The beauty of Jewel Cave inspired its name.

Jewett *Cumberland County.* The place-name probably traces to an 1870 local resident, Charley Jewett Jr., or his father.

John Sevier *Knox County.* The namesake of this hamlet was the state's first governor, General John Sevier, described in one source as "a Huguenot frontiersman." Sevier died in 1815.

Johnson City *Washington County.* The earlier designation for this community was Hainesville. In 1879, however, it was renamed in honor of a respected citizen who became its first mayor, Henry Johnson (1809–1874). Johnson came to the locality in 1834, establishing a store adjacent to the railroad's right-of-way. It should be noted, however, that one printed source contends that the city was named for Andrew Jackson.

Johnson's Crossroads *Sumner County.* The 1850 census records reveal many Johnsons residing in the vicinity of this intersection. Among them were two named Elizabeth, two named Margaret, Silas, Thomas H., Thomas P., Barodill, Leonidas, Rebecca, Richard E., Richard M., James H., James J., James S., George, David T., David M., Francis, Burwell, two Williams, and Benjamin.

Jonesboro *Washington County (seat).* One source claims that this community was laid out in 1779, which seems implausibly early, although it also is said that Jonesboro was the first incorporated town in the state. The Watauga settlements dispatched delegates to North Carolina, where they were received graciously by Governor Caswell and a person named Willie Jones, described as "a friend of John Paul Jones." Jonesboro's name honors Jones—presumably, John Paul. The place-name is seen styled both as Jonesboro and as Jonesborough.

Jones Cove *Sevier County.* The name stems from the John Jones family from Virginia. Early in the 1790s, the family settled in the cove, which is tucked between the Great Smoky Mountains and English Mountain. In 1794, Stephen Jones was killed by Indians and is buried near the New Salem Baptist Church.

Jones Mill *Henry County.* A number of Joneses were nearby citizens in 1870; one or more of them was probably involved in the operation of a mill. Among those residing locally were Ann, John, A. B., E. J. B., Daniel, H. S., J. S., Isham, J. H., and J. M. Jones. At that time, the eldest of those mentioned was A. B. at 64, and the youngest was Daniel at 23.

Jones Valley *Hickman County.* The first merchant in the valley was Thomas Jones; so the locale took on his surname.

Joppa *Grainger County.* An area historian recounts this version of the Joppa place-name story: "In the community, there was a church called Spring House Baptist Church. A black minister came and preached a series of sermons [there]. It is said by those who attended that each sermon was centered around the 'city of Joppa.' [The minister] made the statement that 'Joppa was a Sabbath-day journey from Jerusalem.' There was a young man, noted for his humor, who heard these sermons and started a saying, 'Let's all go over to Joppa.' Others picked up the line, and the place came to be called Joppa." Another source states that Joppa may refer to a Hebrew word meaning "beauty," or to a biblical seaport.

Kagley *Blount County.* Several Kagleys were associated with this area. Included were Joseph Kagley and Will Kagley.

Kansas *Jefferson County.* The Native American term *kansa* may have translated as "people of the south wind" and is believed to be Siouan in origin.

Kansas *Sumner County.* See preceding entry.

Karns *Knox County.* The East Tennessee census of 1880 identified a number of individuals with surnames pronounced the same as this one. Some spelled it Karns and others as Karnes. The former included Charles, age 60; James, 45; John, 27; John, 87; Michael, 60; and William Karns, 32. Those using the alternate spelling were Elebeth, 73; Jackson, 52; William, 21; and Ranson Karnes, 43.

Kedron *Maury County.* This name is usually bestowed because it occurs in the Bible. It is considered the proper Greek form of *Kidron,* as with Brook Kidron, a stream that flows near Jerusalem.

Keefe *Lake County.* In 1870, William, age 31, and Thomas Keefe, 55, resided in the area. It is likely their surname became associated with this site.

Keeling *Haywood County.* Most of the land at this site was held by a Mr. Keeling; so it became known by his surname.

Keenburg *Carter County.* This place-name traces back to the several Keens residing here in 1850. They included Enoch Keen, age 61; William, 32; and Jonas H., 55.

Keith Springs *Franklin County.* A gentleman recalled only as Mr. Keith owned the land where several springs were located; so the place became known as Keith Springs. A native remembers that three springs were located in close proximity to one another, each containing water of a different taste. One was freestone water, one was limestone water, "and one produced what the older people called 'cleavit' water."

Kellertown *Bedford County.* Local citizens in 1870 included W. G., age 33; F. M., 26; Ransom, 25; J. W., 48; and Henry Keller, 77. The community takes its name from their families.

Kellum *Giles County.* Thomas J. Kellum lived here in 1840. His family name adhered to the site.

Kelly's Creek *Lincoln County.* The site probably owes its name to John Kelly and a steam running through the place. Kelly was one of the earliest residents, purchasing land prior to 1817.

Kelso *Lincoln County.* See following entry.

Kelso *Moore County.* There is a Kelso in Roxburgh, Scotland. Sites using this name often were named or settled by those of Scottish heritage.

Keltonburg *DeKalb County.* The post office was named for James Kelton, who erected a mill at the site in 1875.

Kempville *Smith County.* At the time of the 1830 census for the central portion of Tennessee, two Kemps are shown to have resided in this area—Cynthia and Richard. It is not unlikely that one or both of these Kemps gave the site its name. At probably a later time, fifteen Kemps are known to have resided locally. W. L. Kemp Jr., born 1842, was one of thirteen children, served in the Confederate army, and dealt in timber. Asa, Claude, Sarah, Eddie, and Hettie were other local Kemps.

Kenneytown *Greene County.* In 1870, numerous Kenneys resided in this vicinity. They included James D., age 37; Harvy, 34; William, 31; Elizabeth, 50; William, 24; and two named George, ages 65 and 36, respectively.

Kenton *Gibson and Obion Counties.* Like Kenton, Ohio, this community traces its name back to the noted Indian fighter Simon Kenton. The year 1899 marked the town's incorporation.

Kerrville *Shelby County.* The 1850 census for the state recorded a William A. Kerr in Shelby County, probably providing a good clue as to the origin of this place-name.

Key *White County.* According to the *History of Tennessee Illustrated: White, Warren, DeKalb, Coffee, and Cannon Counties,* the first (1809) mercantile enterprise in the county seat of Sparta was known as Keys & Clemmons. The reason for the discrepancy between "Key" and "Keys" is not evident. The individual with this surname may have had a connection to this map designation.

Kilgore's Station *Robertson County.* Thomas Kilgore and some associates are credited with having established this place as early as 1780. The "Station" portion of the name was probably appended much later, unless it was assigned for other than railroad-related reasons. One source claims that Thomas Kilgore lived to be 108 years old.

Kimball *Marion County.* Incorporation took place in 1962. The designation derives from the name of an individual, H. I. Kimball, who in 1880 organized an ill-fated enterprise known as the Kimball Town Company. When the Cherokees still occupied the location, it bore the name Crow Mocker's Place.

Kimberlin Heights *Knox County.* According to the volume *The French Broad-Holston Country,* this community dates its founding to 1786. Its first several place-names were Green's, Manifold's Station, and Gap Creek. In 1787 Jacob Kimberlin discovered lead deposits and provided lead to local citizens. It was not until 1887 that the place became known as Kimberlin Heights.

Kimbro *Davidson County.* W. P., John, J. N., and Samuel Kimbro were county citizens in 1870. It is likely they settled at the place that bears this name.

Kimbrough Crossroads *Jefferson County.* This locality was dotted with Kimbroughs in 1840. Bennona, Bradley, Duke W., Daniel, two Thomases, Robert G., and John were among them. The "Crossroads" portion of the name stems from the location at intersecting thoroughfares.

Kimery *Weakley County.* The Kimery brothers operated a store at this location, and eventually the whole community took on the Kimery label.

Kimsey *Polk County.* The Kimsey family played an important role in the early settlement and development of this (Turtletown-Copper Basin) area of the county almost since earliest times. "Buttermilk John" Kimsey established the Kimsey Dairy Farm on a 410-acre tract. In 1852, the Kimsey Store and Post Office opened, under the management of Matthew S. Kimsey. In 1888, Walter S. Kimsey was postmaster a year before the office was moved to Ducktown, where Erastus Kimsey became postmaster briefly in 1901.

Kinderhook *Maury County.* This site bears part of the nickname of President Martin Van Buren (1782–1862), who was sometimes known as "Old Kinderhook."

Kingsport *Sullivan County.* According to *Historical Sketches of the Holston Valleys,* the city takes its name from James King, who was born in London, England, in 1752. In about 1773, King came here and built a mill at a site known variously as King's Mill or King's Station. King also spent several years as a soldier, attaining the rank of colonel. However, another version may be more credible. It holds that the name refers to William King, a Virginian who came here and operated William King's Boatyard on the shore of the Holston River. The site apparently had a procession of names. First it was Peace Island, after which it was called Great Island, Island Flat, Fort Robinson (in 1761), Fort Patrick Henry (in 1776), The Boatyard, Christianville (in 1802), Rossville (in 1818), and finally, in 1822, Kingsport.

Kingston *Roane County (seat).* A prominent landholder and soldier during the American Revolution, Major Robert King, left his surname with this town. (One source refers to him as Major Roger King.)

Kingston Springs *Cheatham County.* Incorporation took place in 1965. The name refers to sulfur waters and mineral waters emanating from several springs near some local caves. At some early year, a family having the Kingston surname settled in this locality, accounting for the balance of the place-name. The springs became quite an attraction in the surrounding vicinity, and the hamlet that eventually grew up took the Kingston Springs label.

Kinney *Robertson County.* Richard Kinney was involved in a land transaction in Robertson County in 1806, according to early records. The site name relates to him or his family. A local source states that the place is named for the Mr. Kinney who at one time managed a large distillery here. The label is sometimes seen styled as Kinney's.

Kinzel Springs *Blount County.* A hotel and resort grew up here around two clear mineral springs and cold streams. E. J. Kinzel purchased the property from Colonel Wade Tipton, and it was under Kinzel's ownership that the place became a popular destination. Some refer to the locality as Sunshine, because at one time Kinzel gave a piece of property to the International Sunshine Society, a women's group.

Kirby *Macon County.* At some time during the post-1840 years, a business named M. L. Kirby & Co., Drugs, existed in this vicinity. The Kirby for whom this community is named was probably the same one involved with operation of the drugstore.

Kirk *Fayette County.* At about the time of the Civil War, some members of the John Kirk (1802–1870) family relocated from eastern Shelby County across the Warren County line, to this site. A second John Kirk (ca. 1837–ca. 1911) founded this community in the 1880s. He was a storekeeper and, in 1896, postmaster.

Kirkland *Lincoln County.* George, Thomas, John, and William Kirkland populated this locale in 1850. This label on the map may trace back to them, or at least one of them. Other sources, however, state that the site went by the earlier designations of Frogville and Oak Grove. The Frogville name seemed a natural, since the amphibians would set up quite a din after dark. It was so dubbed by a man named Mount McMillan. The Kirkland name was adopted in 1937 when Pauline Towry asked for, and received, permission to change the town's label from Frogville, to give it a more "dignified" designation. At some point, a Rev. John Kirkland had staged revival meetings, or "brush arbor meetings," at the site. It is not known if he is the same John Kirkland mentioned above, or a different one in the family chain. The Towry family has been closely identified with this community, having operated cotton gins at the location.

Kite *Hawkins County.* At the time of the 1840 census, a number of Kites populated the neighborhood. Henry, James, John, and Martin were among them, as well as two named George and one named George Sr. When the 1850 census was compiled, George A. Kite and Hannah Kite resided in the vicinity. It is likely one or more of these Kites gave their surname to the site.

Knob Creek *Sevier County.* This community is located in a region of hills often described as "knobs." A Baptist church was organized here in 1868. Knob Creek is also the name of a stream flowing through the hamlet.

Knox *Shelby County.* Several Knoxes are mentioned in burial records of the county's Magnolia Cemetery, one of them being Mary D. Knox. F. M. Knox is recorded as having passed away in August of 1874.

Knoxville *Knox County (seat).* The city took its name from the nation's first secretary of war, Major General Henry Knox, who served under George Washington. Knox (1750–1806) was a soldier during and after the Revolutionary War, and served as commander in chief of the army. Knoxville was laid out in 1791; for a time, it served as the state capital. The Knoxville name was assigned by the state's governor. Captain James White settled the site.

Kodak *Sevier County.* According to *American Place-Names,* this locality derives its name from the trade name of a well-known camera.

Kyle's Ford *Hancock County.* "Ford" usually denotes a site where a river or stream crossing was convenient. This site is on the Clinch River. When the 1870 census was taken, Robert, age 64, William, 35, and Asbury Kyle, 28, were local citizens. The name probably traces to one or more of them, or someone in their ancestry.

Laager *Grundy County.* A family with the Laager surname resided in this area, near Gruetli. Like many others in the area, they were Swiss. In 1980, the two towns joined and were incorporated as one, called Gruetli-Laager. (See Gruetli entry.)

Laconia *Fayette County.* According to some sources, this label is sometimes assigned to places on lakes or large bodies of water. However, there are no significant bodies of water near this Laconia. For unknown reasons, it may have been named for a small city in central New Hampshire, or the Laconia that in ancient times was a country that is today southern Greece.

Lacy *Hardeman County.* In 1870, 57-year-old James Lacy resided in this area. It is likely that his surname became associated with this site. With a variant spelling of the surname, Sam Lacey, 28, was also a local citizen in 1870.

Ladd's *Marion County.* This site is also known as Ladd's Cove. Early histories mention Balis and Virginia Reed Ladd, Jennie Ladd, and W. R. Ladd as having ties to this locality. Balis was a son of George Washington Turl Ladd (b. 1808). Amos, Constantine, and Noble Ladd lived nearby at the time of the 1830 census of East Tennessee.

Lafayette *Macon County (seat).* Virtually every place in the country with this name took it in honor of the Marquis de Lafayette (1757–1834), French general and statesman, who volunteered during the American Revolution and served under General Washington. The city was laid out in 1842.

LaFollette *Campbell County.* The city owes its name to the president of one of its early industries, the LaFollette Iron & Coal Company. Harvey LaFollette presided over the business.

LaGrange *Fayette County.* The rural estate of the Marquis de Lafayette (1757–1834) was called LaGrange. Many U.S. places use the name, due largely to the fact that Lafayette was held in very high regard in the United States. This site was once known as LaBelle Village. A charter was issued in 1829.

Lake City *Anderson County.* Originally called Coal Creek (or Cole Creek), the settlement was incorporated in 1909. The name officially became Lake City thirty years later. The change may have been due, in part, to the establishment of Norris Dam in the vicinity by the Tennessee Valley Authority (TVA), creating a lake. Although the earliest white settlers may have been the family of John Cole, in the early 1800s, accounting for the Cole Creek spelling, coal was later discovered in great quantity, possibly inspiring the name *Coal* Creek.

Lakeland *Shelby County.* A number of lakes dot the vicinity; so this community acquired the Lakeland name. An individual named Louis Garner had visions of the place becoming a resort community.

Lakemont *Blount County.* This name is said to have been inspired by the remarks of Albert Kinser in 1936. Kinser was a member of a community club that met at McGinley Garage, and made an observation about the Fort Loudoun waters encroaching on Little River as he looked toward the mountains. Julian McGinley and Bill Law, who attended the meeting, attribute the name to Kinser's comments.

Lakeside *Monroe County.* The location is near Tellico Lake, on the Little Tennessee River.

Lakesite *Hamilton County.* Incorporation came in 1972. The name was inspired by the site, on Lake Chickamauga.

Lake Tansi Village *Cumberland County.* This community grew up around Lake Tansi.

Lakeview *Franklin County.* Lakeview is located on a body of water dubbed Lakeview Lake.

Lakewood *Davidson County.* At the time of settlement, this was a densely timbered area adjacent to a lake; so the name was a natural. Today, Lakewood is classified as a city.

Lakewood Village *Rhea County.* Bordered on two sides by water, this community overlooks Watts Bar Lake and has nearby access to a wide spot on the Piney River.

Lambert *Fayette County.* William Lambert, 40 years of age at the time, resided locally in 1870. Some might assume that the designation on maps therefore traces in some way to him. However, a separate source contends that the community takes its name from Levi Lamb, a store operator here until 1881. The same source states that the town known as Lambert came into being during the 1870s.

Lancaster *Smith County.* Several persons having the Lancaster surname resided nearby in 1850. They included Michael, William, William H., and two named Thomas. When the *History of Tennessee Illustrated* was compiled, sixteen county Lancasters were mentioned. Michael was a Ninth District farmer, born 1815. Others included Ira, Frances, Elizabeth, Jane, Wade, and West.

Lancing *Morgan County.* The community is thought to have been founded in the 1860s. It may have been in 1860 that the first settler, John White, constructed a house. Its series of names included Triplet Hill, Triplett's Gap, Kismet, and the current Lancing. The Kismet name adhered to the post office until 1894. It is sometimes seen styled as Kismit. The railroad people always referred to the site as Lancing; they are believed to have so named it, but for reasons now lost.

Lane *Dyer County.* When the 1850 census was taken, George W. and E. Lane were local citizens. By 1870, other Lanes were listed as residing nearby. Included were Elizabeth, age 42; Charles (Chalmers?), age 50; Thomas, 37; John, 30; and Sarah, 33. They, or their families, were probably connected in some direct way to the name of this site.

Laneview *Gibson County.* The descriptive "view" was apparently appended to the Lane surname, which was held by many county residents in 1850, many of whom resided in the Eleventh Civil District (Absolom, Elizabeth, and William). Other local Lanes were Abner S., Mary, Owen, M. B., and another named William.

Langford *Wilson County.* Thomas N. Langford was a local citizen at the time of the 1850 census. The label probably is tied in some way to this individual or his relatives. The longer version of the name, Langford Cave, is still seen on some maps.

Lanier *Blount County.* The place-name traces back to the Lanier clan, including Sterling Lanier of Georgia, and the poet Sidney Lanier. Some of Sidney Lanier's writings had local settings; he was also a musician. A local school board member, Sam Johnson, is credited with suggesting the Lanier name for local schools, established in 1922. A note of interest: Clingman's Dome, the highest point in North Carolina (and very near the Tennessee border), was named for Thomas Lanier Clingman.

Lantana *Cumberland County.* This name is derived from that of a flower. It is probably given to places for its suggestion of beauty or attractiveness.

Lascassas *Rutherford County.* Some say this label was given to the site by a Spanish priest, while others hold that it referred to a Native American encampment along the Trail of Tears followed by the Cherokee people on their forced journey west. The original form may have been Las Casa, or (roughly) "the house," in Spanish. A related account cites a tribal chief who assumed the Lascassas (or equivalent) name from a priest in de Soto's party.

Lassiter Corner *Obion County.* This locality is situated at an intersection on Foothill Road. The Lassiter to whom the label traces may have been an ancestor of E. Lasetter, a local citizen who was 22 years of age in 1870. Several variants on the spelling of this surname are found in county annals. Some may have been merely transcription errors when census data were collected.

Latham *Weakley County.* E. P. Latham, who arrived in the vicinity from North Carolina in about 1850 and settled nearby, is the hamlet's namesake.

Laurel Bloomery *Johnson County.* The "Bloomery" part of the place-name refers to the term for a forge or furnace in which wrought iron "blooms" were produced from cast iron or ore. (A more modern term for one type of steel mill is a "blooming mill.") It is uncertain why the site has the "Laurel" in its name. Perhaps there was a profuse growth of mountain laurel in the vicinity.

Laurelburg *Van Buren County.* An abundant growth of mountain laurel in this vicinity suggested the name.

Laurel Hill *DeKalb County.* The post office on Wolf Creek took on this name by 1856, probably owing to mountain laurel growing profusely on the surrounding hills. Later, the school assumed the same name.

Lavergne *Rutherford County.* The community took the name of an individual who was born in France in 1767 and eventually arrived in this county. His name was Francis Leonard de Roulhac de La Vergne, but later he shortened it to Francis Roulhac. The town did not adopt the name until after Roulhac's death in 1852.

Lawrenceburg *Lawrence County (seat).* Both the county and town names commemorate Captain James Lawrence (1781–1813), a naval commander from New Jersey who fought at Tripoli from 1801 to 1805, and in the War of 1812. He is best recalled for uttering the memorable words, "Don't give up the ship," as he commanded the *Chesapeake* against the *Shannon.* Lawrence was mortally wounded in the encounter.

Law's Chapel *Blount County.* A local family with the Law surname gave its name to this site, and to a place of worship.

Laws' Hill *Marshall County.* This elevation takes its label from the surname of one or several individuals who settled here in an early year: Isaac, Lee, John, and Julia Laws. Lee and Julia Laws were African Americans.

Lawson Crossroads *Blount County.* Residing in this area in 1850 were Daniel B. and Mary Lawsin (relationship, if any, uncertain), as well as Matilda and William A. Lawson (relationship, if any, uncertain). The locality probably owes its name to one or more of these individuals or families. A second source states that the intersection took its name because "Billy Lawson's house" stood there.

Lawton *McNairy County.* The location is said to have been known as Chicken Bristle until about 1916. One day, a man from Lawton, Oklahoma, came through, and apparently applied the Lawton name to this site, or inspired local residents to adopt the designation. The "original" Lawton, now referred to as Old Lawton, was situated on the main road between neighboring communities. In 1925, when U.S. Route 64 was constructed, the town's focus began shifting toward the new thoroughfare. This site is now often referred to as New Lawton, or simply Lawton.

Leach *Carroll County.* When the census of West Tennessee was taken in 1830, William, James, John, and Thomas Leach were residents of this county. It is likely one or more of them resided at this location and gave to it the family name. Numerous Leaches lived in this vicinity in 1870, according to census data. Some of them, and their ages, follow: Linsey, 49; Thomas, 57; Smith, 48; Thomas 39; James, 66; William, 42; Faster, 28; Gaynes, 34; John D., 42; Lucinda, 36; Joseph, 35; and John, 40.

Leadvale *Jefferson County.* A correspondent who is a native of this area writes that a lead mine was once located here, and the bullets made from it were shipped by flatboats to help Andrew Jackson win the Battle of New Orleans in 1812.

Lea Lakes *Grainger County.* This site takes its name from medicinal spring waters located here, and from Major Lea, who in 1792 obtained a grant from North Carolina to some two thousand acres. Major Lea was impressed by both the region's natural beauty and by the quality of the waters. Since he was a land appraiser for the government, he was a good judge of location.

Lea Springs *Grainger County.* The name Luke Lea was on tax lists for this area in 1805. The springs may take their name from him, a descendant, or an ancestor. (Also see preceding entry.)

Lebanon *Hardin County.* See entry for Lebanon, Wilson County.

Lebanon *Rutherford County.* See following entry.

Lebanon *Wilson County (seat).* Biblical mentions of the "cedars of Lebanon" inspired this place-name. Locally grown red cedars went into the manufacture of pencils, slats, handles, and spokes, among other products. According to the *Illustrated Dictionary of Place Names,* the label is derived from the Semitic *laban,* "to be white," possibly for some chalk-white cliffs.

Ledford's Mill *Moore County.* The *1880 Moore County Census* reveals at least eighteen Ledfords residing in the vicinity. They included S. V. Ledford and his wife, Arie. He was a farmer; they had three sons and a daughter: Harrold, Homer, Hubert, and Jesse Ida. Other Ledfords listed include A. E., A. T., E. V., G. G., J. A., J. L., L. I., L. S., Roberta, W. A., N. A., and R. A. One or more of them must have operated the mill.

Lee *Bledsoe County.* In the minutes docket for 1841–1846, a Burdle Lee is mentioned. Other local Lees mentioned in early records include William Lee and Edmund J. Lee. The place-name probably relates to one of these Lees.

Leesburg *Washington County.* Michael Fraker and the Campbells—John and Abraham—founded the town in either 1795 or 1796. The three set aside ninety acres from their property holdings to create the site. The state chartered the town in 1799. First it was known as Washington, or New Washington. The current name leads back to a prominent citizen, Leeroy Taylor, who was honored when the name was changed.

Leeville *Wilson County.* The town owes its name to General Robert E. Lee. The railroad hamlet began to come into its own in about 1871. The Reverend D.C. Kelley held deed to the property. Other place-names have included Kelley's Church and Stringtown.

Leftwich *Maury County.* Martha, Susan, and Thomas A. Leftwich were present in this area in 1850, as well as six other individuals spelling the surname Leftwick. In 1840, the Leftwiches listed on the census rolls included Thomas A., Susan, John B., and Joel.

Legate *Stewart County.* This may be a variant spelling inspired by local residency of one or more of several individuals: Archibald Legett, John Legett, or Daniel Leggit. Or, these names may have been misrecorded in the 1830 West Tennessee census. Variations often occurred between the spoken version and the written version. The county historical society states that, "When the community petitioned the government for a post office, there were more Legate signatures than any other name, so the post office was named Legate." This occurred in the 1870s.

Leinart *Anderson County.* Leinart was the family name of some folks who took up residence here, the name being applied to the railroad station.

Lenoir City *Loudon County.* Incorporation took place in 1907. The town is the namesake of General William Lenoir, whose family was given land in this area in return for his service during the Revolutionary War. The general's son, William B. Lenoir, was engaged in the development of five thousand acres here when the claim was disputed by Alexander Outlaw. This contention went on for some years, with the Outlaws eventually selling their claim to the Lenoir heirs. Lenoir City cites 1840 as its founding year and William Ballard Lenoir as founder.

Lenow *Shelby County.* James, Joseph, and Henrietta Lenow resided in Shelby County at the time of the 1850 census. They were the only Lenows listed in the entire state of Tennessee at the time of that census. A separate source cites a James Lenow (born 1809 in Virginia) of this county as being engaged in the mercantile business and having a brother, Joseph.

Lenox *Dyer County.* At sites where this name has been applied, those naming it usually were looking for a short name with a favorable ring to it. It harks back to a district in Scotland.

Leoma *Lawrence County.* This site was settled in the 1820s. It was called Dean's Switch in the 1880s, when the Dean brothers burned chestnut wood into charcoal and built a railroad spur to service the business. The community began to flourish somewhat starting in about 1893. At some point, it was discovered there was a Dean, Tennessee, so the name was changed to Leoma. Supposedly, it was so named for the daughter of a railroad postal clerk.

Leonardtown *Sullivan County.* A number of Leonards resided nearby when the 1870 census was taken. They included Newel, age 34; Andrew, 30; John, 40; John, 22; Jackson, 30; Jordan, 31; William, 40; and Jacob, 39.

Lewisburg *Marshall County (seat).* Incorporated in 1837, Lewisburg was named in honor of Captain Meriwether Lewis, of Lewis and Clark fame. A large and prominent Lewis clan resided here. One of them was Colonel James Henry Lewis (b. 1837), an attorney. Members of this family were probably related to Captain Lewis, the explorer.

Lewis Chapel *Sequatchie County.* Some historians think the place-name here is in some way connected to the Reverend Edgar R. Lewis, of Chapel Hill.

Lewis Park *Lewis County.* This site, centrally located in the county, probably takes its designation from the county, which was named for the explorer Captain Meriwether Lewis.

Lewis Store *Coffee County.* An Abraham Lewis is listed on 1870 census rolls as having been a county resident at the time. However, contemporary local residents give this account of the map designation: "The Lewis Store was originated by Tom Lewis. He and his son, Clebert, ran it with a Johnny Davis . . . for a period of time. Tom Lewis and Clebert, and . . . two or three other family members were killed in an auto accident in 1939. Jess Phelps later bought the store [which] has now been in the family for two generations and over 50 years. [It] is in the community of Gnat Hill, at the crossroads. . . . The Phelps family has been trying in recent years to get the maps changed from Lewis Store to Phelps Store." In a second, and possibly dissenting, account, the daughter of the store owner wrote to explain that her father, John Lewis, operated the business. "That was . . . where people came for their groceries and sat on the porch and chewed . . . their tobacco," she recalled.

Lexington *Henderson County (seat).* The city takes its name from the Massachusetts village that gained renown at the outset of the American Revolution. Samuel Wilson was the real estate proprietor.

Liberty *DeKalb County.* Incorporation dates back to 1831. The community began to arise in 1807. The first settler was a Revolutionary War veteran, Adam Dale. The place-name honors those who struggled for liberty.

Liberty *Washington County.* The hamlet is thought to have taken the name from the nearby Liberty School or the Liberty Freewill Baptist Church. In all probability, the concept of liberty, or freedom of religion, influenced the choice of name.

Liberty *Weakley County.* According to *History of Weakley County,* this community assumed its name because all of the people were "at liberty" to worship in the open arbor built by people of all faiths. A community began to arise about 1827. About that time, a log house was erected for educational and religious purposes. It is said that all the local citizens recognized the benefits of religion and schooling, so all denominations were welcome to use the facilities.

Liberty Hill *Fayette County.* This designation probably persists due to the fact that the Liberty Baptist Church was organized here in 1824.

Lick Skillet *Decatur County.* According to local lore, a group of campers had cooked up a large meal and proceeded to devour it. One camper, arriving late to eat, found everything gone, and began to lick the skillet. From that time on, the place was known as Lick Skillet.

Light *Hawkins County.* Residents of the county in 1840 included Vachell, James, William, Stacy, Michael, John Sr., John Jr., and Joshua Light. Thus, the community probably took on the surname of the Light family or families. Probably at the same site—and still found on certain maps—is Light Mill, indicating that one or more family members operated a mill of some sort.

Lightfoot *Lauderdale County.* A family with the Roberson surname is believed to have first settled this site, which was initially known as Union. In the early 1860s, Margaret Wilson Bragg Lightfoot came here to reside, and it was from her family that the community took its current name. Apparently, at some point residents signed a petition in an attempt to acquire a post office. The Post Office Department selected the Lightfoot name for the office from the list of signers.

Limestone *Washington County.* Freedom was the previous name of the hamlet, but during the Civil War it was changed to Limestone because Big Limestone Creek flows through it.

Linden *Perry County (seat).* The first name applied to this site was Milton, in honor of Judge Milton Brown, a popular member of Congress from this district. Later, it was realized that another Tennessee place carried the Milton name. The new name settled upon for this community was Linden. It was suggested by Major Thomas Magruder Brashear, and so named by David R. Harris (1808–1873), proprietor of the land. Brashear is said to have been inspired by the poem "Hohenlinden" by Thomas Campbell, who was present at the battle of Hohen-Linden. The author referred to Linden throughout the poem.

Linsdale *Polk County.* In about 1923, a local Lindsey family donated land for a school. The Linsdale name was adapted from their family name. A preceding community was known as Columbus, or Old Columbus.

Linton *Davidson County.* Silas Linton received a North Carolina land grant here and resided in the county as early as 1830, according to one source. Another—the *1770–1790 Census of the Cumberland Settlements*—also cites a Silas Linton possessing a North Carolina land grant. These references may be to the same individual.

Little Barren *Union County.* Just across the county line, in Claiborne County, is a counterpart hamlet known as Big Barren. Both communities are believed to be named for creeks running through them. Little Barren Creek is the one flowing through this town.

Little Cherokee *Washington County.* Little Cherokee Creek borders this hamlet. The Cherokee Indians once occupied the area.

Little Emory *Roane County.* The hamlet is adjacent to the Little Emory River.

Littlelot *Hickman County.* The land proprietor was Hugh McCabe, who emigrated from Maryland in 1810. As the story is told (in *A Patchwork History of Hickman County*), in 1814 other residents asked McCabe to donate sufficient land for a church and schoolhouse. McCabe, the owner of hundreds of acres, responded magnanimously with a quarter-acre. The church and school were erected on the lot; then citizens puzzled over what to name the church. As the yarn is spun, Parker Tyler observed, "It's such a darned little lot, we can't give it a big name." So the label Littlelot (or Little Lot) became firmly affixed to the site.

Little River *Blount County.* This community takes its name from the aptly named stream flowing by. The Little River drains much of the Tennessee portion of the Great Smoky Mountain range and park.

Livesay Mill *Hancock County.* Numerous Livesays populated this area in 1880. Among them were George W., age 67; Debba, 52; Claborn, 40; S. W., 50 (a male); Wilborn, 43; William, 19; Milum, 16; Richard, 32; and M. D., 35 (a male). In 1870, local Livesays recorded by the census were John, Jefferson, George W., Jackson, A. J., Aaron, Claibourne, Elizabeth, Enoch, Stephen, Thomas, Evan, Mary, Milum, and Peter W. In all probability, one or more of them, or some of their ancestors, operated a mill at this juncture.

Livingston *Overton County (seat).* President Andrew Jackson's secretary of state, Edgar Livingston, was the individual for whom this community was named.

Lobelville *Perry County.* Lobelville was established in about 1854 as a post-village on the banks of the Buffalo River. Its name derives from a French immigrant who operated a local tannery, Henry DeLobel.

Locke *Shelby County.* Several Lockes are buried nearby in the Winchester Cemetery. It is probably to one or more of them that this label refers.

Lockertsville *Cheatham County.* Eli and William Lockert were Montgomery County citizens in 1850. A few years later, portions of Montgomery were taken to help constitute Cheatham County. This map site is probably attributable to Eli, William, or their ancestors.

Locust Grove *Dyer County.* The hamlet that arose in this shady grove was undoubtedly named for the abundance of honey locust trees present at the site.

Locust Mount *Washington County.* Considerable locust and oak timber stood at this site. After 1909, when the Oak Hill Missionary Baptist Church was constructed on a hill in the midst of tall oak trees, the place may have been better known as Oak Hill. However, current maps carry the place-name as Locust Mount. Black locust trees were known to flourish in Washington County.

Locust Springs *Greene County.* As in neighboring Washington County, black locusts were found in this county. Kelsey locusts are also found in Greene County. Together with the presence of bubbling springs, the trees gave the site its name.

Lodge *Marion County.* Local cemetery records mention several Lodges in this neighborhood: William J. (1856–1937), Elizabeth W. (1865–1940), Elizabeth M. (1888–1983), and Richard Leslie (1838–1966). The last year mentioned would appear to be a misprint. Joseph Lodge, age 32, is listed in local census records for the year 1880.

Lofton *Rutherford County.* Eldridge and Ann *Loftin* are mentioned in the 1830 census records as being Rutherford County residents. An incorrect spelling of the surname probably evolved as the local designation of the site.

Lois *Moore County.* This place-name came into being around 1892, when a post office was established. It was named for Lois Tolley, a music teacher at the nearby Union Hill Academy, which later became Lois School. The schoolteacher married Ben Tolley, a local farmer and distillery operator. Before the post office opened, the site was known as Union Hill. Earlier still, in the mid-1850s, it went by the name of Call's Store. The store was operated by Daniel Houston Call, also a distillery operator, who owned a good deal of land, which he farmed, and was a Lutheran minister. Call's Store was begun by his father, Joseph Call. It is said that it was Daniel H. Call who taught Jack Daniel the secret of making the whiskey that became famous under the name Jack Daniel's.

Long Branch *Lawrence County.* A stream called Long Branch flows through the town, giving it its name. The stream may have been the "longest branch" of whichever waterway supplies it.

Long Creek *Cocke County.* This is the name of a stream emptying into the French Broad River a little over a mile west of Del Rio. It is unclear whether the name is the result of the length of the creek, or of someone named Long.

Long Rock *Carroll County.* The name of the community of Oak Grove was changed to Long Rock in 1869, by J. M. J. Moore. It was inspired by the presence of an extremely long rock that stretched from a few yards in back of the schoolhouse to the spring. Much of the rock is hidden underground, but schoolchildren often sat on the aboveground portion while eating their lunches.

Longtown *Fayette County.* In 1840, William, E. M., Darling, and John Long lived nearby. Ten years earlier, the locale was home to John, Albert, and two Longs named Alexander. As a result, the site took on the Longtown label.

Lookout Mountain *Hamilton County.* This elevation may have been utilized for surveillance purposes, providing a good vantage point above the surrounding area. One source from 1817 or 1818 was quoted as observing, "It overlooks the whole country." However, other sources elaborate on possible reasons for the name. One states that flatboatmen needed to "look out" for robbers when they passed Ross Landing. Apparently, boatmen would pull out for the evening instead of negotiating the rough passage in the dark. When they did, robbers would descend upon them. Another observer simply felt the name was assigned because rivermen needed to beware the rough waters in the mountain gorge (or, "look out").

Loretto *Lawrence County.* According to one source, the community derives its name from the Loretto section of Italy and was founded in 1872. Information found elsewhere states that a stagecoach stand began business here in the 1820s, operated by a Mr. Glen. Thus, for a time it was referred to as Glenrock. Much later, in 1870, the German Catholic Homestead Association acquired land here for German families from Indiana and Ohio. A new name was desired, and the name Loretta, for a sainted nun, was adopted. Later, perhaps through careless pronunciation or spelling, it became Loretto. It is said that Andrew Jackson frequented a racetrack that operated here for a time.

Loudon *Loudon County (seat).* The fourth earl of Loudon, a British soldier named John Campbell, is credited with inspiring this place-name. Early in the French and Indian War, Campbell was in charge of British troops.

Louisville *Blount County.* Some speculate that founders of this early river settlement aspired for it to become as large as a better-known river town, Louisville, Kentucky, on the Ohio River. (This one is situated on the Tennessee River.) However, a newspaper account speculates that it was "apparently named for" Louis Philippe, a king of France, who visited the region in 1797. The site was once known as Gillispie's Landing. Original incorporation took place in 1851.

Louse Creek *Moore County.* The stream called Louse Creek begins near Lois and empties into Mulberry Creek. One version of the name states that an army officer in the War of 1812 led his troops to the banks of this stream to let their horses drink. There had been recent rains and the creek was quite muddy, prompting the officer to remark, "This is a lousy creek." Another version has a doctor traveling down the road and passing a house where he observed a woman on the porch picking lice from her child's head. The physician is said to have remarked to no one in particular, "This must be Louse Creek."

Lovelady *Pickett County.* This name is sometimes styled Love Lady. There is a good chance that it traces back to a chain carrier for a surveying party that came through the area, Phillip Lovelady. It is also said that a Lovelady family resided in nearby Overton County when it was being settled. However, popular legend has it that the location received its name as a result of an informal meeting of some local ladies, who were trying to come up with a name for the new school. A number of names were suggested, but one elderly woman said, "Let's name it a place where the men love the ladies." The group supposedly liked the idea and settled on Lovelady (or Love Lady).

Lucky *Warren County.* An authority on county history states that a subscription school by this name was operated here, dating to pre–Civil War days. By the 1890s, the local post office also took up the name. Located about nine miles northwest of McMinnville on the Yager-Short Mountain Road, it was observed that "you were lucky to get in, and lucky to get out," due to terrible road conditions that made it difficult to reach.

Lucy *Shelby County.* In early times, a family surnamed Duncan owned a plantation here. One of the females in the family was named Lucy, and the community that sprang up at the site is said to have been named for her.

Lupton City *Hamilton County.* John Thomas Lupton was an attorney in the Chattanooga area in about 1900. He had come from Virginia. Another person with this surname, Thomas Cartter Lupton, was a pioneer in the local Coca-Cola bottling business. One of these individuals probably inspired the place-name.

Luray *Henderson County.* This term is of vague derivation. According to the *Illustrated Dictionary of Place Names,* places named Luray may trace back to Luray, France; to the name Lorraine; or could be a shortened form of Lewis Ray.

Lusk *Bledsoe County.* W. G. Lusk purchased the mines here, and subsequently made some important contributions to the community. He donated a parcel of land and gave a sum of money to help make possible the building of the first consolidated school for the area. This may have been as late as 1923 or 1924. He was held in such high regard that the town was named for him.

Luskville *McMinn County.* Sarah and Fielding Lusk were 1850 citizens of the area, while Jonathan Lusk resided in the county in 1840. The place-name likely is traceable to these individuals.

Luttrell *Loudon County.* James H. Luttrell was a local citizen at the time of the 1880 East Tennessee census. It is likely that the place takes its name from him, or one of his ancestors. James was 29 in 1880.

Luttrell *Union County.* Cedar Fork was an earlier name for this locality. An early settler, S. B. Luttrell, was the founder and family patriarch. Incorporation took place in 1890. It was reincorporated in 1925. Between 1909 and 1925, it was unincorporated.

Lutts *Wayne County.* The town's first postmaster, John D. Stricklin (1849–1905), suggested the Lutts label for the community. Authorities told Stricklin that the name would have to be short. His physician and good friend was Dr. Alexander Lutts; so Stricklin decided to call the post office by that name, with the town becoming similarly known. As of December 1995, an Elmer Lutts still resided in Lutts, Tennessee. Previous names at this location included Pinhook, Madisonville, and Taylorsburg.

Lynchburg *Moore County (seat).* A local man of slight stature, Thomas Lynch, is thought to be the individual from whom the community takes its name. In early days, when local lawbreakers were sentenced to be lashed, Lynch was the person responsible for administering the punishment. A second source sides with the version that holds that the town was named by former Virginians for Lynchburg, Virginia. Still another version claims that convicts were lynched from a nearby beech tree. Incorporation took place in 1833, with a charter amendment in 1872.

Lynn Garden *Sullivan County.* The "Garden" part may be a relatively recent addition, perhaps by developers promoting the area. A number of Lynns traditionally lived in the county, however. Included were Anthony, G. Rogan, James, Joseph, Samuel, and Charles Lynn.

Lynn Point *Gibson County.* Lynn Point is sometimes referred to simply as Lynn. Its first postmaster was Joe Alexander. The name may honor early citizen Michael Lynn (1809–1891).

Lynnville *Giles County.* Incorporation came to Lynnville in 1838. Settlement here began about 1800. Lynn Creek ran nearby, which may have been named for its lining of linden trees. Residents may have wished to name the site Linden, but there was already a town of that name in Tennessee; thus, it may have evolved to Lynnville. A separate source states that emigrants from Lynn, Massachusetts, may have been among early settlers here, resulting in the name being borrowed from the New England city. An earlier name at this place was Waco. Early wayfarers who decided to remain here were headed west, and may have first named the locality for Waco, Texas.

Lyons View *Knox County.* The name undoubtedly traces to Captain William Lyon, who arrived from Baltimore in 1809 or 1810 and put down roots. He became very widely known and prominent. Six other Lyons are mentioned in early chronicles of the county.

Lyonton *Knox County.* The 1830 census records of East Tennessee mention William Lyon as a local citizen. (See preceding entry.)

Macedonia *Carroll County.* As for most places bearing this name, the name was probably biblically inspired, being a reference to an area of southeastern Europe that was a country in ancient times. (See entry for Macedonia, McMinn County.)

Macedonia *Haywood County.* See following entry.

Macedonia *McMinn County.* The name was widely known, both from the Acts of the Apostles and from Alexander the Great, and was often applied to churches. The ancient Macedonia was a region of the Balkan peninsula.

Macedonia *Obion County.* See preceding entry.

Macedonia *Sumner County.* See entry for Macedonia, McMinn County.

Macedonia *White County.* See entry for Macedonia, McMinn County.

Macon *Fayette County.* Most sites using the Macon name refer to American Revolutionary patriot and political figure Nathaniel Macon (1757–1837). He also served as a senator and representative from North Carolina.

Maddox *Hardin County.* Mary, William, and Dan Maddox resided in this vicinity in 1840. It is likely the place-name is derived from their family or families.

Madison *Davidson County.* This city takes the name of the fourth President of the United States, James Madison (1751–1836). Madison was instrumental in framing the Constitution, and also served as a U.S. representative and as secretary of state.

Madison Hall *Madison County.* The first word of the place-name is for the county, while the second refers to a two-story edifice constructed by the Grange, an agricultural organization, after the Civil War. The first floor was utilized for school classes, while the Grange used the second floor. The Grange also emphasized education.

Madisonville *Monroe County (seat).* The community, according to one source, traces its name back to the nation's fourth president, James Madison (1751–1836). Another school of thought holds that the city takes its name from an individual who once served as a state legislator from this county, James Madison Grunway. The place is said to have previously been the Native American encampment called Tellico.

Maggarte *Smith County.* This designation is probably a corruption of the family name Maggard (or Maggart), which occurred commonly in the county during the 1850–1870 period. In 1850, Jimmy, John, and Mary Maggard were listed on census rolls, while twenty years later, John Maggart, age 23, resided in the vicinity.

Magnolia *Houston County.* The site took its name from locally occurring magnolia trees—probably of the umbrella or bigleaf varieties.

Major *Wilson County.* At the time that the 1850 Tennessee census was recorded, John Major resided nearby. This map designation probably grew out of his being identified with the location.

Malesus *Madison County.* Until sometime between 1880 and 1885, the town was known as Harrisburg. It is believed there was another Harrisburg somewhere along the Illinois Central rail line, and confusion between the two was arising. One account states that a Mr. Samuels, who owned orchards locally (or grew strawberries, depending on which records you are reading), was a popular and respected citizen, and that other residents desired to name the community Samuels in his honor. His humility, however, prevented him from endorsing the plan. After some persuasion, Samuels compromised, stating that if a suitable name could be composed from the letters in his surname, that would be acceptable. The result was Malesus. The site had settlers from several families as early as 1830.

Mallory's *Williamson County.* In 1832, a Revolutionary War pensioner named Roger Mallory was residing in this vicinity. The place likely takes its name from him. A Thomas Mallory also resided locally in 1830; he was probably related to Roger. Sometimes the place-name is seen styled as Mallory.

Maloneyville *Knox County.* This place-name may relate in some manner to Judge George L. Maloney or the family of which he was a member.

Manchester *Coffee County (seat).* According to the *Illustrated Dictionary of Place Names,* the community was so named in the hope that it would become a manufacturing center not unlike Manchester, England.

Manila *McMinn County.* Names of larger venues were often assigned because the larger place was prominently in the news at the time. Manila, capital of the Philippines, or the battle of Manila Bay, may have been in the news when this site needed a name.

Mankinville *Rutherford County.* The label leads back to James, Jessee, Jno., or Selia Mankin, who resided in this vicinity in 1830.

Manlyville *Henry County.* At the time of the 1870 census, several Manlys resided in the county, probably accounting for the label on this site. They included Isaac W., James B., Martha T., William C., and two named Richard.

Mansfield *Henry County.* J. R. Mansfield called this county home in 1870. The name of the location probably relates to him or members of his family.

Mansfield Gap *Jefferson County.* Catharine Mansfield, age 80, and William Mansfield, age 44, were local residents in 1880. The family name, coupled with a gap between mountains or a stream flowing between hills, probably accounts for the label on this site.

Maple Hill *Sullivan County.* The trees that distinguished this elevation were of the silver, sugar, black, or red maple variety, or a combination of these.

Marbledale *Knox County.* Marble-quarrying firms operated here, including the Appalachian Marble Company and the Tennessee Marble Company.

Marble Hill *Blount County.* A reference to numerous "nearby marble quarries" in a Blount County history provides a clue to this place-name. Previously, it was known as Frogsville.

Markham *Lake County.* The county's largest pre-Depression cotton grower, Colonel Albert Edward Markham, named this site for himself or his family. He had previously resided in Dyer County, and in 1908 married Bessie Harris.

Marlborough *Carroll County.* Most places so named trace the name back to John Churchill, a British military figure who was the first duke of Marlborough.

Marlow *Anderson County.* Early citizens of this community included the Marlows, whose surname became associated with the location.

Mars Hill *Rhea County.* This promontory may bear an adaptation of the surname of one of two local men. Lloyd Marr served in the military from this area, while Aaron Marrs is recorded as having sold property in the county in 1875.

Martha *Wilson County.* There is a chance this designation traces back to a Martha Davis, who in 1812 married William Parrish, or that it honors a Martha McAdams (or McAdow?), who exchanged vows with Byrd Smith in 1812.

Martha's Chapel *Montgomery County.* A Methodist church was organized here in 1869, during the pastorate of the Reverend John Reynolds. Land was donated for the original church by Jesse Bumpus. The church was named in honor of Miss Martha Mills, who was the largest contributor toward erection of the building. She also was a prime mover in organizing the church. Completion and dedication of the building took place in 1872. The day that the cornerstone was laid, Martha Mills and another local Methodist minister, the Reverend Lewis Lowe, were united in marriage at the site.

Martin *Weakley County.* Marshall Presley Martin, George Washington Martin, and William Hartwell Martin inherited real estate here from their father, Captain William Martin (d. 1859). The town was established in 1873, the sons honoring their father by naming it Martin. It was platted and surveyed by Thomas Little. In earlier times, the site bore the names Green Briar Glade and Frost. The latter was in honor of an official of the Nashville, Chattanooga & St. Louis Railroad. When other rail lines or branches having other names entered the area, the Frost name was dropped and Martin came into being.

Martin Creek *Hancock County.* Thomas, William, William J., and Wesley Martin were local citizens in 1880. Their respective ages at the time were 63, 26, 20, and 19. It is likely the site and creek were so named by being closely identified with the location. However, a source close to this community believes the Martin name may have originated "over the border," in Virginia. The name is often styled as Martin's Creek.

Martin Springs *Marion County.* The same correspondent as for the Comfort entry discloses that the site "was named for my paternal grandfather's brother, Thornton Herbert Martin. He was originally the postmaster of the Dove post office . . . but evidently changed the name when he built a store, turned his home into a boarding house, built tourist cabins, and named the business Martin Springs." The new label was said to have been inspired by the clear, pure water running out of a cave on the property.

Maryville *Blount County (seat).* The city was named for Mary Grainger, wife of Governor William Blount. It grew up around a frontier fort erected by a pioneer, John Craig, in 1785. Incorporation took place in 1837.

Mascot *Knox County.* John Erwin was probably the first settler, in 1796. For a time, the place was designated Meek. But in the post-railroad development of the town, the name fell into disfavor, and railroad officials requested a change. It is said that a Mrs. McMillan suggested—for reasons that remain obscure—the Mascot name, which was accepted.

Mason *Tipton County.* One of the pioneer families to reside at this location bore the surname Mason. The 1850 state census recorded John J. and Lucinda W. Mason in Tipton County. However, one historian credits Dr. James Mason as being the place's namesake, claiming that the physician founded the community and contributed several acres for a railway station (Mason Station). Incorporation came in 1869.

Masonhall *Obion County.* A Masonic lodge hall became somewhat of a landmark here in the early years. As a result, the site became known as Mason Hall, or Masonhall, as it is often styled.

Mason Grove *Crockett County.* At the time of the 1830 census of West Tennessee, Sion Mason was a local citizen, probably influencing the name of this site.

Masseyville *Chester County.* Chester County was formed in 1875 from areas of Hardeman, Henderson, Madison, and McNairy Counties. The 1850 census rolls reflect the residency in Madison County of Caroline Massey and two Stephen Masseys. In McNairy County records, we find Thomas and Pinkny Massey. Since sections of these counties were among the land later absorbed to create Chester County, it is possible, even likely, that some of these Masseys were responsible for the Masseyville place-name. J. H. Mitchell operated the first store here.

Matheny Grove *Weakley County.* A shady site coupled with the surname of an early settler (Matheny) resulted in this label.

Maury City *Crockett County.* Like Maury County, this city utilizes the surname of Abram Maury (1801–1848), an editor who served at various times as a state legislator and U.S. representative. It is said that Maury helped to lay out and survey some of the western Tennessee counties. Incorporation took place in 1911.

Maury Junction *Crockett County.* In the absence of a railroad at this site, this designation may refer to a junction of roads, such as the points where Maury Junction Road is intersected by Welch Road and/or Percy Tucker Road. (See Maury City entry.)

Maxwell *Franklin County.* Old Winchester & Alabama Railroad timetables from the 1860s and 1870s reveal that this is the site then referred to as Jones Station. Apparently, an individual named William R. Jones sold much of the land in this vicinity. Afterward, a new stationmaster arrived, whose surname was Maxwell; so he referred to the stop as Maxwell.

Maxwell *Knox County.* The town's namesake is thought to be an engineer, bridge builder, and manufacturer of the 1850s, Anthony Leggett Maxwell (1824–1904).

Maxwell Chapel *Overton County.* Several Maxwells resided here in 1840. Included were Mary, David, Joel, George, and two each named Thomas and James. By 1870, Maxwells residing locally included Thomas, age 80; Simeon, 48; Bender, 33; J. M., 48; and B. M., 42. One or more of them may have been associated with a place of worship here, or donated land for the church.

Mayday *Washington County.* A settlement was established here as early as 1771 by Colonel Jacob Brown. It was referred to as the Nolachuckey Settlement. The later name was intended to be Mayberry, for families named May and Berry. Somehow, in time, it evolved to Mayday (or May Day).

Maymead *Johnson County.* Explaining this name admittedly involves some speculation. George W., Elizabeth, and Jefferson May lived in the area at the time of the 1870 census. Their surname could have been joined with *mead*, referring to meadows prevalent at this site, to form the place-name.

Maynardville *Union County (seat).* The name honors Horace Maynard, who served as a member of Congress. Incorporation took place in 1958.

McAllister's Crossroads *Montgomery County.* Mary J. McAlister resided near this intersection in 1850. It is likely she—or someone in her family—caused the designation to stick. The more common way to spell the surname is with two *l*'s; so this style may have been adopted over time.

McBurg *Lincoln County.* McDowell's Mill was located here. In 1886, the post office serving the area was moved here from Reuben, and, using the "Mc" from "McDowell," was renamed McBurg in 1892.

McCain *Maury County.* This place-name is sometimes seen styled as McCain's. It derives from the Hugh H. and Sarah McCain family; they arrived in this locale around 1810. Hugh was originally from Waxhaw, North Carolina, in what was then Mecklenburg County but is now Union County. He lived from 1792 until 1881. Both McCains are buried in the cemetery of the McCain's Cumberland Presbyterian Church. A separate source of records reveals that an Elizabeth McKain [sic] assumed ownership of some property in Maury County in 1814.

McCainsville *Jackson County.* In 1870, two Thomas J. McCains were local citizens. Their ages were 53 and 23; they were probably father and son. The hamlet takes its name from this family.

McCloud *Hawkins County.* In 1870, Daniel McCloud, 21, and James M. McCloud, 56, resided close by. The place-name probably refers to this family.

McCoinsville *Jackson County.* In 1840, Wilbon McCoin resided in neighboring Smith County. Since portions of Smith County went to help constitute Jackson County, the name of this site no doubt traces back to the family of Wilbon McCoin.

McConnell *Obion County.* According to the *Obion County History*, McConnell was so named in honor of a railroad official in approximately 1880. But prior to that, it bore the name North Edgar. Two of its earliest settlers were Willie Polk and W. S. Scott.

McDaniel *Williamson County.* Collin McDaniel was a local resident when the 1830 Middle Tennessee census was recorded. This place-name likely stemmed from his family surname.

McDonald *Bradley County.* Unanimity does not prevail in attempts to explain this place-name. According to *The History of Bradley County*, it "may" have been named for a Scots trader named McDonald, who maintained a trading station nearby. Or, it may have been named "for John Ross's mother's family." Still others trace the label to M. W. McDonald, who played a role in construction of the railroad. The settlement of McDonald began in about 1850.

McElroy *Van Buren County.* A. J. McElroy was a local citizen at the time of the 1850 census. In 1917, a Bertram E. McElroy of McElroy, Tennessee, is recorded as having enlisted for military service. The place-name undoubtedly relates to these individuals or the family in general.

McEwen *Humphreys County.* Incorporation took place in 1907. The site was settled largely by persons of Irish heritage. One was John McEwen, a civil engineer, a respected citizen for whom the community took its current name. The place during earlier periods was known as Little Ireland and Buttermilk. The latter was due to the fact that local farmers often supplied Civil War soldiers with buttermilk, selling it to them by the cup. Many of the Irish settlers were employed in the building of railroads.

McGlamery's Stand *Wayne County.* Isaac McGlamery and John McGlamery were county residents in 1870. A strong likelihood exists that one or both gave the family surname to this locality. The term "Stand" in a place-name usually indicates that the individual operated a tavern or stage stop at the site.

McIllwain *Benton County.* John McIllwain is described in one source as "one of the earliest settlers of the southern end of Benton County." (This community is in the extreme southern sector of the county.) John's eldest son, born in 1822, was Henry T. McIllwain. Another early citizen, from the Holladay area, was James Israel McIllwain. Numerous McIllwain entries dot the index of *Benton County, Tennessee Families & Histories.* In the 1850 census rolls, Henry and Alexander McIlwain's names appear, while John McIlwain is listed in the 1840 rolls. The surname of these three was spelled, rightly or wrongly, with one *l*. The first post office opened in 1890; David M. Gossett was the postmaster.

McKenzie *Carroll County.* One source states that the city traces its name back to Colonel John D. McKenzie, and was incorporated in 1869. (It had been laid out in 1865.) A second source, a McKenzie family scion, claims that Captain John McKenzie and his wife, Martha (Patsy), came to the county in 1826 and developed much of the land on which their sons were to live. James Monroe McKenzie owned some land where two railroads converged and donated a parcel for right-of-way requirements; so the site was referred to as McKenzie Station (later, McKenzie). Captain W. H. Hawkins, a brother of Governor Alvin Hawkins, was the town's first mayor.

McKinnon *Houston County.* A post office opened at this locality in 1888. It was located in the rear of a general store on the banks of Cane Creek. The store was owned and operated by Norman McKinnon (1825–1899), who became the first postmaster, according to one of his descendants. Norman was married to Cornelia Outlaw. Norman held a number of local offices in county government and the Masonic Order.

McLemoresville *Carroll County.* This place may have been named Carrolton (or Carrollton) before receiving its current name. The landsite belonged to Robert E. C. Daugherty. The current name probably honors Colonel John C. McLemore. He may have been the same J. C. McLemore who operated a tavern and store at this site. The name was conferred by the state's general assembly, which enacted the town's incorporation in 1833. Daugherty was postmaster at this location. Incorporation took place in 1833.

McMillan *Knox County.* This place-name may in some way relate to J. A. McMillan, a delegate to the Knoxville Convention in mid-1860, or someone in his family. Another source provides a vague reference to a family of early landowners named McMillan, and a Major McMillan.

McMinnville *Warren County (seat).* The name traces to a member of the territorial legislature of 1794, Joseph McMinn (1758–1824), who also served a term as the state's governor and assisted in framing Tennessee's constitution.

McNairy *McNairy County.* Like the county, this community takes its name from Judge John McNairy. Until 1884, it was better known as McNairy Station, due to the Mobile & Ohio Railroad.

McPheeter Bend *Hawkins County.* All three McPheeterses recorded in the state's 1840 census—Samuel, Lucretia, and George—were identified with Hawkins County and resided locally. So it is highly likely one or some of them resided near this major curve in the course of the Holston River, or at the bend of Valley Road near Goshen Creek. The place-name is sometimes seen styled as McPheeters' Bend.

Meadorville *Macon County.* The place-name probably refers to Pleasant Meador, who resided in Smith County at the time of the 1840 census. (Smith County and Sumner County contributed area to form Macon County in 1842. The Smith County line currently is only two miles from this community.) Later, a Captain Meadors, of Macon County, was placed in command of a company of Federals. The inconsistency in the spelling of the surnames is not explained. He may have been Captain Green Meador, identified in the *History of Tennessee Illustrated* as having served in the Union army. The same volume cites Lewis Meador of Macon County as having been a justice of the peace in 1842, and goes on to mention Thomas and Moses Meador. Thomas was a constable in 1842.

Medina *Gibson County.* According to local lore, several Egyptian workers labored here on the Illinois Central Railroad track when it was being laid in 1873. They hailed from Medina, on the Arabian peninsula, about a hundred miles from the city of Memphis on the Nile. When the workers learned that this Gibson County site was about a hundred miles from Memphis, Tennessee, being homesick, they made a crude sign saying "Medina," and affixed it to a boxcar that was being utilized as a temporary depot. A permanent depot was eventually erected at the site, and adopted the Medina name. The town was incorporated in 1902.

Medon *Madison County.* *What's in a Name?* provides an anecdotal—if suspect— story of the name: As the story goes, an Irishman returned here from his job and threw down his tools with the remark, "Me done." At an earlier time, the place is said to have been labeled Frozen Oak, supposedly because a hunter caught in a blizzard froze to death here, in the hollow of an oak tree in which he took refuge. A separate source elaborates on the name anecdote. Apparently Clover Creek was the name of a post office located here in 1834, but residents weren't satisfied with the designation. So they decided to use the first two words uttered by the popular Irishman when he returned from his labors. Settlement of the place began in about 1825. The town's lots were platted by William Boyd and William S. Wisdom in 1834.

Memphis *Shelby County (seat)*. It is believed that when the discoverers or settlers of this site looked out upon the Mississippi River, they considered it "the Nile of America." Thus they were inspired to christen the place Memphis, after an ancient city on the Nile. Founded in 1818, it was laid out the following year by John Overton. Memphis was incorporated in 1826. Those who founded and named the site are believed to have been James Winchester, Andrew Johnson, and Overton.

Mentor *Blount County*. In about 1900, the Louisville & Nashville (L&N) Railroad established a station here. One source states that local resident James Gillespie requested that it be named for Mentor, Ohio, the birthplace of President James A. Garfield. Gillespie was one of the earliest residents of the area, which had been known as Gillespie Station. If this attribution is not valid, the name may have some connection to an E. H. Menter, listed under Blount County in the 1850 census rolls. This individual or his/her family could have influenced the place-name in some manner. The variant spelling is probably the result of misspelling or misunderstanding.

Mercer *Madison County*. Thomas Bonard Mercer and his son, Thomas Erasmus Mercer, liked the site where the stage road crossed the Tennessee Midland Railroad, according to information found in *Historic Madison*. In 1888, they erected a store there. Six years later, when the rail line established a station there, the superintendent asked permission to put "Mercer" on the timetable, and the request was granted. Along with the Mercers, Frank M. McGlathery was credited with being one of the town founders. He was the son-in-law of the elder Mercer.

Michie *McNairy County*. Incorporation dates to 1961. A former name of the site was Pea Ridge. Postal authorities desired Monterey for the name; but when they discovered another place in the state by that name, they acceded to the surname of a long-residing local family (Michie).

Middle Settlement *Blount County*. Sometimes styled Middlesettlements, this name is believed to have grown out of the Cherokee designation for one of their geographical divisions, relating to others with names like Overhill Towns and Lower Towns. This site has also been called Fort Middlesettlements. It was approximately halfway between Fort Sanders and the site of Fort Loudoun, and about equidistant from Ish Fort and Gillespie Fort. Another reason for the name could have been that it was the central stop on the road from Friendsville to Maryville. Abraham Wells may have been the first white settler at the location, in about 1786.

Middleton *Hardeman County.* The community adopted the surname of a prominent family residing locally. The town was incorporated in 1856. In 1870, Middletons residing in the area included J. M., age 22, and J. T., age 37.

Midway *Blount County.* This location is said to have been named by the Reverend A. J. Rowland and his wife, Jo, for its situation midway between Mentor and Louisville, Tennessee.

Midway *Greene County.* Prior to the advent of the modern highway system, this site was probably so named because it was approximately equidistant from Bristol and Knoxville, Tennessee.

Midway *Warren County.* This name was arrived at because the site was approximately equidistant from Green's Crossroad School, Derigo School, and Cambridge School, when the three were consolidated in 1948.

Mifflin *Chester County.* This name, for some reason, was applied here but stems from a former governor of Pennsylvania, Thomas Mifflin (1744–1800). At least two communities in Ohio, Mifflin and Mifflinville, also use the governor's name. It seems more justified near Pittsburgh, Pennsylvania, where West Mifflin is a suburb.

Milan *Gibson County.* This name probably was given during a period of U.S. history when sites were often named for classical places—in this instance, the province and city of Italy.

Milburnton *Greene County.* In 1840, one of the citizens in this vicinity was Nancy Milbourn. It is likely her surname became the basis for this place-name, with a slight modification, plus the terminal *ton,* usually construed as "town."

Miles Crossroads *Clay County.* There is probably a connection between this place-name and persons named George, John H., and Noah Miles, who resided in this vicinity in 1870. In census records, they were noted as residing in Jackson County. Clay County was not formed until 1870, with Jackson County contributing a portion of the land that formed the new entity.

Milky Way *Giles County.* Located at this site, Milky Way Farms was a complex at one time consisting of 2,700 acres, 38 barns, numerous houses, and a spectacular mansion. It was the brainchild of Frank C. Mars, founder of the Mars Candy Company, who established the estate. (Mars Candy Company made Milky Way candy bars.) In its heyday, the farm operated almost like a small city, and was equipped with its own railroad siding. As of 1997, the grounds featured a bed and breakfast, facilities for weddings, a gift shop, and tours.

Mill Brook *Washington County.* Land grants along Mill Creek in 1782 and 1783 resulted in the first white settlement nearby. At one time, the stream was called Carson Creek, after John R. Carson ("Big John"). However, Mill Creek was later designated Mill Brook, with the community including the mills, shops, and houses along the waterway.

Milledgeville *Chester, Hardin, and McNairy Counties.* Incorporation took place in 1983. The name may have been adopted from a place of the same name in the state of Georgia.

Miller *Fayette County.* This site takes its name from early landowners, including Alex, Simon, and Abraham Miller.

Millersville *Sumner County.* The local *Fact Book* issued in July 1994 states that Miller was the surname of a revenue officer who frequently stopped at a store here for crackers and cheese before searching for illegal stills in the more remote surrounding areas. After one such stop, he failed to return from his foray. Later, his body was found at the bottom of an old well. Friends at the country store eventually decided to honor his memory by naming the town Millersville. A somewhat varying account states that the *storekeeper's* name was Miller, and that he had a son named Arthur.

Millican Grove *Sevier County.* A pioneer family having the Millican surname left its mark on this area. A founding year is not known, although the Millican Grove Baptist Church was established in 1875. The Millican Post Office opened in 1889, with Joshua Atchley as postmaster. Millican Creek flows nearby.

Milligan College *Carter County.* Several academic institutions operated here. The first was Buffalo Institute, prior to the Civil War. Later, in 1881, Joseph Hopwood of Kentucky founded Milligan College, naming it after a former teacher at Kentucky University (University of Kentucky?), Robert Milligan. A hamlet grew up around the school.

Millington *Shelby County.* At one time, several water-powered mills operated on nearby streams. Some feel the community's name comes from them, thus meaning "milling town."

Milton *Rutherford County.* As early as (approximately) 1790, a man named Roach and one named James Doran resided here. Much later—in 1830—some land here was purchased by Howard and Benjamin Morgan, and the men laid out a town. The name was conferred upon the community apparently out of admiration for the poet John Milton.

Mimosa *Lincoln County.* The term is used to identify certain trees, shrubs, and plants having small flowers and belonging to the legume family. It is unclear why it was applied to this site.

Minor Hill *Giles County.* One source claims the designation was suggested by the orientation of the village on a modest elevation, or "minor hill." However, another claims that an eventual settler, John Minor, gave his surname to the promontory. An earlier name of the place was Nail Hill, for Kallist Nail. The town was chartered in 1968.

Miser Station *Blount County.* The "Station" portion of the label is by virtue of the community's situation on a railroad line. The "Miser" portion owes to the surname of a local German family, some of whom spelled it Meiser. Its first members arrived about 1799. Henry Meiser had three sons, John, Henry, and George, in addition to two girls, Catharine and Mary Elizabeth. Luther Miser taught school, and Gordon M. Miser operated a grocery store. John Miser is said to have died at age 105, and not of natural causes.

Mitchell *Robertson County.* This hamlet probably traces back to one or more of these individuals listed in 1870 census records: C. M. Mitchel, age 35; S. F. Mitchell, 64; James Mitchel, 38; and W. F. Mitchel, 22. Unless copied in error, some of these persons apparently spelled the surname the less-common way, with one *l*. Mitchells, however, historically resided in this county. As early as 1820, records reveal that John Mitchel, James Mitchell, and William Mitchel (or Mitchell) were local residents.

Mitchellville *Marion County.* Numerous Mitchells resided in this locality in 1840, including Samuel B., George W., Howell, Hawkins, John D., and John. By 1870, Joel D. and William C. remained on county census rolls. Nineteen sixty-two marked the year of incorporation.

Mitchellville *Sumner County.* This locale was settled sometime before 1852, with some of the earliest citizens having the Mitchell surname. The year 1909 marked its incorporation.

Model *Stewart County.* The county historical society advises that, about 1850, an iron manufacturing operation went into production here. Towns usually arose around such furnaces, and the one here was "planned" as a model community. Thus, it retained the name Model. The furnace remained in operation only until 1856.

Mohawk *Greene County.* A native of Mohawk and the granddaughter of James Riley writes that the community first was known as Lick Creek Siding, and later as Pane. She states that during the Civil War "some Indians came through, so they changed Pane to Mohawk, for the Mohawk Indians." This was a story passed down from her father, who was born in 1866. James Riley was from Meath County, Ireland. He may have been born about 1840; he entered this valley and settled at the spot now known as Mohawk.

Molino *Lincoln County.* A contributor believes this place-name to be traceable to Molino del Rey, a Mexican fortress stormed by U.S. troops near the end of the Mexican War. Not everyone subscribes to this account, however. Some say a woman of Spanish heritage once passed this way and, upon learning the site had no name, gave it her own—Molina. In time, this became styled as Molino. The hamlet dates to

1810. Surnames of some of its earliest residents include Kidd, Wiley, Drennon, Phagan, Sloan, Stewart, and Wheffield.

Monteagle *Grundy County.* Eagles are said to have once proliferated in this locale. The "Mont" part of the name probably refers to its relatively high elevation.

Monterey *Putnam County.* Incorporation came in 1901. The Cumberland Mountain Coal Company brought about this community in 1893. The company's president, J. E. Jones, is believed to have conferred upon it a name that translates from the Spanish as "mountain of the king."

Montezuma *Chester County.* This hamlet uses the name of the ruler of Mexico and Aztec Indian chief, born in an uncertain year and killed in 1520 by forces under the leadership of Hernando Cortez. Montezuma ruled from 1479 until his death. The first store here went into operation in 1830, with J. R. Wambler as proprietor.

Montvale *Blount County.* The site is also known as Montvale Springs, because of sulfur and mineral springs located here. The name may have been applied by Sam Houston. *Montvale* means "mountain valley." In 1831 or 1832, D. D. Foute purchased property here, built a hotel, and opened for business.

Moodyville *Pickett County.* Pickett County was formed from portions of Fentress and Overton Counties. Moodys residing in those counties in 1870 included Benjamin Moody, age 36 that year; Greene Moody, 37; Robert Moody, 29; and Peter Moody, 46. As portions of the two counties were absorbed into Pickett, the location where one or more of the Moodys resided took on the Moodyville name.

Mooneyham *Van Buren County.* The site probably owes its label to one or more of the Moonyhams residing in the county when the 1870 census was taken. Andrew was 42 years of age at the time; Jessee, 50; Daniel, 32; William, 45; D., 28; C., 30; and J., 53. The place-name uses an *e* in its spelling, while the family name, in the census book, did not. However, in another source, the name of Clarence Mooneyham is found. He enlisted in the armed forces in 1917.

Moon's *Henry County.* Jefferson Moon resided locally, in the Fifteenth Civil District, when the 1850 census was recorded.

Mooresburg *Hawkins County.* Early historical records of this area reveal thirteen page references to Moores. Elizabeth Moore passed away in 1826. Susan Moore Mountcastle lived from 1788 to 1868. Yancie Moore was born in 1843 and lived until 1905. J. A. Moore lived from 1869 until 1964.

Moore's Chapel *Gibson County.* In 1830, Benjamin and George B. Moore were among the early settlers here. One of them may have ministered to a congregation here, or donated the land for the place of worship.

Moore's College *Warren County.* Allen, Carlant, and John Moore are listed as citizens in 1830, according to census records. Probably, someone in one of these Moore families established an academy at the site during the 1800s. Warren County Moores mentioned in another source include W. H. Jr., M. D., and Willie A. The last named was partner in the Cunningham & Moore mercantile goods business.

Mooresville *Marshall County.* Samuel Moore purchased land here in 1815; so his surname adhered to the location. Another individual with this surname who is said to have resided here in an early year was Ashley Moore.

Mooring *Lake County.* Andy and Eli Mooring, ages 35 and 33, respectively, resided in the vicinity in 1870. This label on maps probably refers to them or their family.

Morgan Springs *Rhea County.* The chalybeate spring at this location, and two hundred acres surrounding it, were purchased jointly by Charles Morgan and Joshua Riddle. Earlier names of the site included Riddle Springs and Scarborough Springs. Cool mountain air and the spring waters were major attractions, and many persons flocked to the facilities erected near the springs. In 1888, a post office was opened, with George Morgan serving as postmaster from 1888 to 1900 and again from 1909 to 1917.

Morgantown *Rhea County.* The many Morgans residing nearby in the community's early years suggested the name. Calvin, Washington, and Gideon Morgan were brothers. Lewis was one of the family elders, and great-grandfather of Dr. A. M. Morgan, who later became a well-known dentist in nearby Dayton. Rufus Morgan and his father, Lewis, also lived nearby. James Morgan was nominated for a position as postmaster here in 1890, but records fail to disclose whether he ever served in that capacity.

Morley *Campbell County.* A grading contractor on a railroad right-of-way here was known as Mr. Morley. The year may have been about 1930.

Morris Chapel *Benton County.* In 1883, property for a school and church was donated by a William P. Morris, whose surname remained with the site.

Morris Chapel *Hardin County.* The namesake of the place is Nimrod Morris, who settled in the vicinity during the 1820s.

Morrison *Warren County.* Some of the early Morrisons in this neighborhood were E. J. and Alvo, both of whom served in the military, and Jane, who married Henry R. Etter. There is probably a connection between this place-name and the families of one or more of these individuals. Morrison was incorporated in 1905.

Morrison City *Sullivan County.* Peter Morrison was a local citizen in 1850. There is an excellent chance the name of this site relates in some manner to him.

Morristown *Hamblen County (seat)*. Three brothers who received land grants here settled the site at an early time. Their names were Daniel, Gideon, and Absalom Morris.

Moscow *Fayette County*. The capital of Russia gives its name to this small town, which was incorporated in 1860.

Moss *Clay County*. Clay County was formed from parts of Jackson County and another county, after 1850. The state's 1850 census rolls list thirteen persons with the Moss surname in Jackson County. One or more of these families probably settled at the place called Moss (later to be in Clay County). Given names in the census index include Amanda, Archibald, Elizabeth, three Jameses, two Johns, Joseph, Joshua, Robert T., Thereson, and William.

Mountain City *Johnson County (seat)*. The community comes by its name quite naturally, situated as it is in a valley circled by mountains.

Mountain Home *Washington County*. A longtime resident of the vicinity explains that Mountain Home was established in 1903 as a home for disabled veterans. It is situated in the mountains of east Tennessee at an altitude of 1,700 feet.

Mount Airy *Sequatchie County*. At an earlier time, the site was known variously as Madison or Old Madison. The Jonathan Pope family, from Mount Airy, North Carolina, is said to have named the town. They also referred to their farm here as Mount Airy Farm. At various times, four different Popes served as postmaster for the Mount Airy post office.

Mount Ararat *Cannon County*. The name was probably assigned by settlers of strong religious belief. The *Eerdmans Bible Dictionary* sheds some light upon the term: "The 'mountains of Ararat' cited as the resting spot of Noah's Ark (Gen. 8:4) refer to the mountainous region as a whole. . . . Later Christian tradition focused on one of these peaks, Agri Dag in northeastern Turkey . . . as the site of that landing." Standing alone, the name Ararat referred to a country or kingdom in the Lake Van region of Armenia. *Urartu* is the Hebrew form of the name, which referred to a people.

Mount Carmel *Decatur County*. See Mount Carmel, Washington County.

Mount Carmel *Hawkins County*. See, in part, the information contained in the following entry.

Mount Carmel *Washington County*. A place of worship called Mount Carmel Methodist Church was located here. It was organized before 1850. Also present were a school, shops, and a sawmill. Mount Carmel in the Bible is the site in Jerusalem where Elijah addressed the issue of the worship of either Yahweh or Baal. Communities named Mount Carmel exist in New Jersey, Ohio, and Indiana, and many other states.

Mount Gilead *Henderson County.* See following entry.

Mount Gilead *White County.* The site may be named after another Mount Gilead; there are ones in Ohio, Kentucky, and North Carolina. Ultimately, the name traces to the Bible. *Gilead* may mean "rugged" or "stronghold." It is the ancient designation for a mountainous region of the Transjordan plateau, between the Dead Sea and the Sea of Galilee, according to the *Mercer Dictionary of the Bible.*

Mount Hermon *Weakley County.* Mount Hermon is a biblically inspired name for this site. The "real" Mount Hermon is located in the Anti-Lebanon Range, towering above the upper Jordan Valley at around 9,300 feet. The source of the Jordan River, one Bible dictionary terms it—or translates it—as "consecrated mountain." Mount Hermon is mentioned in Judges and Joshua.

Mount Hope *Wayne County.* This site was named for a church or cemetery (or both) of the same name.

Mount Horeb *Jefferson County.* Horeb is a variation of Oreb and Orab, the last being probably the most common style. The name refers to a passage in the Bible (Judges 7:25) in which the Midianite prince Oreb is slain on a rocky elevation.

Mount Joy *Maury County.* In an unknown year, a local church administered services here on a hillside campground. Folks attended from miles around. Accounts state that "shouts of joy" arose from the grounds as citizens were converted; so the site became known as Mount of Joy, and eventually Mount Joy. Located on a knoll, the church assumed the name Mount Joy Cumberland Presbyterian Church. The church was organized in 1825 (campground meetings took place here before that year). David C. Mitchell donated the land for the church building.

Mount Juliet *Wilson County.* One account states that the community acquired its name out of respect for "Aunt Julie" (Julia Gleaves), who lived atop a nearby hill and assisted soldiers during the Civil War. An admittedly less likely explanation is that the current name evolved from "Mint Jullip," because settlers often stopped at a tavern here to sip mint julep drinks. The Mt. Juliet-West Wilson County Historical Society adamantly maintains that the Julia Gleaves explanation is a myth that should not be perpetuated. The society points out that, although Gleaves deserves respect as a "guardian angel" of the community during the Civil War, she did not reside in the town until after 1850; the place-name first appeared in print in 1835, when the community was founded. The society goes on to offer the explanation that the site was named for the Mount Juliet Estates, in County Kilkenny, Ireland. The manor house there was established between 1757 and 1761 and named for the wife of the earl of Carrick, Juliet Boyle.

Mount Lebanon *Decatur County.* Such names are usually applied for their religious connotation, or a nearby church using the name. Biblically translating in part as "white mountain," *Lebanon* was the designation for a mountain range near the

Mediterranean Sea, north of Israel, some peaks of which were snow-capped. The Bible contains a number of references to Lebanon, or the equivalent, and the cedars that grew on the slopes.

Mount Lebanon *Tipton County.* See preceding entry.

Mount Moriah *Benton County.* See entry for Mount Moriah, Fayette County.

Mount Moriah *DeKalb County.* See following entry.

Mount Moriah *Fayette County.* The name is of biblical origin, referring, by one account, to the location of the Jerusalem temple. On one of the mountains of the land of Moriah, Abraham was commanded by God to sacrifice his son Isaac.

Mount Nebo *Lawrence County.* See following entry.

Mount Nebo *Maury County.* Such a place-name is usually applied to an elevated site or a place where a church is built, or both. Mount Nebo was the promontory from which Moses viewed the Promised Land (Deuteronomy 32 and 34).

Mount Olive *Grundy County.* The site was no doubt named by persons of strong religious beliefs for the biblical Mount of Olives, the setting for Jesus' entry into Jerusalem. It is also believed the Mount of Olives was the site of his ascension.

Mount Olive *Marion County.* See preceding entry.

Mount Pisgah *White County.* The biblical Pisgah refers to the rugged headlands of the Abarim range between the Dead Sea and Jericho.

Mount Sinai *Dickson County.* The Mount Sinai of the Bible (also called Horeb) was a place of vital significance to the Israelites, being the site where Moses was called by God. There, also, the covenant and the law were received by the Israelites. Scholars have been unable to agree on the exact location of the Mount Sinai of the Bible. The strong religious beliefs of the settlers were usually what inspired them to choose this type of name for their community.

Mount Vinson *McNairy County.* One of the early families settling here bore the Vinson surname.

Mount Zion *Cheatham County.* See entry for Mount Zion, Montgomery County.

Mount Zion *Lawrence County.* See following entry.

Mount Zion *Montgomery County.* A Bible dictionary describes Mount Zion, in Jerusalem, as "a favored abode of God." It is mentioned in Psalms more than once. This location was probably settled by persons of strong religious convictions, who may have had a church named Mount Zion here.

Mount Zion *Sevier County.* See preceding entry.

Mount Zion *Warren County.* See entry for Mount Zion, Montgomery County.

Mowbray *Hamilton County.* This place-name is undoubtedly linked to the founders of the Alpine Academy, Mr. and Mrs. William Mowbray. The academy was later torched by Federal soldiers.

Mulberry *Lincoln County.* The red mulberry grows throughout Tennessee, and this site was named for those evident at this place.

Mulberry Gap *Hancock County.* Some credit the assignment of this name to Elisha Wallens, while others credit it to Josiah Ramsey. Near Powell Mountain, a gap ran between mountains and a trail ran through the gap. Huge mulberry trees lined the path, their limbs overhanging the trail. Travelers would time their trips to arrive in the gap when the mulberries were ripe. Mulberry Creek flows nearby.

Mulberry Hill *Stewart County.* The elevation took its name from the red mulberry trees that marked the location.

Mulloy *Robertson County.* James S. Mulloy was a local citizen in 1850. The name of this hamlet is probably related to him in some manner.

Munford *Tipton County.* Munford was incorporated in 1905. At about that time, or a couple years earlier, local citizens applied for a post office under the then-incumbent name of Mount Zion. Advised that there was another Mount Zion in Tennessee, they then decided to use the surname of a leading county official and prominent citizen of the community, R. H. Munford.

Murfreesboro *Rutherford County (seat).* A land speculator with generous holdings in mid-Tennessee, Hardy Murfree, is the city's namesake, according to the *Illustrated Dictionary of Place Names.* Murfree (1752–1809) had been an officer in the American Revolution, rising to the rank of colonel. The city served as the state's capital from 1819 until 1825.

Murray Store *McMinn County.* Gilbert Murray, age 32, was a local citizen of the county in 1870. It is probable that he or a member of his family operated a store at the site, giving the place its name. However, that distinction may be owed to John Murray, who resided locally as early as 1830.

Nance *Crockett County.* At the time of the 1830 census of West Tennessee, Peter Nance was a citizen of adjacent Madison County, a portion of which later was taken to help make up Crockett County. The adherence of this place-name in what is now Crockett County is probably due to Peter Nance or his family.

Nance's Ferry *Grainger County.* John, Jefferson, and Clement C. Nance resided in this area when the 1870 census was taken. One or more of them—or some earlier member of the clan—may have operated a ferry service on the Holston River. At least one map designates the place as Nance Ferry.

Nance's Grove *Jefferson County.* In the volume *Jefferson County, Tennessee: Families & History, 1792–1996*, this passage is found, referring to a couple named Hickle: "The beginning of their life together was spent working for the Nances [loggers] and living on the banks of the Holston River, near the shoals just above Nance Ferry." The Nances were identified as Tom and Bert.

Nankipoo *Lauderdale County.* An account found in *Lauderdale County from Earliest Times* goes like this: Thomas G. Bomer established a store and applied for a post office under an unknown name. However, authorities discovered there was already a post office of that name elsewhere in Tennessee. Someone—possibly Bomer—then suggested that the name should be Nanki-poo. Apparently, this was prompted by the fact that Gilbert and Sullivan's *The Mikado* was popular at the time. In the opera, the Mikado's son is named Nanki-Poo.

Napier *Lewis County.* Gilbert Napier, 50, and William C. Napier, 49, were county residents in 1870. This place designation probably stems from the family or families to which these men belonged.

Nashville *Davidson County* *(state capital).* At one time known as Nashborough, in 1784 the city adopted its name from General Francis Nash (ca.1720–1777), a noted Revolutionary War figure.

Natural Bridge *Cocke County.* The community assumed this name because of natural phenomena created by Oven Creek—natural bridges referred to as the Little Oven and the Big Oven.

Nauvoo *Dyer County.* The explanation for this name comes from a booklet on Nauvoo, Alabama. One passage states that *nauvoo* is a Hebrew word meaning "beautiful place," and that the root word *na'ah,* means "to be at home" or "be beautiful." Another passage from the same source states that the word comes from the Hebrew adjective *naveh,* said to mean "pleasant."

Neely *Madison County.* Five persons with this surname resided here in 1840: James W., Thomas J., two named James, and Samuel. This site undoubtedly was called home by one or more of these individuals.

Neely Crossroads *Clay County.* There were two Robert Neelys residing in Overton County when the 1850 census was taken. Overton contributed some of its area to the formation of Clay County; so these individuals probably became "Clay countians" and resided at this site. Much later (1925–1944), a gristmill and general merchandise store were operated by an Albert B. Neely, who died in 1944.

Nemo *Morgan County.* Why this place was so named remains open to speculation. The Latin term means "no one." In Jules Verne's *Twenty Thousand Leagues under the Sea,* a prominent character is named Captain Nemo. Sometimes, short place-names were other names or words spelled backward. If such an origin applies in this instance, the label would have come from *omen.*

Nenny *Hamblen County.* There was a place of worship here called the Catherine Nenny Church, suggesting that a Nenny family resided here and gave its name to the location.

Neptune *Cheatham County.* Presumably, for reasons unknown, this community was named after the Roman god of the sea.

Neubert *Knox County.* The 1880 index to the census of East Tennessee lists Harman and Frederic Neubert as local citizens. Harman was 53 at the time, and Frederic was 20.

Newbern *Dyer County.* Bern, Switzerland, is believed to be the namesake of this small community.

Newcomb *Campbell County.* An individual identified as Captain Newcomb provided a good deal of employment to area persons; so in 1883 the place-name was changed to Newcomb from Emmet.

New Fly's Village *Maury County.* This community probably relates in some way to one or more of the many persons with the Fly surname who resided in the county. In 1840, Caleb, Caleb Sr., George, John, and John Jr. resided nearby. (Also refer to entry for Fly.)

New Herman *Bedford County.* A church using this name opened here, with the surrounding community taking on the designation.

New Hope *Marion County.* In 1975, this community was threatened with annexation by nearby South Pittsburg, a move that the majority of citizens opposed. Thus, they voted to incorporate, using the name of a neighborhood cemetery and church, New Hope. The previous name of the locality—Antioch—was also inspired by the religious convictions of residents, for a site mentioned in the Bible.

New Hope *McNairy County.* The community was known earlier by the name of a pioneering settler named Caffey, who donated land for a church. The church was christened New Hope; so in time the town was also called New Hope. The site may at first have been known as North Carolina, since most of the settlers came from that state. William Blanton and Robert Churchwell were two of the initial settlers.

New Johnsonville *Humphreys County.* This community is thought to derive its name from a man named Johnson, about whom little detail could be located.

New Lawton *McNairy County.* See Lawton entry.

New Loyston *Union County.* Loy was a very common surname in this county in the year 1880. A sampling of Loys off the census rolls includes S. Greene, age 32; Freeling H., 34; Isaac, 25; Alfred, 38; Emanuel Jr. and Sr., ages 29 and 55; Elbert, 25; Henry, 54; and two Williams, 41 and 62. "Loyston" probably indicates "Loys' Town." Why the "New" would have been applied to the place-name is unclear.

New Market *Jefferson County.* For a period, this place was referred to as Lost Creek. With the advent of mercantile and business opportunities at this location, it took on the name New Market.

Newport *Cocke County (seat).* This city arose alongside the French Broad River, at a navigable point, making it a port and resulting in this name. Many Newport sites also refer ultimately to Newport, England, located in Monmouthshire.

Newport Camp *Rhea County.* This settlement was begun by the Newport brothers, who (according to one source) came from Ohio about 1858. However, a relative of the brothers, Asa Newport, resided in the vicinity when the 1850 census was taken. It is said that the land was owned by Asa Newport from about 1835 to 1870.

New Salem *Scott County.* The name was undoubtedly applied out of religious inspiration and may be the founders' way of saying "New Jerusalem." *Salem* means "peace" or *shalom.*

New Tazewell *Claiborne County.* The community is thought to be named for Littleton W. Tazewell. In 1821, Tazewell was serving in the U.S. Senate from Virginia. (Also see Tazewell entry.)

Newtown *Bedford County.* This village was described by a local historian as one of the county's "late communities." Thus, for those times, it was a "new town."

Newtown *Polk County.* This name probably came about simply because the town was new when it was established. It came about when a copper mining company operating at nearby Copperhill built the company houses that first formed the community.

New Victory *Washington County.* In the 1780s, a number of families began to immigrate into this vicinity. A school was eventually deemed necessary, and land for one was donated by George W. Sprinkle, who in gratitude was given the privilege of naming it. He decided upon New Victory. Exactly why he selected this name is not known, but it caught on and stuck, although local citizen Davey Renfro, who liked to assign everything a nickname, preferred to call the community Shake Rag.

New Zion *Macon County.* The locality was undoubtedly settled by individuals of strong religious persuasion. (See Mount Zion entry.)

Ninth Model *Coffee County.* Refer to entry on Sixteenth Model.

Niota *McMinn County.* Once known as Mouse Creek, this hamlet's designation caused confusion for the Post Office Department with another place called Mossy Creek. So railroad agent James Burn attempted to have the label changed to Movilla. His reasoning was that the Morse code station call letter of "MO" would not need to be changed. However, John Boggess, a local resident, suggested the name Niota, said to have been the name of an Indian chief in a novel he had read. As the enduring name of the town, Niota prevailed. The story is recounted in *McMinn County,* by C. Stephen Byrum.

Nixon *Hardin County.* Mary Nixon was a local citizen in 1850. This location may have obtained its designation from her surname.

Nolensville *Williamson County.* One of the oldest families of Williamson County—the Nolens—are commemorated in this place-name. General L. Nolen, a surveyor, is known to have been in Williamson County in 1823.

Nonaville *Wilson County.* According to the *History of Wilson County, Tennessee,* for nearly a century this site was referred to as Prosperity. In 1895, local residents desired a post office, but the Prosperity name was found to be in use at another site not that far distant; so it was necessary to select a different name. Nonaville is believed to have been construed to mean "not a city."

Norma *Scott County.* The exact reason for this place-name is unclear. A town referred to as Skullbone once existed here. That was changed to Norma and later to Norcross (after Norcross, Georgia?). Later still, it was changed back to Norma.

Normandy *Bedford County.* The community is thought to have been named after nearby Norman Creek, in turn thought to have been so designated for a family with the Norman surname—possibly that of John Norman, who settled in the area in an early year. Some, however, feel the designation was taken from the coastal region in

France. Locals pronounce it Nor*mandy*. It was not until 1921 that Normandy was incorporated.

Norris *Anderson County.* The village's namesake is George W. Norris, U.S. senator from Nebraska.

North Chattanooga *Hamilton County.* This community, as the name implies, is somewhat north of Chattanooga. (See Chattanooga entry.)

Northcutt's Cove *Grundy County.* Margaret and Mariann Northcutt are listed in the county's 1850 census rolls. They were probably members of the family for which this site was labeled.

North Etowah *McMinn County.* The location is a short distance north of Etowah. (See Etowah entry.)

North Knoxville *Knox County.* This Knoxville suburb, as its name implies, lies just north of the larger city. (See Knoxville entry.)

North Riverside *Lewis County.* This hamlet is named for its location about a quarter-mile from the Buffalo River.

Nough *Cocke County.* Once known as Slabtown for the many slabs lying around, discarded from a local sawmill, Nough is a shortened version of Goodnough. A family having the Goodnough surname resided nearby.

Nunnelly *Hickman County.* The community is the namesake of W. S. Nunnelly and his family. Mr. Nunnelly was a farmer-businessman. Sometime following the Civil War, he built a store in nearby Vernon, which family members operated for many decades thereafter. The community of Nunnelly sprang forth from the year 1882 and became a busy mining town. One source states that the name came from Lawson H. Nunnelly, said to have arrived in 1810 from North Carolina. The Nunnelly Ore Mines were a vital industry at the site.

Oak City *Sevier County.* This was once a thriving, industrious company town, founded by Andrew Jackson Temple and three sons—John, Robert, and Albert. At one time, it was home to a broom factory, a chair factory, a flour and feed mill, general store, and lumber factory. It also boasted a church, a school, tennis courts, a park, and a ball field. The name was inspired by the many stately oaks on the premises.

Oakdale *Morgan County.* A profusion of oak trees dotted this locality. At one time, it was known as Honeycutt. (One source spells it Hunnicutt.) The earlier name honored Allen Honeycutt, who, with Wylie Goldston, made land available to the Cincinnati Southern Railroad. The name change to Oakdale is said to have been made by Martha Jane Buttram Goans, later than the year 1900. Mrs. Goans was the local postmistress, although her husband, David, was listed as postmaster. Her adoption of the Oakdale name for this site may have had some connection with the cessation of operations of a Roane County firm named the Oakdale Iron Works.

Oakfield *Madison County.* According to a newspaper article, hundreds of oak trees at this location gave the site its name. Prior to that, it went by Norwood, the maiden name of the postmaster's wife.

Oak Grove *Carter County.* This community takes its name from one or more of the locally growing varieties of oak. Northern red, chinkapin, black, southern red, post, blackjack, and chestnut oaks all do well in this region.

Oak Grove *Chester County.* The site was given this name due to the number of oaks dotting the landscape. Among the varieties present were pin oaks, black oaks, post oaks, willow oaks, northern red oaks, blackjack oaks, white oaks, and overcup oaks.

Oak Grove *Clay County.* A former student at a schoolhouse here recalls the large oaks growing along the creek and providing much-appreciated shade. A church and community also arose at the site.

Oak Grove *Loudon County.* The oaks for which this grove was named were of the white, southern red, chinkapin, blackjack, northern red, post, and chestnut variety.

Oak Grove *Madison County.* Pin oaks, willow oaks, northern red oaks, and black oaks are among the varieties found in this region, to which the place-name is attributed.

Oak Grove *Monroe County.* This was a very common designation for sites where oaks grew. Among the types growing in this area were the black, post, northern red, white, scarlet, blackjack, southern red, and chestnut oak.

Oak Grove *Overton County.* There were numerous groves of oak flourishing locally. Some of the varieties probably included southern red, scarlet, white, blackjack, chinkapin, black, post, pin, and northern red oak.

Oak Grove *Union County.* This settlement grew up within a grove of oak timber.

Oak Grove *Warren County.* A school existed here in an early year, as well as a Church of Christ, the latter being located in the midst of a large grove of oak trees. Large stands of these white, red, and post oaks still dot the area.

Oak Hill *Morgan County.* The state is heavily forested with oak trees, accounting for the name at this elevation in the Cumberland Mountains. Among the varieties occurring here were white oak, scarlet oak, southern red oak, blackjack oak, chinkapin oak, post oak, willow oak, black oak, and northern red oak.

Oak Hill *Overton County.* See entry for Oak Grove, Overton County.

Oakland *Fayette County.* Settlers from North Carolina and Virginia came here about 1830. James A. Hunter, a medical doctor from North Carolina, is credited with founding the town. His father, Samuel, and two brothers, Charles and John, also came here, opening a dry goods store the same year that James was building the first house, in 1830. A large grove of oak trees at the site inspired the name.

Oakland *Jefferson County.* At the current time, contrary to what one might believe, this site has no oak trees. A local citizen reports a shadeless schoolyard, save for a lone elm, "a few straggly black locusts," and one or two walnut trees. However, it is reliably reported that, many years ago, there was a one-room schoolhouse near the church. The church was erected in a lovely grove of oaks, accounting for the place-name.

Oakland *Washington County.* Organized in 1850, the Oakland Presbyterian Church gave its name to this community. It may also have been influenced by the presence of oak trees at the location.

Oakley *Overton County.* This place-name undoubtedly derives from a surname. Robert Oakley was a local citizen in 1850. In 1870, John, age 50; Millie, 74; Thomas, 39; and Robert Oakley, 55, were area residents. The site probably takes its name from one of these individuals or a relative.

Oakplain *Cheatham County.* This name is sometimes seen styled as Oak Plains. There were several oak trees here, surrounded by farmland, probably inspiring the name.

Oak Ridge *Anderson County.* The upland area of Oak Ridge was dotted with post, black, northern red, white, scarlet, blackjack, chinkapin, and chestnut oaks. The city was incorporated in 1959.

Oak Ridge *Roane County.* Chestnut oaks dotted this ridge, as did northern red, black, post, white, southern red, blackjack, and scarlet oaks.

Oak View *Blount County.* Among the tree varieties that may have inspired the label on this scenic vista were the white, chinkapin, southern red, blackjack, chestnut, northern red, black, scarlet, and post oak.

Oakridge *Montgomery County.* Southern red oaks, pin oaks, Shumard oaks, post oaks, black oaks, willow oaks, northern red oaks, blackjack oaks, and scarlet oaks dot the ridges and valleys in this region, accounting for the name.

Oakview *Sullivan County.* See entry for Oak View.

Obey City *Overton County.* The hamlet derives its name from its location on the east fork of the Obey River. However, historians have been unable to ascertain the meaning of *Obey,* which may be of Native American origin.

Obion *Obion County.* William Mitchell (Billy) Wilson is credited with founding this city. It may have been known as Crescent City at an earlier time. Incorporation took place in 1888. The term is probably Native American, meaning "many forks," although some subscribe to the theory that Obion was a personal name.

Ocoee *Polk County.* "Apricot-vine-place" is the translation of this term from the Cherokee, according to *American Place-Names.*

O'Connor *White County.* In spite of the slightly variant spelling, M. F. O'Conner, an 1870 resident, likely is the individual to whom this place-name traces.

Officer's Chapel *Putnam County.* At the time of the 1870 census, Alexander Officer, age 56, and William Officer, age 35, resided nearby. One may have been a clergyman and/or donated land or materials for a place of worship.

Offutt *Anderson County.* Members of the Offutt family were early settlers here.

Ogden *Rhea County.* The vague attribution information available states that the location was labeled Ogden by an unnamed man after a place where he had once resided. The Loyd family were the site's largest landowners in the early years.

Oglesby *Davidson County.* The only early individual with the Oglesby surname who could be placed in this vicinity at the "late" date of 1870 was Richard, age 45. However, as early as 1820, William and Harris Oglesby were local citizens. The place-name no doubt relates in some way to these individuals.

Old Antioch *Jackson County.* It is not known why "Old" was prefixed to this common place designation. Possibly, it was done for no other reason than to distinguish it from the many sites in Tennessee and other states labeled Antioch. (See entry for Antioch, Montgomery County.)

Old Fort *Polk County.* The site takes its name from Fort Marr, an ancient blockhouse that stood here. In 1830, the fort served as part of the stockade that housed thousands of Cherokees prior to their forced trip to Oklahoma. It was originally built in about 1812. The fort has had several subsequent locations, and currently stands next to the jail in Benton.

Old Glory *Blount County.* A hamlet grew up around an intersection here where a gasoline station was located. The original log cabin-style station was owned by Viven Phelps, a patriotic individual, who painted it red, white, and blue and displayed the U.S. flag out front. So residents and travelers dubbed the spot Old Glory.

Oldham *Sevier County.* The name of this hamlet is sometimes seen as Oldham's Creek. The creek has its source near a mountaintop and joins Bird Creek on land settled in 1807 by Stephen Oldham. The Oldham Creek Baptist Church was organized in the 1850s.

Old Hickory *Cumberland County.* Andrew Jackson, nicknamed "Old Hickory," inspired the name of this town.

Old Hickory *Davidson County.* The town utilizes the nickname of Andrew Jackson, who resided nearby and built The Hermitage. The name of this site did not become Old Hickory until 1923. Prior to that, it had been called Jacksonville, but because mail delivery became confused with other Jacksonvilles, it was changed.

Old Lawton *McNairy County.* See Lawton entry.

Old Salem *Franklin County.* As late as 1926, the site continued to be referred to in news items by its original name of Salem. A correspondent writes, "Older citizens only recall that people just began to refer to the town as 'Old Salem,' the only reason given being that the town was so old, in their minds." For the "Salem" part of the name, refer to the Salem, Cocke County, entry.

Old Springville *Henry County.* This designation distinguishes the community from nearby Springville. (See entry for Springville.)

Old Zion *White County.* There is a site called Zion in this county. (See entry for Zion, White County.) This community may have been the older of the two and thus qualified for the "Old" prefix.

Oliver Springs *Anderson, Morgan, and Roane Counties.* Part of the name stems from nearby sulfur springs. They were developed into an attraction by John Oliver.

Olivet *Hardin County.* Undoubtedly bestowed by those with strong religious convictions, this designation is another way of referring to the Mount of Olives (mentioned in the gospels of Matthew and Mark and the Acts of the Apostles). The biblical site was on a ridge east of Jerusalem.

Oneida *Scott County.* The label traces back to the Native American Oneida people.

Only *Hickman County.* A local "armchair historian" advances the notion that this settlement derived its name from a family residing there. The family surname was Lonlly, or had a similar spelling, and when the town was named, for some reason the initial *L* was left off. However, in *A Patchwork History of Hickman County,* another explanation is provided: it seems the local storekeeper, Tom Sutton, when asked the price of an item, would habitually preface the reply with the word "only." Thus, he was often heard to answer, "only five cents," or "only a dollar." Customers humorously referred to the businessplace as "the Only store." This appellation became generalized to the surrounding area, according to this source, until Only supplanted the community's previous name, Dreamer. When postmaster Allen Hunt Brown owned the store and hosted the post office there, he had the name officially changed to Only. A still-earlier place-name than either of the preceding was Mount Zion, for a Mount Zion Primitive Baptist Church that was established here. The initial settlers may have been the Wilkens family, in the early 1800s.

Ooltewah *Hamilton County.* "Resting place" may be the translation of this Native American term, thought to be of Cherokee origin.

Orgain's Crossroads *Montgomery County.* Although there were persons in nearby counties with the Orgain surname, it is believed this particular designation is a corruption from the Organ surname. Benjamin Organ was in Montgomery County as early as 1830, and by 1840, census records reveal the presence of Peter, Thomas, and Griffin Organ, plus two with the given name William. In 1870, numerous Organs were still on county census records.

Orlinda *Robertson County.* Incorporation took place in 1965. The place at one time was dubbed Crocker's Crossroads, a reference to local land proprietor H. J. Crocker. Post accounts reveal that he applied for a post office under this label, but because of the proximity of *Tucker* Crossroads, it was rejected. Centerville was advanced as a name possibility, but there was at least one other Centerville; so postal authorities, in their quest for a "unique" name, came up with Orlinda, claiming that it would be the only Orlinda in the country. Local citizens went along, and Orlinda became the new name.

Orysa *Lauderdale County.* Shadrach and John P. Rice were some of the earliest landholders in this vicinity. The first store in the area was operated by a Mack Rice, in 1880. The site was given the name Oryza—Greek for "rice"—by Professor Case, since a place called Riceville already existed in the state. Later, the spelling was altered to Orysa.

Osage *Henry County.* The location may have been so named for an Indian tribe, or for the osage orange tree or shrub. According to *American Place-Names,* the term *Ouchage* was used in a French context as early as 1673. The term is commonly applied in Oklahoma, Missouri, and other Central/Plains states.

Ostella *Marshall County.* The reason for this place-name is uncertain. Some speculate that it relates to the Latin *stella,* for "star."

Oswego *Campbell County.* One of the earlier place-name applications of this Iroquoian term may have been for a city in New York. It has been repeated in a number of states. Some scholars feel the Native American term was *osh-we-ge* and could be interpreted as "the outpouring." According to *American Place-Names,* it may describe a place at the mouth of a river and translate roughly as "flowing out." Another source speculates that it may indicate a site at which a valley widens.

Overall *Rutherford County.* Settling in the county in about 1800 was Nathaniel Overall, one of the signers of the Cumberland Compact. Records also show that an N. D. Overall became a school superintendent in the county. They may have been the same person, or merely related; references to the names in historical sources are vague. Another source states that the site was settled in 1805 by Robert Overall. At one time or another, the locality bore the Beesley designation.

Ovoca *Coffee County.* Sources close to this community provide the following account. "The Order of the Knights of Pythias bought land in 1908 . . . to establish a home for orphans and widows . . . and for an assembly grounds. Walter Dennis Fox . . . of near Murfreesboro, was Grand Keeper of Records and Seals for the Knights . . . and was the founder of Ovoca. He gave the site the name . . . after the river Ovoca in County Wicklow, Ireland, where his father was born. Frank Avent Gumm came from Murfreesboro in 1909 to be secretary to W. D. Fox. Frank and his sister, Mary, lived in Tullahoma, but [Frank] later left and married. His daughter was the actress, Judy Garland."

Owens Chapel *Robertson County.* When the 1870 census rolls were compiled, there were several persons residing nearby having the surname Owens or Owen. Included were George Owens, age 65; James Owen, 72; J. W. Owen, 42; and Jonathon F. Owen, 35. Without knowing which of these individuals was the namesake of the place, it is impossible to know how the place-name should be styled—Owen's Chapel or Owens Chapel. Such a designation was often given when the person donated land for a church, was the minister of the church, or both. However, a Robertson County source attributes the place-name to a Revolutionary War soldier said to have settled the site, James Owens.

Owl Hoot *Lake County.* At the extreme southern edge of the county, where Owl Hoot Road meets Lower Owl Hoot Road, this hamlet was once so remote that the hooting of owls could be heard in the after-dark stillness.

Ozone *Cumberland County.* The clean, pure quality of the air here is said to have inspired the name of this mountain settlement.

Pactolus *Sullivan County.* This is the name of a small river in Asia Minor, in ancient Lydia, noted for the gold washed from its sands. Those who named this site Pactolus may have believed it to be a place where they could settle and prosper.

Pailo *Bledsoe County.* An early resident of this place—Pailo Gates—is said to have given his name to this community.

Paine Springs *Rhea County.* Once known as Mathis Spring, the site now bears the name of Major F. J. Paine's parents. One or both families operated a summer camp near the mineral springs found here.

Palestine *Henderson County.* This designation was sometimes given by settlers who felt they had reached the "promised land." The biblical Palestine is interpreted as the land along the Mediterranean Sea's eastern coast. Its southern boundary is the Sinai Desert, with the Euphrates River to the east. The name derives from the Philistines. The area is also referred to as the Holy Land, Land of Canaan, and Land of Israel.

Pall Mall *Fentress County.* A resident of the town explains that the name was assigned by one John M. Clement, terming him "the father of Samuel Clement (Mark Twain)." (Reference is to Samuel Clemens.) The source goes on to explain that John Clement [sic] was a young lawyer and thought Jamestown would be a good place to practice law, arriving there five years after the county was established. In 1832, he moved to the Wolf River Valley, where Pall Mall is located, erecting a log cabin and storehouse. In the storehouse, he opened the county's second post office and named it Pall Mall after an English town. Our informant states that the original Clement house was still standing on his property in 1995, when he gave it to John Rice Irwin, who marked the logs and moved the cabin to his Museum of Appalachia in Norris, Tennessee. John Clement moved to Missouri in April of 1835, selling his cabin to Barry Gatewood. Seven months after the move, Samuel Clemens (Mark Twain) was born in Missouri.

Palmer *Grundy County.* This city was the center of a thriving coal mining industry for many years. It takes its name from a Fort Wayne, Indiana, native, Clarence William Palmer (b. 1850). Palmer is said to have grown up with Tom Thumb, the midget who became a circus attraction, and is said to have been present at Ford's Theatre in Washington when President Lincoln was assassinated. When Palmer came to Tennessee, he married Alice Rogers, of Dunlap. When coal was discovered on the land where they had settled, they sold most of it to Tennessee Consolidated Coal Company. In 1917, a local historian advises, "they opened a mine at the site, built a town, and named it Palmer in honor of Mr. Palmer."

Palmersville *Weakley County.* Palmersville was established in 1842 on a parcel owned by its first merchant, Smith Palmer.

Palmyra *Montgomery County.* The name Palmyra was selected from the Bible. Along with Nashville, Knoxville, and Clarksville, it may be one of the four oldest towns in the state. Lots were laid out by Dr. Morgan Brown, and it was incorporated by the legislature in 1796. In 1797, Palmyra was designated as a "port of entry" by the federal government. It is situated along the Cumberland River and Deacon Creek.

Papaw Ridge *Dyer County.* This topographical feature was probably dotted with papaw trees. These North American trees, or shrubs, are characterized by a large, edible fruit, purple flowers, and big, obovate leaves.

Paperville *Sullivan County.* This is one of the oldest towns in this section of the state. Its name resulted from a paper manufacturing plant that was operated by George Burkhart, who arrived from Maryland in about 1794. Mention of Paperville is found in records as early as 1816. An 1834 gazetteer adds that, in addition to the paper mill, there was a blacksmith, a wagonmaker, a physician, two saddlers, one tavern, and a Presbyterian church in town.

Parker *Henderson County.* Turner, Samuel S., Jeptha, and John Parker all were county citizens in 1840. It is likely their name became associated with this very site.

Park Headquarters *Henderson County.* The community grew up around the headquarters for the Natchez Trace State Park and Forest.

Park Station *Maury County.* In 1870, George W. Park, age 30, was a local citizen. John A. Park, 57; William Park, 62; and William Park, 71, also lived near this place. It is likely they were all related, and the town took the surname.

Parksville *Polk County.* A store and mill on the Ocoee River at this site were operated by the Parks family. In 1854, a Parksville post office opened with James Parks as postmaster. Succeeding postmasters included Alexander C. Parks, James B. Parks, and Samuel Parks.

Parrottsville *Cocke County.* The individual or family who founded the community is believed to have had the surname Parrott, or Parrotts.

Pate Hill *Greene County.* This elevation stands at 1,112 feet and owes its name to John Pates, who was 45 in 1870.

Patmos Chapel *Coffee County.* The Old World Patmos is a rocky isle in a part of the Aegean known as the Icarian Sea. It was once a place to which criminals were banished. It was there that the apostle John received the inspiration for the Book of Revelation. Apparently, there was a chapel at this site in Coffee County.

Patterson *Rutherford County.* When the census was recorded in 1870, local citizens included the following Pattersons: John, age 45; Benjamin, 55; Clina, 20; James, 23; and John, 46. The place-name probably relates to these persons or their ancestors.

Pattersonville *Fayette County.* John T. Patterson is identified as the founder of this early county settlement, in 1820, when he constructed the first house. It may have been the first house in the entire county. Patterson was a blacksmith and farmer.

Pattie Gap *Roane County.* In 1870 records, the sole Pattie who can be placed nearby was John. He may have been a member of a family that lived near this passage between mountains.

Paulette *Union County.* The community apparently takes its name from a local family with the Paul surname. The elementary school was also named Paulette. Some members of the Paul family still resided here in the late 1990s.

Payne's Cove *Grundy County.* Benjamin F., George W., and Cleaveland Payne lived in this area in 1850. The place-name probably relates to them.

Payne's Store *Trousdale County.* Trousdale County was constituted from parts of Smith, Wilson, and Macon Counties. Many Paynes resided in those counties. In 1850, Smith County was home to Absalom B. Payne, two Paynes named Benjamin, Andrew, two having the given name William, Nancy, John, Hamilton, and Larkin. Daniel and Jane Payne lived in Wilson County, while Wily Payne was a Macon County resident. One or more of the Paynes apparently operated a store at this location. Also, in nearby Hartsville, there was a hardware store by the name of Payne & Dayton. One of the incorporators of another well-known county business, the Willard Tobacco Company, was E. S. Payne.

Peach *Giles County.* John Peach, an early immigrant to this place, ran a wool carding factory. He was deceased by 1831.

Peak *Anderson County.* Peak was the surname of a family identified with this town.

Peakland *Meigs County.* Several Peaks, or Peakes, are mentioned in connection with this locality. Luke Peake is described as a pioneer settler of the 1830s or early 1840s. Jacob Peake is also mentioned in historical chronicles. The Peak spelling appears as a variant.

Pea Ridge *Clay County.* According to folklore, the soil here was so poor "it would not sprout a pea."

Pearl City *Lincoln County.* This town is said to have been so named for the pearly appearance on the inside surfaces of mussels that were found in a local creek.

Peavine *Cumberland County.* In settlement times, cattle here flourished on the wild turkey vine that proliferated at this site. Apparently, the vegetation was also known as peavine, giving the place its name.

Pebble Hill *McNairy County.* A collection of tiny settlements were situated among a cluster of hills in this locality. They included Sand Hill, Spring Hill, Pebble Hill, and Gravel Hill. There were gravel pits at Pebble Hill.

Peckerwood Point *Tipton County.* Dictionaries define the term *peckerwood* as Southern and Midlands slang for a woodpecker. In the same areas, it can be an adjective meaning "insignificant" or "small." Thus, this rural venue could have been considered by its namer as a "small, insignificant place," or it could have been a location where woodpeckers were common—or both!

Pedigo *Knox County.* The name of this site is probably attributable to Elijah or Elijah P. Pedigo, who resided locally in 1850.

Pegram *Cheatham County.* Pegram was incorporated in 1974. In 1814, George Scott Pegram emigrated from Virginia, putting roots down in this area. His acquaintances in the area named the locale Pegram, out of respect for Mr. Pegram.

Pelham *Grundy County.* A local historian supposes that Pelham takes its name from an area family with that surname. The family is said to have been residing here prior to 1844, when Grundy became a county.

Pennine *Rhea County.* The late Hattie Beard, who once operated a store here, told a longtime resident the settlement was first known as Sheffield. However, its name caused confusion with Sheffield, Alabama, for trains carrying Civil War supplies. A man visiting the area then observed that the mountains in the area reminded him of the Pennine Mountains in another country. The designation caught on. He may have been referring to the Pennine chain of Alps on the Italy-Switzerland border or the Pennine hills of northern England. Another earlier name of the site was Miller's Station.

Pennington Chapel *Union County.* Land for the local church was donated by Shelby Pennington, who also operated a water mill nearby.

Perrin Hollow *Dyer County.* John, Nancy, James H., and William Perrin were all local citizens in 1850. All resided in the Seventh District of the county, probably at this locality. The dictionary definition of *hollow*, as used in place-names, equates it with a valley or depression.

Perryville *Decatur County.* The oldest town in the county, Perryville was formerly a part of Perry County, which was named for Oliver Hazard Perry. The county seat added a *ville* to the name. Perryville was incorporated in 1825. That same year, Perryville Academy was established here. Twenty years later, the town lost its title of county seat when two hundred interested citizens petitioned to form a new county, and persuaded the general assembly to ratify the act. Decatur County was born, formed from the piece of land called Perryville, located west of the Tennessee River.

Persia *Hawkins County.* An unauthenticated account submitted by a Persia resident states that the community was given its current name out of respect for a railroad worker from Persia (the current Iran). About 1840, so the story goes, the Southern Railway was building a line from Rogersville to Bull's Gap, utilizing quite a few foreign nationals in its labor crews. A man from what was then known as Persia was among them. An accident occurred, taking the life of the worker from Persia; so the place was dubbed Persia to commemorate "the man from Persia." A diverging opinion comes from another source, which states that the Reverend Lewis Monroe Arnott and several other residents called a meeting, since the community seemed to be growing and was in need of a name. Some of the others present may have included members of the Lauderback and Reynolds families. The Reverend Arnott was an avid reader of every book he could lay his hands on, and the country then called Persia held a special fascination for him. When the question of what to name the site was submitted, the clergyman advanced the label Persia, reasoning, "We are so far from any other place, [why don't we] name it Persia?" The others present agreed. Lewis Monroe Arnott was born in 1835 and died in 1917.

Petersburg *Lincoln and Marshall Counties.* The inspiration for this place-name is vague. It may have been named for a major Russian city or for a Petersburg in Virginia. It is thought to have been named by the first settler here, George L. Lenord. Some believe Lenord named the site for a black man who came to this area with him; presumably, if this is so, that man would have been named Peter or Peters. The town incorporated in 1837.

Peters' Mill *Knox County.* At the time of the 1880 East Tennessee census, N.J. Peters and William Peters were residents of this vicinity. N.J. was a 53-year-old male and William a 66-year-old African American. One of them—or ancestors of one of them—apparently operated a mill here.

Petros *Morgan County.* Speculation in *Tennessee: A Guide to the Volunteer State* leans toward the theory that the name was an unusual consolidation using portions of the first name of Governor Peter Turney and the surname of a friend named Ross.

Petway *Cheatham County.* Mary E., John, Hinchey, F. S., Susan C., William, and George W. Petway in 1850 resided in an adjacent county that was among those (Davidson, Dickson, and Montgomery) that, in 1856, surrendered land to help form Cheatham County. It is likely the place-name traces back to one or more of these individuals.

Philadelphia *Loudon County.* The City of Brotherly Love, Pennsylvania's largest city, suggested the name for this tiny hamlet. Laid out by a pair of Quakers (William Knox and Jacob Pearson) in 1822, the two decided to honor the eastern city by using the Philadelphia name. One of the first residents (perhaps the first) was James Price. The year of incorporation was 1968.

Philippi *DeKalb County.* This is the name of a Church of Christ established about 1938, taking its name from the New Testament church at Philippi. The hamlet that arose here also used the Philippi name.

Phillippy *Lake County.* Traveling from southern Illinois in about the year 1907, the Charles L. Phillippy family beheld this area of Lake County and decided to make it their home. Initially, Mr. Phillippy acquired a sole acre of land, from James L. Harris; later, however, he was able to purchase tracts of timber that brought family holdings up to one thousand acres. Phillippy descendants continued to hold real estate here for many decades.

Phillips *Monroe County.* Census records reveal that in 1880, Frank M. Phillips, age 52; Joseph M. Phillips, age 27; and Milla Phillips, age 30, resided nearby. The place-name is probably linked in some manner to one or more of them.

Philpot *Lincoln County.* Joseph and M. B. Philpot are listed as having been local residents in 1870. Joseph was 39 at the time, while M. B. was 60. Earlier—in 1850— John G. and William Philpot were recorded as having been local citizens.

Pickwick Dam *Hardin County.* The *Pickwick Papers,* by Charles Dickens, inspired the use of this name locally.

Pickwick Village *Hardin County.* (See preceding entry.) The village and dam are located at Pickwick Lake, on the Tennessee River.

Piedmont *Jefferson County.* In the mid-1800s, a community began to arise in this neighborhood. John Mount owned the land that was to become this townsite. For a period, it was referred to as Mount's Crossroads. At a time when Samuel Cate was postmaster here, a letter arrived from the Nashville post office suggesting that a new name for the post office (community) might be in order. The reason given was that a great deal of mail was being misdirected due to the existence of so many places ending with the word "Crossroads." Mr. Cate convened a meeting of the residents at the local general store. The name Piedmont was submitted by Wesley Carter, who cited its meaning as a flat area at the base of a mountain. Bays Mountain loomed above; so it seemed a logical selection and was accepted.

Pierce *Carter County.* This place may have adopted the surname of one or more of the following Pierces listed on the county's 1880 census rolls: Mary, age 20; William A., 50; William C., 44; Sarah, 16; Louis, 35; July, 10; William, 24; and Lillie, 4. In the 1870 census rolls, the following Pierces and their ages were given as Mary, 12; Tennessee, 52; Samuel, 28; Lewis, 25; William, 49; and Nathaniel, 29. The discrepancies in their ages from census to census are not explained.

Pigeon Forge *Sevier County.* This city takes its name from the adjacent Little Pigeon River and from an iron foundry that once operated locally. The forge was established in 1820 by Isaac Love, completing the community's name, since the Native Americans earlier had named the river for the numerous pigeons that populated its banks. Pigeon Forge was incorporated in 1961.

Pikeville *Bledsoe County (seat).* The city was founded in 1807 and for a time was known as Thurman. One source states that John Bridgman renamed it Pikeville after his mother's town of Pikeville, North Carolina. However, it may have been named for Zebulon M. Pike, for whom Pike's Peak is named. Pike was an explorer and distinguished himself in the War of 1812. If Pikeville, North Carolina, was named for Z. M. Pike, then both explanations are correct. A minority opinion holds that the label referred to a road, since for a period most roads were referred to as pikes.

Pillowville *Montgomery County.* At the time of the 1850 state census, an individual named J. M. Pillow resided in the vicinity. It is likely the community takes its name from this person, or the Pillow family in general.

Pilot Knob *Greene County.* From the Cumberland River, this promontory appears as the highest hill around. Riverboat pilots are credited with conferring the label, which enabled them to identify their location by using the "pilot knob" as a reference point.

Pilot Mountain *Morgan County.* A correspondent in the vicinity writes that this place-name may not have come into usage until after a mishap he believes occurred about 1936. He states, "The . . . name, I think, came from a plane wreck on the mountain. It was a mail-carrying plane. I had two uncles who saw it burning and went over; they were among the first there."

Pine Crest *Campbell County.* This elevation owes its name to the eastern white pines, Virginia pines, and pitch pines that proliferate in this region.

Pine Grove *Greene County.* This site took its name from a grove of pine trees, probably loblolly pine.

Pine Grove *Loudon County.* This Pine Grove was so named for the presence of pitch pine, shortleaf pine, Virginia pine, or eastern white pine, or some combination of these varieties.

Pine Grove *McMinn County.* Loblolly pine flourished in this area, as did shortleaf pine, pitch pine, and Virginia pine, accounting for the label.

Pine Grove *Sevier County.* Table mountain pine occurs in Sevier County, as did eastern white pine, Virginia pine, and shortleaf pine, accounting for the name.

Pine Haven *Fentress County.* The hamlet sprang up among an abundance of eastern white pines, pitch pines, and Virginia pines.

Pine Hill *Bradley County.* This elevation takes its name from the pitch pine, shortleaf pine, and Virginia pine trees that dotted the area in settlement times.

Pine Hill *Clay County.* A native and longtime resident of Pine Hill states that the first school and church were about a half-mile distant, at a site known as Chestnut Mound. (There were a lot of chestnut trees there.) Both the school and church went by the name Chestnut Mound. "Then they built a new building about a half-mile to the east, where there were a lot of pine trees, and named it Pine Hill," the correspondent advises. It is unclear just when the names were implemented. The local source states that her mother was born in 1895 and went to school at Chestnut Mound, and she, herself, was born in 1922 and schooled at Pine Hill.

Pine Hill *Marion County.* Virginia pine and other pine varieties were found at this location.

Pine Hill *Scott County.* Pine Hill was covered with pitch pine, shortleaf pine, and eastern white pine, inspiring the name conferred by early settlers.

Pineland *Meigs County.* This label recognized the prevalence of the Virginia and pitch pines growing locally.

Pine Top *Loudon County.* The Virginia pine and pitch pine flourish in this area, undoubtedly accounting for the designation for this community.

Pine View *Perry County.* Pines were indeed "in view" when this community was named. The variety found locally was probably the Virginia pine.

Piney *Loudon County.* This site was named for the proliferation of pine timber growing nearby, including Virginia, shortleaf, eastern white, and pitch pine.

Piney Flats *Sullivan County.* Pine trees once covered the "flats" along the river here.

Pinson *Madison County.* The town was founded on a parcel belonging to A. S. Rogers. This may have been in 1866. Forty-five years earlier, five surveyors—Joel Pinson, Memucan Hunt Howard, and three others—encountered an apparent Indian mound, six or seven feet high, "large enough to build a house upon," according to one source.

They dubbed the elevation Mount Pinson. Mount Pinson was a short distance from the site later to become the "downtown" of Pinson. At the time of the discovery of the mounds, the party was surveying old grants for Colonel Thomas Henderson.

Pioneer *Campbell County.* Early in the 1800s, settlers entering the vast, open sectors of Campbell County discussed the "pioneer conditions" under which they would have to live. As a result, the locality became known as Pioneer.

Piperton *Fayette County.* Incorporated in 1974, Piperton owes its name to the person who, in 1837, purchased the tract and laid out the community, Samuel Piper.

Pisgah *DeKalb County.* See following entry.

Pisgah *Giles County.* The biblical place of this name is said to have been the prominence from which Moses viewed the Promised Land. (See Deuteronomy 34:1.) It is a mountain range of ancient Moab.

Pisgah *Shelby County.* See preceding entry.

Pisgah *Weakley County.* See the Pisgah entry for Giles County.

Pittman Center *Sevier County.* This mountainous enclave was the site of a mission school developed in an early year by Dr. Eli Pittman, who spent heavily on the project and basically made the school's success his life's work. Out of respect for him, the town's citizens later attached his name to the community. Pittman Center was incorporated in 1974.

Plant *Humphreys County.* Plant was the surname of one or more families residing here. Families named Plant still live in the area. In a chronicle of early marriages in the area, the Bride Index lists Alma, Bessie, Della, Flora, Jennie, Mattie, Stella, and Willie, while grooms listed include Charley, Eugene Thomas, Henry, James, Walter, and Will. The 1870 census reveals a number of local Plants: James, age 78; Lorenzo, 34; Susan E., 13; Thomas G., 26; and William H., 52.

Pleasant Grove *Bedford County.* This site was historically described in part by "Grove" in all probability because of its shaded situation. At an earlier time, it was known as Cottage Grove. When a Cumberland Presbyterian Church was established here, the place came to be known as Pleasant Grove.

Pleasant Grove *Cocke County.* The Pleasant Grove Baptist Church, situated in this shady, serene environment, was begun in 1838 and probably gave the town its name.

Pleasant Grove *Union County.* One theory regarding this name is that it was inspired by one or more local families having the Pleasant name. It has also been observed that a number of the older residents have "Pleasant" as one of their given names. (See entry for Pleasantville, Hickman County.)

Pleasant Hill *Cumberland County.* Pleasant Hill takes its name from the pleasing setting and flora that greeted settlers at the time when a place-name was bestowed.

Pleasant Point *Lawrence County.* The name dates to an unknown year, but the community came into being when the Andrew Jackson Highway was completed in 1821. At that time, a stagecoach stop sprang up here, and at some later date, it was referred to as Pleasant, no doubt because of a pleasing view or atmosphere. Later, "Point" was appended.

Pleasant Shade *Smith County.* Established at a site where two roads crossed, this community was first called Herod's Crossroads. In 1808, Revolutionary War veteran William Herod Sr. arrived from Virginia and settled on land that was probably a grant for service in the military. He had served under General Washington. The Herods had fourteen children; many of the family members became prominent. This site was still known as Herod's Crossroads as late as 1900, or possibly later. At some subsequent juncture, the name was changed to Pleasant Shade, in order to reflect the ambience of the location.

Pleasant View *Cheatham County.* An account in *Goodspeed's History of Cheatham County, 1886,* states that a group of citizens met at the Bainbridge & Justice store to decide upon a name for the community. This may have been around 1870, when a post office opened here with H. E. Hyde as postmaster. As the story is told, Burgess Bradley and a Mr. Lowe were conversing when one of them said, "What a pleasant view," while surveying the sights from the Jim Evans home, known as Scott Hill. When this expression was recalled, Pleasant Hill became the label for the town. It had been known variously as Bradley's Crossroads or Bradley's Stand. The earliest settlers were probably John Hyde and Howard Alley, in 1790.

Pleasantville *Hickman County.* With its generally pleasing atmosphere, featuring Cane Creek and a grove of beeches, this location is believed to owe its name simply to the pleasantness of the surroundings. It is said to have been named in 1840 by the postmaster, William Bradley Cook, who doubled as a merchant. However, an early (1820) preacher-schoolteacher here was named Pleasant Whitwell.

Plum Grove *Hawkins County.* It is possible that the natural occurrence of the American plum tree extended into this area, inspiring the name.

Pocahontas *Coffee County.* (See following entry.)

Pocahontas *Hardeman County.* It is not known why this site was named for the daughter of Chief Powhatan. Her Indian name may mean "playful" or "radiance." After reaching puberty, according to the *Illustrated Dictionary of Place Names,* she was dubbed *Matoaka,* which is said to translate as "plays with others." Later, as a Christian, her name became Rebecca. Credited with saving the life of Captain John Smith, who was exploring portions of Virginia, she later wed John Rolfe and traveled to England. She contracted smallpox there and died of that disease in 1617.

Poga *Carter County.* The Potter family may have been the first whites to settle at this location. Several versions exist as to why the town was so named. One holds that the original name of the Elk River, which flows locally, was Poga. A second states that it owes its name to a Native American who once lived in the vicinity, Chief Poga. Still another version states that a hunter was lost for several days in the area, and when he eventually emerged, he described himself as having been "pogued up" in the wilderness.

Pomona *Cumberland County.* According to *American Place-Names,* this name traces back to the Roman goddess of fruit trees. It is thought to be commonly applied to places where orchards flourish. John W. Dodge (1807–1891), a portrait artist, is credited with conferring the name upon the community.

Pomona *Dickson County.* See preceding entry.

Pomona Road *Cumberland County.* Maps indicate that two thoroughfares lead to one designated Pomona Road, which leads to the village of Pomona, about four miles away. So perhaps this site was viewed as "on the road to Pomona." (See Pomona entry.)

Pond *Dickson County.* A large body of water existed here, known in Civil War days as Contrary Pond. With the arrival of a railroad, it was used to supply the locomotives. When the Mineral Branch Line of the Louisville & Nashville (L&N) Railroad was constructed from Clarksville to Pond, this site became known as Pond Switch. Before World War I, there was talk of platting the community and naming it Rapid City, but the plan never materialized. It remained referred to as Pond Switch, or simply Pond. A post office at the place was once known as Treswell.

Pondville *Sumner County.* Elizabeth, Richard, and Rachael Pond resided in Sumner County at the time of the 1850 census. In all probability, this place-name relates to one or all of them. The volume *History of Tennessee Illustrated* indexes ten Sumner County Ponds, including John L. and Nannie J.

Poplar Hill *Giles County.* This elevation was covered with yellow poplar, a tree that thrives throughout Tennessee.

Poplar Hill *McMinn County.* See preceding entry.

Poplar Springs *Henderson County.* Near these springs grew poplar trees, probably the variety also known as the yellow poplar, or tulip tree, which sometimes exceeds a hundred feet in height. The Eastern cottonwood (a poplar) also grows in this region.

Poplar Springs *Loudon County.* The poplars near these watering holes were probably of the Carolina poplar (cottonwood) variety.

Poplar Springs *Roane County.* See preceding entry.

Poplar Top *Maury County.* At an early date, this community consisted of a store, blacksmith shop, and one or two houses on one side of the intersection, and on the other side, the Fulton farm, with a grove of poplar trees in the front lot. It was from these trees that the site took its name. A group of boys calling themselves the Zion Tigers used to play baseball near the grove of trees.

Poplin's Crossroads *Bedford County.* This town was probably named for a physician, Dr. Green L. Poplin, or for his father, William Poplin, from North Carolina. However, it is said that when William Poplin sold his farm at Rover and bought land at "the crossroads," the deed described the site as "near Poplin's Crossroads," lending credence to the presumption that the name existed at the site before William purchased it.

Porter *Dickson County.* The first settler at this site was John Porter, from whom the place takes its name. It is not known with certainty if he is the same John (W.) Porter listed as a county resident in the 1850 census rolls, along with William B. Porter. As early as the 1830s, a school was located here.

Porter *Lauderdale County.* Benjamin T. Porter and Dickson Porter were early settlers nearby. The place-name probably traces back to them.

Porter's Chapel *Maury County.* Numerous Porters resided nearby at the time of the 1820 state census. Among them were Charles and Charles M., Redie, three named William, Mimrod, James, Joseph, and Joseph B. It is likely there was a preacher among them, or that they donated land for the chapel.

Porter's Creek *Hardeman County.* At the time of the 1850 census, a number of Porters resided locally, most of them in the Fourth and Seventh Civil Districts of the county. Among them were W. R., Alex T., Nancy, James W., Eleanor, and Elias. One of these families probably gave the waterway its name, which in turn may have been generalized to the community.

Port Royal *Montgomery County.* In 1797, Samuel Wilcox obtained 290 acres of land here, and had part of it surveyed and laid out into lots for a town. It was assigned the name Port Royal; Wilcox had come from Port Royal, South Carolina, which itself was probably named for Port Royal, France. Frontiersmen had come to the site much earlier, and it was probably settled from 1784 on, if not earlier.

Postelle *Polk County.* In 1870, McDoutherd Postell resided at this locality. The name in census rolls is recorded without the terminal *e*. Still, he or his family probably were responsible for this place-name.

Post Oak *Putnam County.* The post oak grows throughout Tennessee and undoubtedly was prominent here.

Post Oak *Roane County.* See preceding entry.

Pottsville *Maury County.* Two John Pottses, Anderson Potts, and George Potts were local citizens in 1840. This place-name is probably related to them in some manner.

Powder Branch *Carter County.* This site may have been settled as early as 1769, by the Hyder family. Later, Mary McKeehan Patton, operating out of an old powder mill on the banks of the creek, manufactured powder to supply the soldiers fighting at Kings Mountain (1780). At some date, Nathaniel Taylor is also said to have operated a powder mill here.

Powell *Knox County.* Jefferson Powell was an early resident of this area, at least as early as 1830. He is likely the person for whom the spot was named.

Powell Chapel *Giles County.* An individual named Lewis Powell resided nearby in 1830. Apparently, the place took its name in part from a church at the site. Powell could have been a minister, the person who donated land for the church, or "none of the above." Information is vague on this place.

Powell's Chapel *Hardeman County.* When the 1830 census of West Tennessee was recorded, two Powells lived in the neighborhood—David G. and Joshua M. Apparently, a place of worship was located here. One of the Powells may have donated the land for it and/or acted as the minister.

Powell's Crossroads *Marion County.* Land and stores at this juncture were owned by a man named Foster V. Powell. (Roads also intersected here.) Apparently, Powell was a busy man: in addition to the store and a "rolling store," he is said to have operated a gristmill, gas station, garage, barber shop, blacksmith shop, and tourist camp. At one time or another, he was also the acting sheriff and coroner. Other Powells in the area included William H. H. Powell (b. 1841), Lewis Powell (b. 1835), Barton Powell (b. 1850), Burl Lamb Powell (b. 1863), John Crawford Powell (b. 1812), and James Powell (b. 1847).

Powell Valley *Claiborne County.* The community is located in the Powell River Valley. In local census records for 1830, 1840, and 1880, several Powells are found. (For some, the surname was spelled Powel, rightly or wrongly.) Joseph Powell was listed in both 1830 and 1840. Other local Powells listed in the 1830 records included Absalom, John, and Jonathan. Also in 1840, the names of George Powel, Jonathan Powel, and Harvey Powell are found.

Powers *Fayette County.* There was a succession of storeowners here, by whose names the site became known. First was the Locke Store, followed by the McKinstry Store, then the Powers Store, and, in recent times, the Teague Store. The label adapted from Robert Powers was the one by which it remains known.

Prater *Cannon County.* On a branch of the Stone River, in about 1820, a mill was operated by Archibald Prater. This label very likely traces back to him.

Primm Springs *Hickman County.* The springs at this site were reputed to contain beneficial amounts of black sulfur, white sulfur, arsenic, calomel, and freestone (or lime). The first person to commercially promote the waters was John T. Primm, in 1836. Primm referred to the retreat as White Sulphur Springs and began to advertise. In the 1860s, Daniel J. Estes spent a summer in an unused cabin nearby, drinking heavily of the spring waters, and was cured of a serious condition. Estes organized a stock company to further promote the springs. The peak of popularity came in the post–Civil War years; often, four hundred to five hundred persons would be camped nearby or staying at the hotel or cottages. Much of these data can be found in *A Patchwork History of Hickman County.* Also present in the county at the time of the 1850 census was an individual named A. M. Primm.

Princeton *Washington County.* The earliest settlers arrived in this area before 1800. In 1876, a school was being constructed. Pupils were asked their opinion on what would be an appropriate name for the school. They replied that it should be called Princeton, for Princeton University, one of the nation's older institutions of higher learning. The name was adopted, and eventually the community in general became known as Princeton.

Prospect *Lincoln County.* This community may have derived its name from the establishment here, in 1871, of a place of worship christened Prospect Missionary Baptist Church.

Pruette *Humphreys County.* In 1840, many persons with an identically pronounced surname lived in this area. However, variant spellings of it were common. Local citizens included two individuals named John Pruett, Shadrick Pruet, James Pruet, David Pruett Jr., and Elisha Pruett. At some point, the geographic designation took on an extra *e* at the end.

Pulaski *Giles County (seat).* As with an Ohio community using this designation, it honors the Polish patriot Kazimierz Pulaski. Fighting in the Battle of Savannah, Pulaski incurred wounds of which he eventually died.

Pumpkin Center *Blount County.* The county historian states only that this site was "named by local jokesters." But pumpkins were probably raised locally, suggesting the name.

Puncheon Camp *Grainger County. Puncheon* is defined variously as a short, wooden upright utilized in structural framing; a pointed tool or dagger; and a cask holding between 72 and 120 gallons. (Other definitions also exist.) There may have been a sawmill or woodcrafting enterprise here that manufactured casks or that prepared raw timber for building applications.

Purdy *McNairy County.* A surveyor for the government, Colonel John Purdy, performed the survey for the town's plat map. The community is named for him. It served as the first county seat in 1823.

Puryear *Henry County.* James T. and Lucretia Fitts Littleton were proprietors at this site, which was initially dubbed Littleton. At this time (1891), the Paducah, Tennessee & Alabama Railroad cut through the location. In 1895, the Paducah, Tennessee & Alabama was purchased by the Louisville & Nashville Railroad, which already had a town named Littleton along its route in North Carolina. Consequently, they desired that the Littleton label be discarded. James Littleton's son is credited with submitting the name Puryear, the surname of one of his close friends, who was a tobacco dealer and chief executive of the railroad branch in question.

Putnam Wall *Bedford County.* Although the "Wall" part of this label is puzzling, William Putnam was a local resident in 1850 and in all likelihood is associated with the place-name.

Pyburn's *Hardin County.* Jacob Pyburn was a citizen residing in this neighborhood in 1840. Very likely there is a relationship between him and this place-name.

Quebeck *White County.* A terminal *k* was appended to the name of Canada's capital city, to form a distinctive name for this site.

Quito *Tipton County.* The name may have been inspired by the capital of Ecuador. But according to *American Place-Names*, the Quito Hill name in Maine may be Algonquian in origin and translate roughly as "long-flow." So perhaps the designation here referred to a stream, spring, or the nearby Mississippi River.

Rader *Greene County.* In the 1870 census book, twenty-nine Raders are named as citizens of the county. Undoubtedly, the label on this site traces to an individual Rader or one or more of the local Rader families. Included among those listed were Lewis, Annis, Jessa, Mary A., and several Williams.

Ragsdale *Coffee County.* Sarah, John, and F. H. Ragsdale were local citizens at the time of the 1850 census. F. H. was probably Frank H. Ragsdale, in 1861 a first lieutenant in Company K of the Twenty-fourth Infantry Regiment. A Frank Ragsdale also served from 1850 to 1854 as a clerk of the circuit court. The place-name can probably be attributed to one or more of them.

Raines *Shelby County.* The origin of this place-name is vague. It probably traces to an early family surname. The only Raines that could be readily located in county cemetery records was a Lena Raines. However, in the 1870 census rolls, references are found to Joseph and William Raines. Joseph at the time was 30, and William was 25.

Raleigh *Shelby County.* Most Raleigh place-names trace back to Raleigh, North Carolina, and ultimately to Sir Walter Raleigh, for his colonizing activities.

Ralston *Weakley County.* Alexander Ralston, the first postmaster at this locale, is the individual to whom the place-name traces. The town was founded in 1860.

Ramah *Lawrence County.* Emigrants from Alabama settled this locality, arriving in the 1870s. With growth came the need for a name; so a competition was held to select one. A Mrs. Phillips submitted Pleasant Ridge, which was accepted and used for some time. But in 1911, with the establishment of a Baptist church in the village, the Biblical name Ramah was adopted. A Bible dictionary describes the original Ramah as a town in the tribal territory of Benjamin, near Saul's home of Gibeah. It was considered of military importance because of its situation not far north of Jerusalem. The label Ramah was also applied to certain other biblical sites.

Ramer *McNairy County.* In 1858, John T. Ramer donated a right-of-way across his land for the Mobile & Ohio Railroad, a site that was designated Ramer Station. A descendant of his reports that Mr. Ramer had great foresight and believed in progress, and was thus inspired to donate the stretch of land, measuring about a mile. Since the trains need a great deal of wood, and passengers needed a place to wait, a wood yard and waiting station were built to accommodate. In 1873, a former Confederate soldier arrived, establishing a huge general store known as A. B. Hamm & Co. It drew a large clientele and helped the town grow. A new depot was then built, with a telegraph office, waiting rooms, and freight facilities.

Ramsey *Hancock County.* A Ramsey descendant advises that the Ramsey settlement and mill were located on Mill Branch, which ran into Mulberry Creek. The same source states that family antecedents arrived near the site in the late 1700s. A number of Ramseys were local citizens in 1880, when the census was recorded. Among them were Jessee, 37; Ruhama, 39; Oliver, 40; Joseh, 44; Nancy, 63; Josah, 38; Clinton, 33; Alviz, 29; and two named James, ages 22 and 35. Ten years earlier, Ramseys residing locally included Riley, Sarah, William, Jesse, two named Josiah, Nancy, Oliver, Florin, and James. The place-name and the presence of these Ramseys in the area is not a coincidence. (Also see Mulberry Gap entry.)

Randolph *Tipton County.* The community is said to have been named out of respect for John Randolph, who hailed from Roanoke, Virginia. In 1870, an individual named John Randolph, age 33, resided near here. It is not known whether he and the above-mentioned John Randolph were one and the same.

Rankin *Cocke County.* Dr. James Rankin gave his surname to the hamlet. A practicing physician, he resided at this site. At times, it was referred to as Rankin's Depot.

Rankin Cove *Marion County.* The cove is believed to be named for David Rankin (b. 1799). Other Rankins identified with the place include Hugh L. Rankin Jr. (b. 1886), whose father was sheriff of Marion County.

Rascal Town *Lawrence County.* Two versions exist of how this place acquired the name. One holds that local lads were raiding storekeeper Orb Brown's watermelon patch and he was overheard saying, "I'm going to have to get them little rascals." Another version states that men used to congregate outside the local store, and some began to refer to the group as a "gathering of the rascals."

Rathburn *Hamilton County.* This designation probably relates to W. P. Rathburn, who came from Ohio after the Civil War and helped organize a local bank. In 1865, he was president of the First National Bank of Chattanooga.

Raus *Bedford County.* A post office called Thompson's Creek operated here from 1833 until 1837, when it moved to Rowesville. In 1892, when this site was granted another post office, the Thompson's Creek name was in use; so it was named Raus. Fred Raus had come to the hamlet a year earlier and reopened a defunct store. His son, Fred Raus Jr., became the new postmaster.

Raven Branch *Cocke County.* This name is sometimes styled as Raven's Branch. A story is told of an aged Cherokee woman named Raven who grew so weary at this site that she could not continue back to North Carolina with her people. They were supposedly in Tennessee gathering chestnuts. A contingent of her people later returned for her, finding her body.

Raysville *Moore County.* In the *1880 Moore County Census,* fully twenty-nine Rays are listed as area residents. This place-name undoubtedly traces back to one or more of them. Among those having the Ray surname were William R., A. G., Ann, Ida B., John H., L. T., Mary, and Tom.

Readyville *Cannon County.* The community owes its name to Charles Ready, who arrived in the area in about 1800.

Red Bank *Hamilton County.* Noting a red clay ridge through the window of her cabin, Mrs. George S. Hartman nominated Red Bank as the new name for this settlement. The year was 1881, and Mrs. Hartman was the wife of the local postmaster. Previously, it had been called Pleasant Hill, but the name was identical to that of another site in the state.

Red Boiling Springs *Macon County.* Edmund Jennings was perhaps the initial settler at the locale, arriving in 1830. Somewhat of a resort arose in ensuing years, based on a bubbling spring containing some type of red sediment that was believed to have healing qualities.

Red Hill *Lawrence County.* This name was suggested by red-hued soil prominent at the site. Local settlement began in the 1820s.

Red Hill *Weakley County.* Soil having a red cast to it inspired the name of the hamlet at this elevation.

Red Oak *Lincoln County.* A large oak tree grew here, serving as a local landmark. When John Redd established the first store to serve the neighborhood, his surname was combined with "Oak" to furnish the place with its name. The post office was located in Redd's store. But southern red oaks were probably the variety growing locally.

Reeder's Crossing *Dickson County.* The reference to a "crossing" is unclear. The only nearby bodies of water are Lake Woodhaven and Beaverdam Creek. In this application, it probably means the intersection of roads. Elisha A. Reeder resided locally in 1870. He was also listed as a local citizen in 1850, when the given name was spelled Elisa. When the 1840 census was recorded, Jacob H. Reeder and Jacob Reeder were listed as residents.

Reed Spring *Loudon County.* Mary Reed, 42, lived in this area in 1880, according to census records. Along with the existence of a local spring, she or her family may have been responsible for this label now found on maps.

Reeves *Washington County.* Peter M. Reeves and William R. Reeves were local residents in 1850, as shown in census records. They were probably identified with this locality.

Rehobeth *Dyer County.* The biblical name Rehoboth (with a second *o*, not *e*) means "broad place" or "roominess." Isaac gave the name to a well he dug (Genesis 26:22).

Reidtown *Cocke County.* At one time, a store was operated at this location by David H. Reid (1853–1938).

Reliance *Polk County.* One of the earliest landholders here was Joseph Dallas Vaughn, who purchased acreage in 1880 and built a home. According to a newspaper article, Sarah Reed Vaughn is credited with naming Reliance and was the first "keeper of the mail." When she began in the post, she received the mail delivered from saddlebags carried on horseback over the wild terrain and across the river. It is said that she so named the community because "Reliance" had a "solid, dependable sound." Several others in Sarah Reed Vaughn's family served as Reliance postmasters. She died at age 94. In 1996, a great-granddaughter of Sarah Reed Vaughn was serving as Reliance postmaster.

Revilo *Lawrence County.* The hamlet is situated along Steadman Ridge, which took its name from the local Steadman family. With growth, a church school was deemed necessary, but when built, it had no name. By one account, some men were enjoying their lunch at a county store when one of them called attention to the Oliver twin-shovel turning plow parked nearby, and spelled out the name backward—"Revilo." The sound seemed to come trippingly to their ears; so they adopted it as the name of the school and community.

Rheatown *Greene County.* This venerable site was settled as early as 1771. The name traces back to an Irishman, John Rhea (1753–1839), who arrived here in 1783. Rhea helped organize the state and write its constitution, and served as a representative from Sullivan County to the state legislature. A well-educated man, Rhea also served in Congress and in the Revolutionary War, and was a confidant of presidents. In 1823, he obtained a post office for Rheatown.

Riceville *McMinn County.* Although he emigrated to Arkansas in 1859, Charles Rice left the legacy of his surname with this community. In the *Tennessee 1850 Census Index,* McMinn County Rices listed include A. G., C. W. (who perhaps was the Charles previously referred to), Henry, John, Lerner, Miller, Tandy S., and Wile L.

Rich *Giles County.* The hamlet was settled about 1820 by the Yokley and Alexander families. It owes its name to an African American resident named James Rich. The 1870 state census rolls list a James D. Rich, age 28, as residing nearby.

Richardson's *Tipton County.* Marcus and Jane Richardson lived here in 1850. J. L. Richardson also resided near here in an unknown early year. The surname probably inspired the Richardson label that is still seen on maps.

Richardson's Cove *Sevier County.* This cove is the site where five people were killed by Indians in 1792, near William Richardson's cabin.

Richmond *Bedford County.* In about 1831, a local merchant from Richmond, Virginia, named this community for his former city.

Rickman *Overton County.* The current name refers to Carney H. Rickman, one-time owner/operator of a large lumberyard alongside the railroad tracks. An active railroad line operated through here from the early 1900s until 1934. A previous place-name was Bilbrey's Crossing, which made reference to the crossroads where "Uncle Bob" Bilbrey's store was located.

Riddle's Store *McMinn County.* Sarah, James, William, Samuel, and Joseph Riddle were counted among the local residents in 1850. Very likely, one or more of them ran a store, and the place became identified with the family name and business.

Riddleton *Smith County.* In the late 1800s, a subscription school was built here. A formal dedication was planned and Congressman Haywood Riddle, of Lebanon, Tennessee, was invited to conduct the ceremonies. At that time, the new school was still without a name. Afterward, it was agreed that the school should adopt Congressman Riddle's given name, and it became Haywood Academy. The town then took on his surname and became Riddleton.

Ridgely *Lake County.* Logically, the site adopted the name due to its situation on a ridge.

Ridgeside *Hamilton County.* The lay of the land here suggested the community's name, it being situated at the side of a ridge.

Ridgetop *Davidson and Robertson Counties.* This hamlet perches atop Highland Rim, at an altitude of 730 feet.

Riggs Crossroads *Williamson County.* Gideon Riggs resided near this intersection in 1840.

Rinnie *Cumberland County.* A grocer here was asked his opinion on a name for a new post office at the locality, and submitted Piney. Somehow, in transmission, it was misspelled and came out Rinnie, which it remained.

Riovista *Carter County.* This locality bears a name that translates from the Spanish as "river view."

Ripley *Lauderdale County (seat).* Soldier-legislator Eleazor Wheelock Ripley (1782–1839) is the town's namesake. He was active in politics in both Massachusetts and Louisiana, and became a general in the War of 1812. One source describes him as a hero of the Battle of New Orleans and of the War of 1812. Incorporations of Ripley took place in 1838 and 1901.

Riverdale *Knox County.* The community is situated in a dale (valley) adjacent to the French Broad River.

Riversburg *Giles County.* Originally dubbed Petersburg, Riversburg traces its current name to the William Rivers family, at one time extensive landowners in the vicinity. The Petersburg label may have referred to Peter Martin, an early settler nearby.

Riverside *Monroe County.* The community's name was inspired by its location, on a branch of the Little Tennessee River.

Riverside *Sullivan County.* Riverside undoubtedly gained its name by virtue of its orientation on the banks of the Holston River.

River View *Claiborne County.* River View is situated on the Powell River.

Riverview *Unicoi County.* This aptly named community has an overview of the Nolachuckey River.

Rives *Obion County.* Rives was incorporated in 1905 and is now a city. Although it is known to have been named for an individual with the Rives surname, his given name seems to have been lost. Pioneers came to this approximate site in about 1825.

Before the place was known as Rives, it was dubbed Troy Station, beginning in 1859. Mr. Rives was the supervisor of the local district for the Mobile & Ohio Railroad. He liked the place a great deal and had numerous friends in the community. A surveyor named Jack Hudgins may have laid out the town. The name was changed to Rives by a vote of the citizens.

Roan Mountain *Carter County.* This community reposes at the foot of Roan Mountain, which may have assumed the name because of iron ore deposits that gave it a reddish (roan) hue.

Robbins *Scott County.* In 1870, Lucinda, age 37; Jonathan, 33; Mary, 36; and Melton J. Robbins resided here. The site probably takes its name from their family or families. The Robbins post office was established in that name in 1880; the year before, it was known as Bianco. In 1906, Alba Robbins became a charter member of a Baptist church located near here.

Roberts *Putnam County.* Several Robertses resided locally at the time of the 1870 census. Included were Mary, age 39; Adaline, 23; J. A., 41; J. H., 44; J. D., 32; G. W., 32; Thomas, 71; Robert, 50; and F. M., 34. The place-name likely is due to one or more of these persons.

Robinson Mill *Loudon County.* Loudon County was not formed until 1870. So when checking 1850 census rolls for Robinsons who may have resided in this area, one must search the Roane, McMinn, Blount, and Monroe County records, for these are the counties that contributed portions of land for the formation of Loudon County. Eighteen-fifty records reveal the following Robinsons and their county at the time: Isaac and Reuben (Blount); two Edwards, James, J. J., Samuel, and John (McMinn); William and two named James (Monroe); and Sally, Wiley, William, and James (Roane). Apparently, there was a mill at this site, and one of more of these individuals may have had a hand in it.

Rockdale *Maury County.* An individual named J. J. Gray owned and operated the Rockdale Furnace here. The business name may have pre-dated the place-name; if so, the site can be said to have adopted the name of the enterprise that was a landmark here.

Rockford *Blount County.* The Little River runs nearby. At one time, travelers "forded" the river at a rocky site adjacent to the community that is now a city. The site was referred to as Rocky Ford at one time. A solid rock bottom enabled horses or oxen to pull vehicles across the river with a minimum of difficulty. One of the first settlers was John M. Clark.

Rock Island *Warren County.* Now home to Rock Island State Park, this locality was the site of Middle Tennessee's last Indian battle, in 1793. The name comes from the location, a rocky island in the middle of the Caney Fork River.

Rockwood *Roane County.* A military figure, Major W. O. Rockwood, gave his name to this town, according to some sources. Others state that it takes its name from a man who provided some capital for the Roane Iron Company, W. E. Rockwood.

Rocky Branch *Blount County.* It is said that the hamlet takes its name from the fact that it was reached via a dirt road and a "rocky branch" leading up a hill to the town. "When it rained, it was difficult to tell which was which," recounts a statement in a newspaper article.

Rocky Valley *Jefferson County.* This community was named for the appearance of the valley there. The valley floor is said to have been covered with rocks, making farming virtually impossible.

Roddy *Rhea County.* A reference is found that the Reverend Jesse Preston Roddy (or Roddey) was in the county as early as 1821, and a reference to Jesse Roddy places him in the vicinity in 1812. An amazing ninety-six entries for Roddys, with a wide assortment of given names, appear in the biographical index of an early source covering Rhea County. A separate source states simply, "Roddy was named for a family by that name who lived in the area."

Roe Gap *Franklin County.* James and Laneson Roe were local citizens in 1850. The site likely adopted its designation from this family. The word "Gap" in a place-named usually identified it as the point of a passageway through the mountains, or where water flowed through.

Rogana *Sumner County.* This is a variant of the surname of Hugh Rogan, an early explorer of the area, who in 1800 erected a place of residence here.

Rogers' Springs *Hardeman County.* Numerous individuals with the Rogers surname resided in the county in 1830. Their given names were Green B., Peter, William, Richard, William R., Stephen, Nathan, John, and Henry. One or more of their families apparently resided near the springs and gave their name to them.

Rogersville *Hawkins County (seat).* A settler in the vicinity in 1785 or 1786 was Joseph Rogers, to whom the city can trace its name. He was a native of Ireland and is credited with founding this city.

Rome *Smith County.* There also being a Carthage in this county, it is likely this name was chosen for its classical connotations. Sometimes, places named Rome were situated in hilly regions, suggestive of Rome's seven hills, according to *American Place-Names.*

Rosser *Carroll County.* Norwood, Atlas, Jederiah, and Arock Rosser were local citizens when the 1870 census was taken. Their respective ages were 26, 61, 50, and 21. Their relationships were not apparent from census data. The name of the community is probably tied in some way to one or more of these individuals.

Rossview *Montgomery County.* This designation may relate to a Reuben Ross, listed on county records from the West Tennessee census of 1830. Reuben also was on the 1850 census rolls, as well as James Ross.

Rossville *Fayette County.* P. B. and Nancy Ross were the only Rosses who could be placed at this site in the year 1850. It is likely the community assumed their family name.

Routon *Henry County.* Several Routon family members resided in this vicinity, so the place-name probably traces back to them, or one of them in particular. An earlier label on the site was Albany.

Rover *Bedford County.* Historians are unsure of the rationale for this name. With tongue in cheek, some local residents suggest that an early settler named it for his favorite dog. Another version suggests that a lot of fisticuffs took place there, "like dogs fighting," and thus it earned the label Rover. The name is thought to have first appeared in the 1840s. A previous label for the locality was Bylor's.

Rowark's Cove *Franklin County.* This cove is located in the southeast corner of the county, in a natural cove of Cumberland Mountain that was settled by a Roark family in 1800. A church was built and called Roark's Cove Church. At least one popular book of county maps styles the name as Rowark. Mr. Roark's grave is in a local cemetery.

Rowland Station *Warren County.* Sometime between 1800 and 1815, a William Rowland settled just over the county line, in White County. This place-name probably traces back in some way to this individual or his progeny. The "Station" part of the name probably relates to the situation of this community on the Caney Fork & Western Railroad.

Royal *Bedford County.* Royal probably took its name from the nearby U.S. Royal Tire Company, later to become Uniroyal. In this "mill village" on the Duck River, the company operated a plant to make cord for tires.

Royal Blue *Campbell County.* A coal seam discovered and mined here was designated the Royal Blue Coal Seam, in part because of the Blue Diamond Coal Company operating here in the 1800s. The current name dates only to about 1940. Among the site's many previous names were Uplands (1870), Morrowville (1871), Buckeye (1883), Titus (1905), and Hickey (1923).

Rucker *Rutherford County.* There were some prominent local Ruckers in this county. The first county court was convened in 1804 at the residence of Thomas Rucker, who had acquired real estate in the vicinity in 1797. In about 1817, a Dr. William R. Rucker established his practice of medicine nearby. This site probably owes its name to one of these individuals, or another clan member. Much later, in 1870, the names of at least forty-four Ruckers dot the census roster. Some of them, and their ages at the time, were Barber, 30; Butler, 30; Osborn, 61; Harriet, 45; Ike, 60; Isaac, 38; Cabet, 70; Rol, 30; Wash, 45; and Isham, 50.

Rudderville *Williamson County.* Eph and Sallie Rudder, age 60 and 40 respectively, called this neighborhood home in 1870. It is not known for certain if they were husband and wife or related. However, the Rudderville designation no doubt relates to the family or families.

Rudd's Crossing *Weakley County.* In 1858, William Granville Rudd immigrated to this locality and put down roots. It is uncertain whether the "Crossing" part of the label refers to a branch of Mud Creek or some other obstacle that was crossed at this site.

Rugby *Morgan County.* British author and social reformer Tom Hughes founded the community in 1880. The name was inspired by the noted British public school evoked in Hughes's *Tom Brown's School Days* (1857). According to the Historic Rugby web site, the Rugby colony in Tennessee "was to be a cooperative, class-free, agricultural community for younger sons of English gentry and others wishing to start life anew in America."

Ruskin *Dickson County.* The Ruskin Cooperative Association settled at Ruskin Cave. An adherent of John Ruskin, Julius Augustees Wayland, is credited with naming the place. The area is characterized by the existence of a number of caves, including Jewel Cave.

Russell Chapel *Sullivan County.* James, John, and Seth Russell were area residents in 1850. One of them may have been a clergyman, or possibly donated the land for the place of worship. By 1880, local census rolls carried the names of Jeremiah and Mary Russel, ages 50 and 18, respectively, believed to be African Americans. Whether the spelling of the surname with only one *l* was a transcribing error or the family's preference is open to conjecture.

Russell Hill *Macon County.* Rebecca Russell is listed as a county citizen in the 1850 census records. It may be that she or her family resided at this location.

Russell Mill *Claiborne County.* Records show that the mill was last owned by Ned Russell.

Russellville *Hamblen County.* Local taxpayers in 1799 with the Russell surname or a close variant included Elizabeth Rusel, James Russel, and James, George, J. R., John Sr., and Mary Russell. The proprietor was Colonel James Roddye (or Roddey), who received it in return for his efforts in the Battle of Kings Mountain. Roddye became very active in state organizational activities. One source believes the community was named for Roddye's second wife, a Miss Russell.

Rutherford *Gibson County.* Griffith Rutherford, an American general who served in the Revolutionary War, is thought to be the individual honored in this place-name.

Ruthton *Sullivan County.* George W. Ruth, age 38 in 1880, may have been related to the Ruths responsible for the attachment of this designation. He was the only Sullivan County Ruth reflected on rolls of the census in that year. The "ton" would simply indicate "town."

Ruthville *Weakley County.* Ruth was the name of the daughter of an early settler here. She was honored by having the site named for her.

Rutledge *Grainger County (seat).* The name traces to General George R. Rutledge.

Rutledge Falls *Coffee County.* The "Falls" part of the name probably derives from falls or rapids on the local waterway. One source refers to the stream as Compton Creek, and one terms it Crumpton Creek. What was later better known as Childress Mill is believed to have been constructed by Arthur Rutledge.

Rutledge Hill *Coffee County.* There were several Rutledges in this general area. One early settler was H. M. Rutledge. The settlement is situated at an elevation. (Also see preceding entry.)

Ryall Springs *Hamilton County.* Evidently, natural springs were discovered here. Lamb Ryall, age 46, resided in the vicinity at the time of the 1870 census. His family's name attaches to this place.

Sadlersville *Robertson County.* Some land in this county was deeded to George Sadler in 1796 by Nicholas Conrad. Sadler was originally from South Carolina. Other Sadlers identified with this general area included George H., Nannie, Elizabeth H., Thomas, and W. R. The last named is shown in census records to have been 46 years old in 1870.

Safley *Warren County.* Early settlers in this vicinity were Jessie and David Safley, of the Fifth District.

Saint Andrew's *Franklin County.* At one time, the place was known as Gipson's Switch, being the site of a railroad siding that constituted the last place where trains could pass before the nine-mile slope leading down the mountainside to Cowan. In about 1900, an Episcopal order of monks (the Order of the Holy Cross) headquartered in West Park, New York, decided to establish a school for underprivileged "mountain boys" in Tennessee, who had no access to school buses or schools close enough to attend. The school became a reality in about 1904; earlier, a school for girls had been established on the opposite side of the mountain. One of the moving forces behind introduction of the schools was Bishop Charles T. Quintard, although he died in 1898 before seeing his ideas germinate into reality. Since Saint Andrew was the patron saint of the monks' order, this name became attached to the location as a place-name.

Saint Joseph *Lawrence County.* Most believe this label is a biblical reference to the Virgin Mary's husband, Joseph. One source states that a German immigrant priest, the Reverend Henry Hueser, founded the hamlet in 1871 as a Catholic settlement, and that the parish patron is Saint Joseph.

Saint Mary's *Franklin County.* This label is usually applied by citizens with strong religious convictions, in honor of Mary, the mother of Jesus and wife of Joseph. Sometimes, a church bearing this name exists at the place before the surrounding community assumes the name as well.

Sainville *Coffee County.* This place-name in all probability relates to G. T. Sain, a businessman in this area at least during the period of 1870 to 1880.

Sale Creek *Hamilton County.* The name is believed attributable to an event: in 1779, Colonel Evan Shelby tarried here long enough to hold an auction of captured horses and other goods, part of the booty of war. A creek flows nearby.

Salem *Cocke County.* This Hebrew term translating as "peace" (*shalom*) is often associated with sites centered around the founding of a church. Biblically, it is often thought to be virtually synonymous with Zion or Jerusalem.

Salem *Lewis County.* See preceding entry.

Salem *Montgomery County.* See entry for Salem, Cocke County.

Salem *Tipton County.* See entry for Salem, Cocke County.

Saltillo *Hardin County.* Between 1820 and 1849, this locality bore several names. In 1849, however, it was dubbed Saltillo, after the site of a battle during the Mexican War. A variant account advances the notion that it was named for a salt lick not far away.

Samburg *Obion County.* The initial name of this hamlet was Wheeling, named for a man with that surname who operated a store here. When the citizens made a bid for a post office, they discovered another Wheeling, Tennessee, was on record. By that time, a gentleman with the Samburg surname operated the same store Mr. Wheeling had previously run; so it seemed only logical to rename the town Samburg. (These data are contained in the *Obion County History*.)

Sanders *Grundy County*. The Sanderses living nearby in 1870 included Catharine, G. C., Henderson, Jackson, James, John R., Jordan, Mathew, Mitchell, Robert, and Silas. The community was probably dubbed Sanders because one or more of these individuals settled there. A reference is also found in Grundy County to a Sanders Crossing, which is probably the same site known as Sanders.

Sandy *Overton County*. The community arose at a site where the soil was very sandy.

Sandy Hill *Weakley County*. An elevated situation and a sandy quality to the earth here gave the community its designation.

Sanford *McMinn County*. According to a passage in a volume authored by C. Stephen Byrum, "Tobe Gettys, owner of a woolen mill, constructed a depot and named it Sanford after a prominent Knoxville family."

Sango *Montgomery County*. *Webster's Third New International Dictionary* describes this term as identifying "a trade language widely used in French Equatorial Africa [and] belonging to the Adamawa-Eastern branch of the Niger-Congo family." Why it would have been applied here is uncertain.

Santa Fe *Maury County*. This name translates from the Spanish as "holy faith."

Sardis *Cocke County*. This designation was probably inspired by a biblical city of that name mentioned in Revelation. The name was given to a campground established for religious purposes near this site.

Saulsbury *Hardeman County*. This name may trace to Burrell Sauls, a local citizen in 1830. However, a second source attributes the place-name to Dr. J. D. Saul, the town's first physician.

Saundersville *Sumner County*. The name traces back to the Reverend Hubbard Thomas Saunders, a pioneer Methodist preacher who built a camp meetinghouse at the site. Saunders was a racehorse enthusiast who maintained a stable of horses there, as well. He fathered fourteen children, one of whom, William Russell Saunders, became the first postmaster and merchant at the village. Sometimes the place-name is seen printed as Sanders, or Sandersville. One source states that this is attributable to a James Sanders, who in 1799 donated the land for the Methodist meetinghouse, but was not related to Hubbard Saunders.

Savannah *Hardin County (seat)*. David Robinson purchased land at this site. The real estate had been part of the original Colonel Joseph Hardin Land Grant. Robinson's wife hailed from Savannah, Georgia; so this city is thought to have been named for the one further south. Savannah, Tennessee, was known at an earlier time as Rudd's Ferry.

Sawdust *Maury County.* This hamlet has gone by several other names during its history. Having been platted by Revolutionary War soldier and statesman Major General Richard Winn, it became known variously as Winntown, Winnsboro, or Winton. Winn purchased five thousand acres in the area in 1794 for 50 cents an acre, and settled here in 1811. The 1830s found the community being labeled Blocken's Shop, in recognition of the blacksmith operations carried on there by Elijah Blocken. In the 1850s, a sawmill enterprise was conducted by W. R. McKennon and S. P. Jones. One result was the accumulation of a large pile of sawdust by-product. The schoolhouse erected in 1858 bore the name Sawdust Valley School. A roller process flour milling operation went on-line in about 1900, and for a time the products bore such names as Sawdust Meal or Sawdust Flour. This proved to be an unwise marketing move, as some consumers assumed that sawdust was used as an extender in the flour or meal. Thus, the mill took on the name Valley Milling Company. The site is also known widely as Sawdust Valley. An early village promoter, George W. Kinzer, was referred to in his 1873 obituary as "the founder of Sawdust." He had owned six hundred acres nearby, and operated a store, gristmill, and sawmill.

Scandlyn *Roane County.* Two individuals having the Scandlyn surname resided in the vicinity in 1880: E. W. Scandlyn and M. Scandlyn. The latter was forty-seven years of age at the time. It is likely that they, or their forebears, influenced this place-name.

Scattersville *Sumner County.* The history section of the county *Fact Book* dated July 1994 recounts that George German, a traveler, suggested this name when he noted that the houses were all "scattered around." The community arose about 1880, and for some unknown reason—or no reason at all—the citizens all settled at considerable distance from one another.

Scoot Mill *Greene County.* When the 1840 census was recorded, David Scoot was a local resident. It is likely that he had something to do with the operation or ownership of the mill.

Scottsboro *Davidson County.* In 1850, this area was a haven for persons with the Scott surname. Among the many Scotts in the vicinity were Madeline, Calvin, George, Frederick, Alfred, Alex, David, Nancy, Thomas, D. T., Cynthia, E., Elvin, Nelson, Winfield, and several named William. Much earlier, however—in 1787—tax rolls showed local citizenship of James Scott and Samuel Scott. Moreover, Marmaduke Scott received a North Carolina land grant in this vicinity in a very early year, and John Scott purchased land in the county in 1788. So the Scott name was inextricably associated with this area over many decades.

Scott's Hill *Decatur and Henderson Counties.* The community is believed to have been named for an emigrant from North Carolina, Micajah Scott. He may have arrived in the vicinity as early as 1825 and later operated a store. W. C., Wyley, and

Wright Scott—possibly relatives of Micajah—resided at this locale when the 1840 census was taken. The elevation probably borrows their family name to form the place-name. Incorporation came in 1917.

Scribner's Mill *Maury County.* It is believed that this community took on the identity of a nearby gristmill operation situated on Foundation Creek. The mill's operator was George W. Scribner.

Selmer *McNairy County (seat).* It is believed that the intention was to name the town for Selma, Alabama, and that the person who submitted the name to the Post Office Department misspelled it.

Sequatchie *Marion County.* Also the name of a Tennessee county, this label traces back to the name of a noted Cherokee chief of the early 1700s.

Sevierville *Sevier County (seat).* According to the *Illustrated Dictionary of Place Names*, this city, like the county, takes its name from a statesman who influenced the formation of the state of Tennessee, John Sevier (1745–1815). Sevier was the first governor of Franklin, the state's previous name, and became the first and third governor after the name was changed to Tennessee. He also became a U.S. representative.

Sewanee *Grundy County.* After the 1857 founding here of the University of the South, the area was generally known simply as University Place. Native Americans in the region (probably Shawnee) were thought to apply the *sewanee* term like the words "south" or "southern" would be used today. The Algonquian version of the term may have been *Saawaneew.* In the *Sewanee Sampler,* Arthur Ben Chitty recounts several other theories as to the derivation of the Sewanee name. One holds that a Creek word, *sawani,* translated as "echo." A second belief was that a similar word signified "lost" in Shawnee. Another Shawnee term is said to have translated as "foggy" or "misty." A fourth notion, totally unfounded, was that "Mother Mountain" was the meaning of *sewanee.* The first-mentioned explanation is probably the correct one, the ones following it having been largely discredited by authorities. It was by chance and timeliness that this site was able to secure the Sewanee name. In 1867, there was a Memphis-area post office using the label, but it allowed the designation to lapse. George Rainsford Fairbanks applied to Washington for permission to apply the name here, and permission was granted.

Seymour *Sevier County.* This map designation traces back to a construction engineer with the Knoxville, Sevierville & Eastern Railroad, D. G. Seymour.

Shackle Island *Sumner County.* In 1900, the Post Office Department finally validated this designation by using it for the name of the community. The July 1994 *Fact Book* reveals its genesis: it seems there was a small shack on an island in a nearby stream, and illegal whiskey could be obtained therein. It was common to hear the suggestion, "Let's go to the shack on the island for a drink." This evolved into the label Shackle Island.

Shacklett *Cheatham County.* John and Ridgway Shacklett were area residents at the time of the 1850 census, probably accounting for this label.

Shady Grove *Hickman County.* When settlers near the mouth of the Dunlap Branch left a sizable stand of trees in the middle of their intended "business district," the site took on the name Shady Grove. When the site obtained a post office, it could not be known by that designation, as it would have duplicated the name of another Tennessee office; so the facility was labeled Duck River.

Shady Rest *Warren County.* This name is a shortened version of the name of a tourist court that existed here along U.S. Route 70 (the "Broadway of America") in the late 1920s and early 1930s. It was known as Shady Rest Tourist Court.

Shallowford *Unicoi County.* Mill Creek and Indian Creek flow nearby. This label was probably adopted because the low water levels enabled a "shallow ford" of the creek or creeks.

Shanghai *Hardin County.* Ultimately, this label must trace back to the name of the major city in China. American settlers went through a period when they named many sites after well-known exotic or faraway places.

Sharon *Weakley County.* Located in a neighborhood once known as Dedham (for Dedham, Massachusetts), this community is thought to have been named for its profusion of althea, the wild shrub also known as the rose of Sharon. One authority states that a conductor on the first train through the site suggested the Sharon name, while another source claims that the place is named *for* the conductor. Still a third opinion advances the notion that Sharon was the given name of a pioneer woman. Incorporation took place in 1901.

Sharp Place *Fentress County.* Several Sharps resided locally in 1850, undoubtedly accounting for this place-name. George, William, John, and Joseph Sharp were among local citizens having this surname at that time. By 1915, William Eddison Sharp was operating a farm nearby. His father *may* have been Ozie Sharp.

Sharp's Chapel *Union County.* Two persons currently residing in the Sharp's Chapel area, both having the Sharp surname, provided the information that the town was founded by a Peter Sharp. Details are lacking. There was probably a place of worship at the site, and Sharp may have been the preacher.

Shaver Mill *Sullivan County.* In 1880, a number of Shavers lived in this locality. Among them were Jacob, age 45; Joshua, 36; Elizabeth, 26; Joel H., 87; and John E. Shaver, 29. This family, or relatives with the same surname, probably operated a mill at the site and gave the place its name.

Shaver Town *Smith County.* The *History of Tennessee Illustrated* lists six persons with the Shaver surname in its index. The Honorable W. R. Shaver, born 1837, was perhaps the most prominent. Others were Lou D., Annie L., Lou C., Hattie (or Hettie), and Susan.

Shaw *Haywood County.* Daniel and Robert T. Shaw resided locally at the time of the 1830 census of Western Tennessee, suggesting that the site assumed their surname.

Shawnettee *Wayne County.* This designation is thought to mean Shawnee Camp. One story holds that a Shawnee campground was located on the creek when the branch was named, probably in the 1780s.

Shawtown *Obion County.* A farm family surnamed Shaw located near this site, accounting for the label that some still use today, although it may appear as Samburg on today's maps.

Shea *Campbell County.* James T. Shea was the postmaster and namesake of the post office at this site. In 1872, a timber processing operation was active here. Its name was the Shea Brothers Lumber Company.

Sheboygan *Cannon County.* A word of Native American origin, its meaning is vague and may refer to virtually any item with holes in it. "Reed-like" or "tube-like" are other connotations of the term. The Algonquians may have coined the word. The city of the same name in Wisconsin is larger and better known; perhaps labeling the Tennessee site was the idea of someone with ties to, or knowledge of, the Wisconsin city. One mention of this (Tennessee) place-name was spelled Sheybogan. Other variant spellings, such as Cheboygan, also are found.

Shelby Farms *Shelby County.* One portion of this designation derives from the name of the county (see entry for Shelby in county section). The "Farms" part probably relates to a bucolic setting and may have been a developer's "promotional" label.

Shelbyville *Bedford County (seat).* Kentucky's first governor, Isaac Shelby (1750–1826), is the city's namesake. Shelby was also a land developer and noted military figure, having distinguished himself during the Battle of Kings Mountain during the Revolutionary War and achieved the rank of colonel. The city dates to at least 1810, and was incorporated in 1819. A dissenting source on Shelbyville's name origin claims it was named for Evan Shelby, who was a prominent individual in East Tennessee. However, most authorities attribute the name to Isaac.

Shelbyville Mills *Bedford County.* Like nearby Shelbyville, the community takes its name from Colonel Isaac Shelby, who commanded a small group of riflemen from the region against the British during the Revolutionary War. Located on the Duck River, the town probably had mills operating on the waterway, accounting for the final portion of the name.

Shell Creek *Carter County.* The name probably traces to one of the initial settlers at the site, Dempsey Shell. The first pioneer to put down roots here is thought to have been a North Carolinian, Barnabus Oaks.

Shellmound *Marion County.* Some of the first human inhabitants of the Tennessee Valley, prehistoric Indian tribes, subsisted chiefly on the abundant mussels found in the Tennessee River. As they ate, they discarded the empty shells, which accumulated in huge mounds that marked the abode of these Native Americans. Shellmound was on the Nashville, Chattanooga & St. Louis Railroad (now the CSX), near Nickajack Cave and Dam. This information is found in the book, *Rivers of America: The Tennessee; Volume 1—The Old River, Frontier to Secession.*

Shellsford *Warren County.* The 1830 Middle Tennessee census records reveal that Mary E. Shell was a nearby resident at the time. In all probability, her family name was assigned to a spot where a stream was forded.

Shepp *Haywood County.* This designation is probably a shortened version of the Shepperd surname. Egbert and Fanny Shepperd lived near here in 1850, and by 1870 David Shepperd was a local resident.

Sherrilltown *Wilson County.* The 1830 census for the central portion of the state recorded several county persons with the Sherrill surname. At least three spelling variations were found; however, these may be attributable to recording errors. Included were Elizabeth Sherrill; Abl., Epraim, and Samuel Sherrell; and Archibald Sherrel. The community assumed the surname.

Sherwood *Franklin County.* Sherwood owes its name to a former lieutenant governor of Wisconsin, C. D. Sherwood, who came here in 1875. In 1870, records show that a B. W. Shearwood was on the local scene; however, it is unclear whether Shearwood is a variant spelling or the result of an error in copying.

Shiloh *Bedford County.* (See entry for Shiloh, Cumberland County.) An old Shiloh School was located here, and later a church.

Shiloh *Carroll County.* See following entry.

Shiloh *Cumberland County.* This name probably was evoked by the religious persuasion of the settlers. Biblical references to a place named Shiloh are found in Joshua and Judges. It was said to be the location of the tabernacle of the children of Israel, on the north side of Bethel (or Beth-el) and the south side of Lebanon.

Shiloh *Grainger County.* See preceding entry.

Shiloh *Hardin County.* Local church founders felt their building was "the dwelling place of God." The town took its name from the place of worship. The bloody Civil War battle was fought nearby. (See entry for Shiloh, Cumberland County.)

Shiloh *Hawkins County.* See entry for Shiloh, Cumberland County.

Shiloh *Jackson County.* See entry for Shiloh, Cumberland County.

Shiloh *Montgomery County.* See entry for Shiloh, Cumberland County.

Shiloh *Overton County.* See entry for Shiloh, Cumberland County.

Shiloh *Sumner County.* See entry for Shiloh, Cumberland County.

Shiloh *Wilson County.* See entry for Shiloh, Cumberland County.

Shiney Rock *DeKalb County.* Many names were associated with this locality. The church was called Whorton Springs, the school was designated Oak Grove, and the post office was labeled Hollandsworth. Shiney Rock itself is often misdesignated on maps as *Shining* Rock. As the story is told, in the 1890s the illegal whiskey trade was flourishing. A customer was instructed to place his money under the shiny rock and leave. When he returned a few minutes later, he would find his whiskey there. If summoned before a grand jury, he could swear under oath that he did not know from whom he bought it.

Shingletown *Johnson County.* A longtime resident reports that the accepted explanation for this name is that paper shingles formerly were manufactured at this location. No further details are available.

Shook's *Knox County.* This designation on maps may in some way be connected to an 1830 local resident, Isaac Shook.

Shop Springs *Wilson County.* One account relates that Elisha Chastain constructed a blacksmith shop on Hugh Bryan's farm, near the spring, which inspired the town's name. The settlement had been referred to earlier as Tubtown.

Sidonia *Weakley County. American Place-Names* speculates that this tag may have been inspired by the Phoenician city of Sidon, mentioned in the Bible, with the addition of a Latin ending. Or, it may have been suggested by the Spanish town of Medina Sidonia. *History of Weakley County* states only that Willie Wilson suggested naming the town for the biblical place, and that "someone else added the 'ia.'"

Signal Mountain *Hamilton County.* The community was developed by Charles James and incorporated in 1919. It was at first known as Signal Point. The current name probably relates to the site's importance during the Civil War.

Silerton *Chester and Hardeman Counties.* When the railroad came through the local area, landowner Joseph Siler donated or sold a parcel of his land to accommodate laying of the tracks.

Siloam *Macon County.* This place-name is biblical. In John 9, the account is set forth of Jesus anointing with clay the eyes of a man blind since birth, telling him to "go and wash in the pool of Siloam." When the man did so, he received his sight. Siloam was a section of Jerusalem. The name comes from the Hebrew verb for "to send." According to the *Mercer Dictionary of the Bible,* it was identified with a tunnel and pool at the southern terminus of a spur where the Jebusite city of Jerusalem was built, from which water was sent to an artificial reservoir inside the city of Jerusalem.

Silver Hill *Rutherford County.* This designation is sometimes styled Silverhill. An unknown person is said to have lost some silver coins in a spring near this site.

Sims Ridge *Lawrence County.* In early years, a number of families named Sims or Simms settled at this locality, resulting in the place-name. By 1870, local Simses included John F., age 24; Marion F., 25; Benjamin A., 34; James A., 28; and Paris L., 43.

Singleton *Bedford County.* In 1870, a number of Singletons were residing at this locality. Among them were Wiley, age 27; J., 50; G., 27; Houston, 42; and E. S., 50. This designation on maps probably leads back to one or more of these persons.

Singleton *Blount County.* Several Singletons populated this locale in 1850—John, Allen, Rebecca, Robert, H., and Elijah. By 1870, Evaline, Enic, Pick, William, Caroline, James, and Harrison Singleton also called this vicinity home. One of them, or the family or families, was probably responsible for this place-name. John Singleton may have been Dr. John Singleton, who owned property in the area through which the Louisville & Nashville (L&N) Railroad came. He may have donated or sold some land to the railroad, or the place may have been dubbed Singleton due to its proximity to his property.

Sinking Cove *Franklin County.* A local resident explains this name as follows: The waters of Crow Creek that drain the valley simply run under the mountain and "sink." The hamlet is in a natural cove.

Sixmile *Blount County.* The name is adopted from nearby Sixmile Creek. Local historians, however, are not certain if the creek was so named due to its length, its distance from some other point, or some other rationale.

Sixteenth Model *Coffee County.* A local history buff believes—probably rightly—that names such as this referred to the model of Sears home that was built here. She also provided a clipping of a reproduction of a rare catalog entitled *Small Houses of the Twenties: The Sears, Roebuck 1926 House Catalog,* which would seem to support the contention.

Skaggston *Knox County.* At least one family of pioneers here had the Skaggs surname. It is known that Eli Skaggs, a clergyman, resided nearby at one time. Eli is listed in the 1830 census rolls, along with Stephen, James, Moses, and Solomon Skaggs.

Skinem *Lincoln County.* W. J. McAlister came to this site about 1902, and it became known as McAlister. With his three sons, McAlister operated several endeavors— wagon wheel repair and the manufacture of chicken coops and wooden chairs among them. Some of these were extremely successful and operated for many years. Local lore has it that many area residents felt the McAlisters overcharged. It became popular to admonish those headed for McAlister's, "Be careful; they'll skin you." And from that is said to have emerged the label "Skinem." Oddly, a no-longer-existing community called Ketchum once was nearby. So residents were fond of joking, "You Ketchum, we'll Skinem."

Skullbone *Gibson County.* This name is sometimes styled Skull Bone, or Skullbonia. It is believed the name was conferred upon this locality because, for a period, it was notorious for mayhem, murders, and feuds, some of which may have been racial in nature. One account states that bare-knuckle fights took place here, in which all blows were required to be struck to the "skull bone." Non-cranial punches were considered fouls. Locals referred to the matches as "fist and skull" contests. Prior to that time, the locality was known as North Gibson.

Slayden *Dickson County.* A local land proprietor in some early year had the Slayden surname. Little else could be discovered about him, but he gave his family name to this site.

Smartt's *Warren County.* According to one account, this designation on maps leads back to James Polk Smartt, or his family in general. James was born here in 1844 and became a soldier and wholesaler of shoes. His paternal grandfather was General William C. Smartt. Another clan member was Will M. Smartt, born 1875. One map gives the designation as Smartt's Station. Information supplied by the county historian credits the name to William Cheek Smartt, identifying him as the county's first sheriff and a prominent plantation owner. In 1852, he provided a good deal of land, as well as financing, for construction of the McMinnville & Manchester Railroad.

Smithland *Lincoln County.* From 1854 until 1885, the town was called George's Store. The community is believed to date to 1840. "George's Store" may refer to an individual named George W. Head, who served as an early postmaster. In 1854, the designation became Arnold's Grocery, but in 1880 it reverted to George's Store. But one of the town's wealthiest residents was Richard Smith III, and after being popularly known as George's Store for many years, in 1885 the place was renamed in Smith's honor.

Smithtown *Bledsoe County.* This community saw post–Civil War settlement, led by a Union veteran named John Smith. From his mustering-out pay, Smith purchased four hundred acres for the princely sum of 25 cents per acre, and apportioned some of it out to other Smith family members, as well as to friends.

Smithville *DeKalb County (seat).* The community was laid out in 1838 and first incorporated in 1843. It was reincorporated in 1919. The name traces back to the family of a settler with the Smith surname.

Smoky Junction *Scott County.* Creeks, roads, and a railroad converge at this site, near Smoky Mountain.

Smyrna *Carroll County.* See entry for Smyrna, Rutherford County.

Smyrna *Marshall County.* See entry for Smyrna, Rutherford County.

Smyrna *Pickett County.* See following entry.

Smyrna *Rutherford County.* Smyrna takes its name from an early center of Christianity, a Greek seaport on the Aegean Sea. Today, that city is known as Izmir, and is located in Turkey. A biblical mention of Smyrna occurs in Revelation.

Smyrna *Warren County.* A Church of Christ was founded at this site in 1857, with the community taking on the name of the biblical city. (See preceding entry.)

Sneedville *Hancock County (seat).* The community takes its name from an attorney who became a congressman, William H. Sneed (1812–1869). At one time, Sneed had served as a state legislator. Greasy Rock was a previous label for the place.

Snow Hill *Hamilton County.* This elevation may have taken its name from William Hill, a nearby resident in 1850.

Snow's Hill *DeKalb County.* This location received its name about 1837, when the Lebanon-Sparta turnpike was being constructed. By 1813, Joseph Snow (1772–1852) was residing in a log house at the foot of the hill, which took its name from him. Joseph had been born in Kent County, Delaware, the son of William Snow and a great-great-grandson of Nicholas Snow and Constance Hopkins, who arrived in 1620 on the *Mayflower*.

Soddy-Daisy *Hamilton County.* The "Daisy" part of the designation is believed to have been a reference to Thomas Parks's daughter of that name. Parks was second-in-charge of a prominent coal firm operating locally. "Soddy" is probably a variant or corruption of the surname of a Welsh immigrant, William Sodder, who operated a trading post at the site.

Somerville *Fayette County (seat).* During the Creek Indian War, a Lieutenant Robert Somerville lost his life. Town fathers honored him by attaching his surname to this hamlet. The site previously bore the name Bowersville.

Southall *Williamson County.* James, John, and a second James Southall resided in this vicinity in 1840, according to census records. Their surname likely became attached to the physical site.

South Berlin *Marshall County.* South Berlin is just about a mile south of the small community of Berlin.

South Carthage *Smith County.* This site is nominally south-southwest of the county seat of Carthage. It was incorporated in 1963. (See Carthage entry.)

South Cleveland *Bradley County.* South Cleveland takes its label from its orientation, nominally south of Cleveland. (See Cleveland entry.)

South Clinton *Anderson County.* This community is south of Clinton. (See Clinton entry.)

South Covington *Tipton County.* South Covington is nominally south of Covington. (See Covington entry.)

South Dyersburg *Dyer County.* This community is south of Dyersburg. (See Dyer entry.)

Southerland *McMinn County.* Macijah and Micajah Southard Sr. are listed on local census rolls for 1850. Unaccountably, there is a variation in the spelling of given names. The name of the community, however, may have been an adaptation of the Southard surname.

South Etowah *McMinn County.* This diminutive community is slightly south of Etowah. (See Etowah entry.)

South Fulton *Obion County.* Fulton, Kentucky, lies just to the north, accounting for the "South" portion of the label. The "Fulton" part is derived from the inventor of the steamboat, Robert Fulton.

South Pittsburg *Marion County.* Early settlers apparently had ambitions of transforming the site into a "Pittsburgh of the South," after Pittsburgh, Pennsylvania, because there was a great deal of coal and iron ore in the surrounding countryside.

Southside *Hardin County.* Although the community is located in the southern portion of the county, and the county is one of the southernmost in the state (the state of Mississippi lies just to the south), these factors apparently had little influence on this place-name. As a local schoolteacher learned upon speaking with an older resident, "The community was named Southside because the people living there fought on the Confederate side during the Civil War, while their neighbors in Savannah [Tennessee] supported the Union side."

South Tunnel *Sumner County.* This community sprang up during construction of the Louisville & Nashville (L&N) Railroad. To reduce the elevation of the line, it was necessary to cut a tunnel through the base of a ridge. Constituting the southernmost tunnel on the line, naturally it was referred to as South Tunnel. Because of its strategic placement, it became a target during the Civil War.

Sparkmantown *Van Buren County.* The 1850 state census rolls list numerous Sparkmans as citizens of this vicinity. Among them were Joseph, Lewis, Martha A., William, William S., Solomon, Oliver, Bryant, two named James, David, two named George, and John. However, another county source claims the place owes its name to a Cliff Sparkman, going on to say that in 1905, property for the local school was purchased from P. H. and Betty Sparkman. Other Sparkmans mentioned in this second source include T. B. and L. D. Sparkman.

Sparta *White County (seat)*. The ancient Sparta of Greece inspired this city's name.

Spencer *Van Buren County (seat)*. An early explorer, frontiersman, and Indian fighter, Thomas Sharpe Spencer, gave his surname to this community. A native of Virginia, Spencer was one of the outdoorsmen who spent months, or even longer, in the wilds. In 1794, he lost his life near this spot.

Spencer Hill *Maury County*. The nearby residency of Ahlmeaz, Frederick, and Francis Spencer inspired the name assigned to this elevation. The Spencers were at this locality in 1820 and perhaps earlier.

Spencer's Mill *Dickson County*. On the rolls of the 1850 census, the names of Daniel, James, and Eleanor Spencer are found. It is likely one or more of them resided at this site and operated a milling business.

Spinks *Henry County*. The railroad designated this location Spinks after the H. C. Spinks Clay Company, which also had cattle ranching operations in the area. Before the site belonged to the clay company, it was the two-thousand-acre Camp Tyson Barrage Balloon Training Center of the U.S. Army. The center's activities ceased in 1942, and the center was dismantled at the war's end.

Spivey *Macon County*. Several Spiveys lived nearby, some of whom were engaged in endeavors across the Clay County line, near Hermitage Springs. Hamilton H. Spivey, a merchant, was well known. Lynn Spivey was another local citizen.

Spot *Hickman County*. An account set forth in *A Patchwork History of Hickman County* states that the manager of the local store and lumber company, Lewis Mathey, was registering at a Chicago hotel when he dropped a blob of ink on the registration form, where it asked for his address. According to the tale, the hotel clerk jokingly inquired if he was from Spot, and when Mathey returned home, he promptly bestowed that name upon this Hickman County site.

Spring City *Rhea County*. Although some believe the place-name was derived from Rhea Springs, most subscribe to the belief that it was inspired by a spring near the Audley Caldwell residence. Railroaders had earlier dubbed the place Rheaville, but local residents discarded it in favor of the more logical Spring City.

Spring Creek *Madison County*. One passage of a newspaper article states that "residents believe the town got its name from a spring-fed creek near the village." The hamlet arose around the gristmill of Colonel Jeremiah P. Haughton, a local farmer who arrived in 1825. The stream named Spring Creek—a tributary of the middle fork of the Forked Deer River—flows through this site. A charter of incorporation was granted in 1854. Four years later, an expanded charter was approved. In 1883, a repeal of the municipal charter was sought and approved.

Springfield *Robertson County (seat).* A prominent spring flowed forth here, inspiring the name of the city.

Spring Hill *Anderson County.* Today, locals describe this site as a subdivision created from what formerly was the Hill family farm. Apparently, a spring existed on the property.

Spring Hill *Maury County* The land here was cleared by Colonel Russell, but the first settler may have been James Peters. Some wished to honor Peters by dubbing the hamlet Petersburg, but Peters opposed the idea. It was then that they turned to their important source of quality water for a place-name. The *History of Tennessee* states that the place was settled in about 1808 and names Abram Hammond as one of the first to reside here. It says Hammond "lived just above the big spring from whence the town takes its name." In a separate source, the information is found that Father James Peters bought land here in 1819 and had a religious camp known as Peters Campground. It adds that, after Peters rejected the notion of naming the town Petersburg (citing a biblical injunction to "call not your lands by your own name"), it was "named for a spring on his property instead." A commonly heard statement was, "I am going to the spring hill for water." The spring may have been situated on the property of Colonel Russell, who was assisted in clearing the land by Abram Hammond (or Hammonds). At a much earlier time, Major George Doherty received some five thousand acres here from the state of North Carolina. However, he died prior to 1806. Doherty's widow, daughter Frances, and son-in-law William Bond actually made the journey to this locality, with the Bond-Doherty family eventually contributing a parcel for purposes of the settlement.

Spring Hill *Williamson County.* One of the local landmarks was a coldwater spring, near—or at the foot of—an elevation; so the location took on the Spring Hill name.

Springtown *Polk County.* A beautiful spring gushed water from the ground in this mountainous sector of Polk County, inspiring the name of the place. A picturesque mill adorned the bank of the creek and was first known as Harris Mill. During another period, it was known as Maggie's Mill; local residents insist that it inspired the ballad "When You & I Were Young, Maggie."

Springview *Blount County.* This hamlet was so named because it had "a view of the spring," being situated above the water source.

Springville *Henry County.* Numerous springs existed here at one time. When the post office and railroad were relocated to accommodate the Tennessee Valley Authority (TVA), the new location was designated New Springville.

Spruce Pine *Hawkins County.* See entry for Big Piney.

Spurgeon *Washington County.* In 1850, William Spurgin was among the local citizens. The way the name was recorded on census rolls—Spurgin—may have been a variant spelling. The label on this site may relate in some way to William or one or more relatives. Individuals spelling the name Spurgen are found on the 1840 census rolls as residing locally. They included Joseph, Samuel, and William Sr. By 1870, local residents using this variant were listed as Ed, age 25; James, 25; John R., 38; Peter, 34; and Robert, 66. A source unrelated to census records attributes the designation to an individual named John R. Spurgeon and puts the settlement time in the late 1800s. This is probably the same location also known as Spurgeon Knob. The "Knob" part of the name was suggested by a topographical characteristic.

Squawberry The squawberry shrub (or tree) is native to the eastern United States. It grew in profusion here, inspiring the place-name. It is also known as the deerberry or squaw huckleberry.

Stacy *Hawkins County.* William, Claiburne, and Miller Stacy lived nearby in 1840. The place-name likely traces back to their residency.

Stafford's Store *Weakley County.* Apparently, a store was operated at this site by someone with the Stafford surname. In 1870, a number of Staffords lived in the vicinity, including Thomas E., Thomas R., John, Phebe, G. B., J. N., and William. John's surname was recorded as Stafferd, which may have been a transcription error.

Staffordtown *Polk County.* In the early 1900s, Jim Stafford operated a livery stable and grocery store at this locality. The community took its name from him or his family.

Stakely Mill *Monroe County.* Several individuals using this surname—or a close variant—were county residents when the 1850 census was taken. Included were Abraham Stakeley and John and William M. Stakely. One or more of them was probably involved in operation of the mill.

Stanley Junction *Scott County.* The junction probably took its name from one of several Stanley families residing locally in 1870. Individuals with the Stanley surname and their ages at the time included William G., 28; Eliza, 51; Rhodes, 55; Rhodes, 21; Ferril H., 32; and James C., 34.

Stanton *Haywood County.* It is said that Joseph Blackwell Stanton arrived from North Carolina in the 1850s, obtaining a land grant and becoming a successful farmer. Stanton erected a large home at the site, which was not far away from the settlement of Westly. Soon, the railroad announced plans to build a line through the area, and Stanton paid the railroad a sum to come through his land instead of closer to Westly. As a result, people moved to the town of Stanton, it flourished, and Westly became more or less of a ghost town. Incorporation took place in 1927.

Stantonville *McNairy County.* Benjamin Stanton is believed to have been the community's namesake. He was accompanying a wagon train from North Carolina that was headed for Missouri, and decided to settle here. One source states that the family was related to Edwin M. Stanton, President Lincoln's secretary of war. The community was incorporated in 1966.

State Line *Lincoln County.* This community is situated just north of the state boundary with Alabama.

Static *Pickett County.* A correspondent from the area recollects this account of the town's name origin: A local contest was held for the purpose of deciding upon a name for the settlement. A gentleman submitted the name of his pet bulldog, Static, and the name was accepted. Another account, however, states that—at the time when a name for the post office was being considered—an individual brought a radio to the site. Most of what emanated from the device was just noise; so town fathers dubbed the post office Static. Another version of the second account goes like this: "My father (Timothy Stephens, postmaster at Timothy) had been called up there to set up a post office and they didn't have a name. A radio was on and naturally, in those days, there was a lot of static. He said, 'If there wasn't so much static around here, we could come up with a name.' Everyone immediately agreed, that was it!"

Stella *Giles County.* One of the first settlers—if not the first—was Elijah Anthony, who came in 1817 and erected Shores Mill, a water mill. Other early families were surnamed Paisley, Barnes, Jones, Browning, White, Davenport, Hopper, Hammonds, Carroll, Boyd, and Riggs. The current name came about in 1868. As the tale goes, a local resident and country physician, Dr. M. S. Waters, named it for the girlfriend of his son, David Waters.

Stella Ruth *Weakley County.* The town's school was erected by Will Dildine, who had a wife named Stella and a daughter named Ruth. Thus, the community became known as Stella Ruth. Although the town is among the county's earliest, the place-name came into being in 1919 and is sometimes hyphenated.

Stephens *Morgan County.* A correspondent from the vicinity advises that a Stephens family resided here, resulting in the place-name. A son became a major in the armed forces, returning to this site to live out his life. He is said to be interred in the local cemetery. Whether he served during one of the wars is unclear, since the period of his military service was not readily available.

Stephenson *Coffee County.* William and Thomas P. Stephenson were county citizens in 1850. It is very likely that this label refers to them or the family.

Stewart *Houston County.* The town is directly adjacent to Stewart County, which was named for Revolutionary War veteran Duncan Stewart. Houston County was formed in part from Stewart County lands.

Stewart Chapel *Warren County.* This designation is said to have been inspired by the families who lived at the site and the church that they built there. In an uncertain year, the James Madison Stewart family emigrated to this spot from Georgia. There were five sons: Charlie, Joe, George, John, and Jesse. With the parents' passing, John moved from the area. Jesse and Charlie assumed the reins of the farm. George and Joe lived with Jesse and his wife. Charlie had a wife and daughter. Church services in the community began in about 1936. Joe E. Stewart conducted them. He had asthma, no transportation, and the nearest place of worship was farther away than he could walk. Services at first were held outdoors in good weather. But in the winter, they were held in a member's house. In 1938–1939, a church was built. Joe E. Stewart and Mr. and Mrs. Jesse Stewart were the founders. Joe wanted to name it for his mother and call it Sarah's Chapel, but for some reason the name wasn't adopted, and it became known as Stewart's Chapel Baptist Church. The Warren County Stewarts listed on census rolls at an earlier time—in 1850—include Archibald, Nathan, Robert, Sarah, James, Mary, and John.

Stinking Creek *Campbell County.* An odor hung in the air here, caused by sulfur springs that ran nearby.

Stivers *Maury County.* In 1840, John Stivers resided in the county, quite possibly at this site, accounting for its name. One map shows the site as *Stiversville*.

Stockton Valley *Loudon County.* Since Loudon County was formed in 1870 from sections of Roane, McMinn, Monroe, and Blount Counties, this place-name may relate to Thomas or Smith Stockton, two persons listed as Roane County residents in the 1850 census records.

Stone *Jackson County.* The 1820 Tennessee census rolls show that Samuel, Thomas, Uriah, and Ireby Stone were already in Jackson County.

Stone's Mill *Campbell County.* In 1897, Joel Edward Stone established and operated a gristmill at this location, which afterward retained the name.

Stony Fork *Campbell County.* This site was formerly known as Clinchmore. Its current name is taken from the rock-strewn character of Stony Fork Creek, which empties into the New River.

Strawberry Plains *Jefferson County.* Although Alexander McMillan resided here for a time before moving in 1778, the first permanent settler was Adam Meek, a surveyor who had come from North Carolina. Meek was making surveys in the region as early as 1785 and in 1788, and settled where Holston River and Beaver Creek converge. A French chronicler who fought in the Revolutionary War, Andre Michaux, made a journal entry that describes this site as being covered (in season) with wild strawberries. He added that "the berries covered the ground as with a red cloth" and "the fetlocks of a horse walking through the fields became red like blood." Referred to as a "barren," the area became known as Strawberry Plains. The Indians created barrens by burning the area to prepare it for cultivation.

Stroudsville *Robertson County.* The site was named for one or more Stroud families populating the area. Robert, Joshua, James, and two Strouds named William are found in the 1850 county census rolls. A post office opened in 1900 and operated for a bit over three years, with James F. Stroud as postmaster.

Sugar Grove *Sumner County.* A brisk trade in maple syrup was once carried on at this site, fed by the numerous maple trees in the vicinity.

Sullivan Gardens *Sullivan County.* The "Sullivan" part of the place-name stems from the same source as that of the county, Revolutionary War hero General John Sullivan. The "Gardens" portion was probably given to suggest a florid setting or appearance, for promotional or aesthetic purposes.

Sulphur Springs *Lincoln County.* A pool of water located here was termed "one of the best sulphur springs in the state." In 1856, a school known as The Sulphur Spring Institute opened here, on land near the Childs and Harris farms. The school operated for several decades. It may have also been known, at one time, as Sulphur Springs Academy.

Sulphur Springs *Washington County.* A nearby sulfur spring having a greenish-yellow cast and giving off a characteristic odor caused this community to be so named.

Sumac *Giles County.* It seems likely that early settlers encountered a great deal of the poisonous wild sumac bush here. Current local historians confirm the continued presence of the plant in this locale.

Summertown *Lawrence County.* This name is sometimes styled Summer Town. It arose as a summer resort, with cottages and hotels. There were mineral springs and a racetrack.

Sunbright *Morgan County.* At an earlier time, this locale was known as Stapleton. With the coming of the railroad, the label Sunbright was attached to the station, and the town adopted it as well. It was probably a tribute to the importance of the railroad, with citizens seeing the event as "the dawning of a new day." The information is disclosed in a book by W. Calvin Dickinson.

Sunset Gap *Cocke and Sevier Counties.* An earlier name of the site was Glenwood. Later, it was changed to Sunset Gap because of the way the setting sun was visible in the evenings, in a gap between the mountains.

Surgoinsville *Hawkins County.* Major James F. Surgoins, described as a French Huguenot, is the community's namesake.

Susong *Hamblen County.* Hamblen County was formed from portions of Grainger County and Jefferson County. According to a census of East Tennessee taken in 1830, a number of Susongs resided in that portion of Grainger County later adjoined to

Hamblen. Included among them were John, Elizabeth, Andrew, and Alexander Susong.

Sutherland *Johnson County.* Joseph Sutherland resided in this area when the 1850 and 1870 censuses were taken. He or his family is probably responsible for the name that remains with the community.

Swann *Jefferson County.* James P. Swann resided in this vicinity in 1850. There is also a site labeled Swann in North Carolina. (Many North Carolina place-names were "imported" to Tennessee with the westward movement of pioneers.)

Swannsylvania *Jefferson County.* Numerous Swanns were local citizens in 1880. Harry, 30, an African American; A. H. (a male), age 61; J. P. (male), 60; V. R. (male), 30; George, 28; and J. B. (male), 28, are known to have been among them, according to census records. One or more of these, or local Swanns who preceded them at the site, probably influenced the name of the place. The *sylvania* suffix is often given to a place having a sylvan setting, or profuse flora.

Sweet Lips *Chester County.* "How sweet to the lips" are said to have been the words uttered by a wayfaring Civil War soldier who came upon a spring here and knelt to partake of its clear, cold waters. The name, obviously, caught on.

Sweetwater *Monroe County.* This label probably indicates that there were "good springs" at the site, providing a source of wholesome water. *Culla saga,* the Cherokee term for the water source, is believed to translate as "sweet water." It also may refer to the Sweetwater River.

Sycamore *Putnam County.* The hamlet was named for the sycamore trees that occur here and throughout the state.

Sycamore Landing *Humphreys County.* It is said that numerous sycamore trees grew here. The "Landing" portion of the name is due to the site's orientation on the banks of the Tennessee River.

Sycamore Valley *Cheatham County.* This low-lying community was named for the local profusion of sycamore trees.

Sycamore Valley *Macon County.* See preceding entry.

Sykes *Smith County.* Details are sketchy regarding this place-name. However, it was found that Sarah Sykes, second wife of J. S. Prowell, had ties to this locality. In all probability, the site was named for her family or a related family. The *1830 Census of Middle Tennessee* discloses that Thomas A. Lancaster and Majr L. Sykes were local citizens of that time, as was Joshua Sikes. It is unclear whether "Majr" is a given name (spelled rightly or wrongly) or the abbreviation of a title or rank.

T

Tabernacle *Tipton County.* One can only speculate that the site may have been so named for a local church or place of worship.

Tabor *Cumberland County.* According to the *Eerdmans Bible Dictionary,* this biblical term refers to a mountain east of Nazareth having an elevation of 1,843 feet. The name was also applied to a Levitical city and to an oak tree where Samuel instructed Saul to meet three pilgrims. Tabor or Mount Tabor is mentioned in several books of the Bible.

Tackett Creek *Campbell County.* Mike, F. M., and James Tacket resided in this vicinity at the time of the 1870 census. As recorded on rolls, the surname was spelled without the second *t* on the end. However, these persons, or their ancestors, probably gave Tackett Creek its name.

Talbott *Jefferson County.* A surveyor named Colonel John Talbott gave his name to this site, at one time referred to as Talbott Station. Colonel Talbott was born in 1801, passing away in 1884. On local taxpayer rolls in the year 1800 was a Parry Talbot (with one *t*). It is uncertain whether or not he was a relative of Colonel John Talbott. The same can be said for Joseph and Ross Talbott, whose names can be found on the 1822 tax list.

Tallassee *Blount County.* This term may mean "beautiful water," from the Native American *talise.*

Talley *Marshall County.* The first postmaster here, appointed in 1879, was Samuel Talley. A town arose around a new rail line and was referred to as Talley's Station, or simply Talley. Marshall County was made up in part from portions of Bedford and Lincoln Counties. In 1830, Abraham Talley was a resident of Bedford County, while Henry and Patrick Talley were Lincoln County residents.

Tarpley *Giles County.* Several persons with this surname, or a close variation, resided in the county at the time of the 1830 census. Included were Thomas, Littleton, W. A., and C. S. Tarpley, and Pascal and A. Tarply. However, current sources in this county suggest the place is the same one better known as Tarpley's Shop, tracing back to an Esquire Epperson Tarpley, who moved to the site in 1869 and erected a carriage and woodworking shop. A blacksmith shop was associated with these enterprises, but occupied a separate building. In 1871, Tarpley was named postmaster, with the result that the office, shops, and community in general became recognized by the label Tarpley's Shop.

Tarsus *Montgomery County.* The apostle Paul was a native of the biblical Tarsus, mentioned several times in Acts of the Apostles. Paul's Jewish name was Saul. Located ten miles from the Mediterranean Sea, Tarsus was an ancient city situated in Cilicia, Asia Minor, on the Cydnus River. The name was probably applied here for religious reasons.

Tasso *Bradley County.* In 1901, this locality became known as Tasso, for Torquato Tasso, a sixteenth-century Italian poet. Why this particular name was given is unclear. Prior to that, there had been postal confusion between the previous name, Chatata, and the larger city of Chattanooga. Before Chatata, the site went by the name of McMillan Station, and at a still earlier time was called Fish Town because of the abundance of fish in nearby Chatata Creek. The name Chatata is of Native American origin.

Tate *Carroll County.* In 1830, local citizens included Henry, J. W., Thomas W., and George Tate. It is likely one or more of them was closely associated with this site, and the place then adopted the surname as its label.

Tate Springs *Grainger County.* Like so many venues in Tennessee, freshwater springs bubbled forth at this location. And many persons with the Tate surname called the area home. They included Able, age 60 in 1870; Allan, 27; Hariet, 34; William C., 30; Edward, 25; and Tates identified only by their initials: D. A., D. N., W. B., S., S. N., E. M., G. W., and W. C. However, the place-name is linked to C. O. Tate, who constructed the first hotel at the springs. The water was said to have been particularly beneficial for eye problems, and, in addition to drawing visitors from a large area, was bottled and sold widely.

Tatesville *Grundy County.* Included on the rolls of county residents in the 1850 census were the following Tates: Andrew J., Davidson, Elisha, Elizabeth, Francis, two Jameses, Jemuel, John G., Robert, Robert H., Sally Ann, and William N. A connection between the place-name and one or more of these persons is quite likely. When the 1870 census rolled around, other Tates residing in the county included Martha, Ferrel, Jackson, Lias, and two named Jazeal.

Tatumville *Dyer County.* Three Tatums—Alx., Andie, and Bryant—were local residents at the time of the 1870 census. There is probably a relationship between them and this geographical designation.

Taylor Crossroads *Dickson County.* Several Taylors are listed on the 1850 census rolls as residing in this county. Included are Ann, Gipson, Johnathan, Thomas, Mary A., and W. R. Taylor. The place-name probably draws from this family name and the proximity of their domicile to an intersection of roads.

Taylor's Chapel *Stewart County.* One account states that, in 1928, a funeral was being held outdoors at a cemetery located here when a heavy rain began to fall. This prompted discussion about the need for a church to worship in, and where funerals could be held. An old church was purchased by the Taylor brothers and moved here, to some land they owned. It became known as Taylor's Chapel.

Taylor's Crossroads *Bedford County.* A family surnamed Taylor lived at this intersection, giving it its name.

Taylorville *Wilson County.* Philander Davis and John N. Taylor were the landholders here. A merchant at the scene, General Paulding Anderson, is believed to have suggested Taylor's name for the place. The town was established between 1836 and 1840, according to an essay by G. Frank Burns, "The Record of a People: An Historical Sketch of Wilson County, Tennessee."

Tazewell *Claiborne County (seat).* Tazewell, Virginia, is the place for which this town was named. In turn, the Virginia site took the name of statesman Henry Tazewell (1753–1799), who served in the U.S. Senate and helped to frame his state's constitution.

Teague *Hardeman County.* John, Joseph, and Joseph B. Teague resided in this vicinity in 1850, providing a solid clue to the place-name. A man named John Teague also lived in the area in 1830, but it is not known whether or not he is the same individual as the first-named John, or an ancestor.

Tekoa *Knox County.* A district or city of this name is mentioned in the Bible, and is the probable source of this Tennessee designation.

Telford *Washington County.* Colonel George Whitfield Telford (b. 1803) is the town's namesake. Colonel Telford was influential in the formation and early progress of the county. He married Amanda Duff Hannah and they produced twelve children—all daughters. The Telford Manufacturing Company and a rolling mill were operated by Colonel Telford. He also served as a state senator. Also on local tax rolls, in 1819, was Mirriam Telford. This area was initially known as Millwood, due to the existence of several mills on the banks of nearby creeks.

Tellico Plains *Monroe County.* This designation stems in part from the local "lay of the land." Tellico was the name of an early Cherokee settlement, sometimes seen styled as Talequah or Tellequah. It is not certain what the term means, but it may have been the name of a Cherokee chief.

Temperance Hall *DeKalb County.* The first settler here was Stephen Robinson. The name stems from the second floor of a town building that served as a meeting place for the Sons of Temperance. The group organized here in 1849.

Templeton *Dyer County.* Richard Templeton, age 24, and James Templeton, age 55, were local citizens when the 1870 census was taken. They probably endowed this site with their surname.

Ten-Mile *Meigs County.* Ten-Mile was so named because it was a reference point ten miles from one or more other area sites. Just which places those were is not clear.

Tennemo *Dyer County.* Some speculation is involved in explaining the name of this site, using its location as a clue. It is less than a mile from the Mississippi River, across which is the state of Missouri. In all probability, the site name comes from using the first five letters of "Tennessee" and a common abbreviation for the state of Missouri, "Mo."

Tennessee City *Dickson County.* Founders probably had high hopes this hamlet would grow into a city. The Cherokee word *tanasi* (or *tanasee, tansi, tenasee,* or *tenassee*), of unknown meaning, gave the state its name.

Tennessee Ridge *Houston County.* The designation combines a local geological characteristic with the name of the state. The ridge is situated on Highland Rim. The town was incorporated in 1960.

Tennga *Polk County.* This town's situation on the Tennessee border with Georgia explains the name, which was compounded from parts of the two.

Terrell *Weakley County.* One of Weakley County's first settlers was John L. Terrell. The town that bears this label was developed on land owned by his son, Benjamin Franklin Terrell. Peleg Terrell was one-time sheriff of the county and a brother of John L. Terrell. John is also described in early records as one of the founders of Dresden, Tennessee. The 1830 area census rolls refer to John and Patrick Terrell as local citizens.

Terry *Carroll County.* Stephen Terry was a local resident when the 1830 census of the western portion of the state was recorded. There is a good chance he lived at this site and that it then became known by the Terry surname.

Terry Creek *Campbell County.* In 1880, Marion and Rosie Terry are known to have resided locally. Marion was 35 and Rosie was 22. The name of the stream and hamlet may relate to this family (or these families).

Theta *Maury County.* It is uncertain why this community took the name of the eighth letter of the Greek alphabet.

The Wye *Anderson County.* According to one source, this location marks a site where the road divides and goes two directions, forming a **Y**. A more likely explanation, however, is that a wye was located here. *Wye* was a railroad term for a **Y**-shaped switch that enabled trains to back up. A railroad line runs adjacent to this community.

Thomas Bridge *Sullivan County.* Numerous Thomases called this area home when the 1850 census was taken. Included were Jacob, John, William, Adam, Elizabeth, George, and Landon Thomas. Apparently, a bridge arched a stream near the home of one or more of these Thomases, and the place became referred to as Thomas Bridge.

Thompson's Store *Clay County.* A country store was located here, run by persons with the Thompson surname.

Thompson Station *Williamson County.* Also known as Thompson's, this juncture was named for someone with the Thompson surname and for its site on the Louisville & Nashville (L&N) Railroad.

Three Oaks *Lawrence County.* According to early records, in 1909 Henry Daws moved southward from Brace, along the Military Road. At the selected site, there were three white oak trees growing almost as one, and he dubbed the place Three Oaks. Mr. Daws operated a store at the site. Soon, ballfields, a basketball court, and a croquet lawn became popular attractions at Three Oaks.

Three-Point *Lauderdale County.* Three roads intersect at this point, accounting for the label.

Throckmorton *Stewart County.* An early (1828) landowner in the area—whose name may have been William Throgmorton or William Thogmorton—gave his surname, or a version thereof, to the community. The first store did not go up until 1873.

Tidwell *Dickson County.* Numerous Tidwells are found in 1870 census listings for the county. Eli, E. W., Margaret, Harvy, Nancy, Moses, Robert, Sarah, Josiah, J. D., A. J., and others are included. However, the granddaughter of Captain Fulton Tidwell writes that this place is also known as Tidwell Switch, and prior to that, may have been referred to as Beulah Land. "He was a captain in the Civil War and got his eye shot out," she recalls. Her grandfather owned a good deal of local timber and had a crew working for him. They processed the timber for cordwood and railroad ties. They had to transport the wood about six miles, where it was loaded onto trains. So the place became known as Tidwell Switch.

Tidwell *Hickman County.* At one time, a school named North Tidwell School existed here. Virtually all of its constituents had the Tidwell surname. Another school not far away was known as the Martin Tidwell School; according to the county historian, neither Martins nor Tidwells resided in its vicinity.

Tiftonia *Hamilton County.* One source states that real estate here was developed by "in-laws of the Jerome Pound family." These individuals hailed from Tifton, Georgia, and possessed the surname Tift. Thus, the name Tiftonia must have seemed like a natural choice for this location.

Timothy *Overton County.* The son of an early postmaster in this area writes, "This [designation] was simply an honor to my father [Timothy Stephens]. He had done a lot to get this small community their post office and they wanted him to get the recognition."

Tipton *Tipton County.* The community may take its name from the Joseph Tipton for whom the county was named, and who died in 1791. However, in 1830 another Joseph Tipton (possibly a descendant) resided nearby, plus Jacob and Isaac Tipton.

Tiptonville *Lake County (seat).* The town is the namesake of a well-known early Indian fighter, Jacob Tipton, according to a source. However, an alternative source states that the village was named for a merchant and early settler named William Tipton. It was founded in 1852.

Tobaccoport *Stewart County.* As the name implies, this site takes its name from a prominent early industry, tobacco raising. The crop was brought by wagon to the landing site, where it was loaded on steamboats and shipped along the Cumberland River to Clarksville. The first settler was Christopher Brandon.

Todd Town *Cumberland County.* Martha and William Todd resided in adjoining Morgan County at about the time Morgan surrendered part of its territory to form Cumberland. Their surname probably contributed in some direct manner to the labeling of this place.

Tolley Town *Carter County.* This place-name probably traces back to an Appalachian pioneer named William Tolley, who was born in Yancey County, North Carolina, in 1824. He passed away sometime after 1900 in Carter County. Possibly related to him was Francis Tolley, who was born in North Carolina about 1796 and died in Tennessee in 1885.

Toone *Hardeman County.* James Toone and his family came to this locale at an early time. Toone had a blacksmith shop at the site and is said to have built a portion of the railroad here. It was first known as Toone's Station. James and the former Elizabeth Lofton resided on Clover Creek. According to *What's in a Name?*, Davy Crockett stayed with the Toones while campaigning for Congress. James Toone is listed as having been a county resident at least as early as 1830.

Top of the World *Blount County.* This designation is given to a hamlet at an elevation in the Great Smoky Mountains, near Chilhowee Mountain. Overlooking Happy Valley, it is said to have been named by Charlie Headrick. The name is sometimes styled as Top O' World.

Topsy *Wayne County.* An authority on local history states: "Rita Duncan tells the story that they were trying to determine a name for the post office. Mr. Meredith suggested they call it Topsy after his old mule named Topsy."

Totty's Bend *Hickman County.* In 1870, this place was amply populated with persons having the Totty surname. Included were Barnett, Daniel, Francis W., two named Harberd, two named William, Zachariah, John, Jones, and Rhoda. The "Bend" part of the designation came either from a nearby bend in the road or a bend in the Duck River, also nearby.

Town Creek *Claiborne County.* The hamlet is situated on a stream named Old Town Creek.

Townsend *Blount County.* A logging firm known as the Little River Lumber Company once operated here. It was headed by an individual named W. B. Townsend. An earlier name of the place was Tuckaleechee Cove. Townsend began operations sometime between 1898 and 1900. (One source puts the year at 1902.)

Tracy City *Grundy County.* The first president of a mining company doing business here—Samuel Franklin Tracy—conferred his family name upon the community. (The name Benjamin Franklin Tracy is listed in one source.) Tracy was from New York and presided over operations of the Sewanee Mining Company. The place-name traces to 1858. Incorporation occurred in 1915.

Trade *Johnson County.* Trade is considered the oldest continuously inhabited town in the state, tracing back well into the 1700s. The area was first surveyed by Thomas Jefferson's father, Peter, in 1749. It was referred to as the Trade Gap area, or Trade Gap, later shortened to simply Trade. Its situation made it a natural passageway to the West from other states, including North Carolina, Virginia, and Kentucky. When travelers made their way through the mountain passages to Trade, they generally stopped and traded with the Native Americans, and later with the white settlers.

Travisville *Pickett County.* David and William Travis resided in nearby Fentress County in 1850. Since later a portion of Fentress became a portion of Pickett, there is a good possibility that these men's surname became associated with the site known as Travisville, Pickett County.

Trenton *Gibson County (seat).* The name traces back to Trenton, New Jersey, and its founder, William Trent. Its previous name was Gibsonport.

Trent Valley *Hancock County.* Quite a few Trents called Hancock County home in 1850. This valley location may have taken the name from David, Cyntha (Cynthia?), James, Richard, Z. G., William, or Thomas Trent. A current map shows Paul Trent Road running nearby.

Trentville *Knox County.* Numerous Trents lived in this area in 1870, probably inspiring the place-name. Included were Robbert W., age 35; William B., 58; James W., 35; Zacariah, 25; and George L., 31.

Trezevant *Carroll County.* The community was incorporated in 1911. According to one account, James Trezevant was the town's namesake. He is said to have been instrumental in bringing the railroad through this locality. Rail activity here began in about 1857. Some referred to the place as Trezevant's Switch. A competing theory is that the community name was combined from the place-names Levant and Trezibond. Levant is a regional name applied to the countries bordering the eastern Mediterranean. Trebizond—probably the same as Trezibond—is a place in Turkey.

Trigonia *Blount and Loudon Counties.* Although the place was settled much earlier, the Trigonia name for this locality dates to 1888. The *tri* part of the designation relates to the location, near the intersection of three counties—Blount, Loudon, and Monroe. Colonel John McGhee was one of the earliest settlers in the vicinity. This may be the same spot that was dubbed McGhee Station in an earlier time.

Trimble *Dyer and Obion Counties.* The name traces to Justice Robert Trimble. He lived from 1777 to 1828 and served on the U.S. Supreme Court. He served as president of the railroad that had its end point here.

Triune *Williamson County.* The town was probably named by those with strong Christian beliefs. The term is used to indicate the Trinity, Godhead, or concept of "three in one" (unity).

Trousdale *Sumner County.* The community derives its name from a Revolutionary War soldier who was prominent in the county at an early time (ca. 1798), James Trousdale. His son, General William Trousdale, became the state's governor in 1849.

Troy *Obion County.* The Troy made famous in the writings of Homer inspired this place-name. The town was laid out in 1823 (Davy Crockett may have had a hand in the process) and incorporated eight years later. The proprietor was William Polk, but Rice Williams is credited with founding the community.

Trundle Crossroads *Sevier County.* This place-name was first applied in 1838, when John W. Trundle became postmaster at the site sometimes styled as Trundle's Cross Roads or a variant.

Tuckahoe *Knox County.* This term may have evolved from a Native American word, *tuckahog,* thought to refer to a vegetable or tuber, probably a potato. The origin is probably Algonquian.

Tucker's Corner *Gibson County.* Tuckers abounded on the rolls of the 1850 state census. John and Mary Tucker were residents of the Thirteenth Civil District of the county, while Joseph Tucker was a citizen of the Tenth District. Other Tuckers in the vicinity were J. M., Edmund V., J. W., and Enoch. Two roads intersect at Tucker's Corner.

Tucker's Store *Decatur County.* When the 1850 census was recorded, local citizens included William A., Rebecca, George W., and J. J. Tucker. It is probable that one of them—or someone in the family—operated a store here and thus inspired the name found on maps even today.

Tulip Grove *Davidson County.* The location takes its name from the state tree, the tulip poplar, which was widely used for a great variety of products. A stand of tulip poplars existed here, near Andrew Jackson's estate, The Hermitage. President Martin Van Buren is credited with suggesting the Tulip Grove name during a visit with Jackson.

Tullahoma *Coffee County.* Part of Tullahoma overlaps into Franklin County. Both the Muskogee and Choctaw tribes of Native Americans use this term, which is said to translate from Muskogean as "red town."

Tumbling *Weakley County.* This hamlet derives its name from a waterway coursing through the site, Tumbling Creek, named for the way it seemed to tumble over and around rocks.

Turner's Station *Sumner County.* This place-name is sometimes seen styled as Turner's, or simply Turner. Only vague information is available on the source. Turner was the surname of a family that resided near the site.

Turnersville *Robertson County.* Local authorities state that the place is named for Major Jack Turner, who settled the area. At the taking of the 1850 census, Turners living in this vicinity included William, Henry H., J. E., two Johns, Joseph, R. C., and Susan.

Turnersville *Sumner County.* The *1770–1790 Census of the Cumberland Settlements* lists a John Turner as having been a signer of the 1780 Cumberland Compact and residing in this vicinity. Daniel and William Turner also were county residents. They may well have given their surname to this hamlet.

Tusculum College *Greene County.* The community is referred to as Tusculum College, or simply Tusculum. According to one account, early founders named the institution of higher learning after the summer home of the Caesars, outside of Rome. The college, said to be the oldest such institution west of the Alleghenies, was founded in 1794, the current entity being the result of a merger of Tusculum Academy and Greeneville College. A second source states that the site was given its name by the Reverend Samuel Doak, after the home of the president of Princeton University, John Witherspoon. Doak had also attended Princeton.

Twinton *Overton County.* This is another small mining community about whose founding we have only vague information. It is believed that the name was affixed because it was considered a "twin" to another small nearby mining town.

Twomey *Hickman County.* According to *A Patchwork History of Hickman County,* Twomey refers to the Maurice Twomey family, early settlers of the area. The Twomeys were farmers. Other industries included phosphate mining and the flour and gristmill.

Tyner *Hamilton County.* Formerly designated Tynerville, the community had its name shortened to Tyner, both names honoring a Confederate soldier, Captain J. S. Tyner. When the local section of railroad was built, he was the chief engineer.

Tyson Store *Gibson County.* In all likelihood, a store was operated at this site by someone with the Tyson surname. At the time of the 1850 census, Malinda Tyson and William R. Tyson were area citizens. It is not known whether either of them was directly associated with the store, but there is a strong possibility they were.

Unaka Springs *Unicoi County.* Freshwater springs were discovered here. The modifier derives from a Cherokee term. (See Unicoi entry.)

Underwood *Sevier County.* Enoch P. Underwood became the first postmaster at this venue, in 1882. However, the site is believed to have been settled many years earlier, in about 1807, by an ancestor, Samuel Underwood.

Unicoi *Unicoi County.* The designation is derived from the Cherokee term for "white"—*unaka.* It may have been inspired by the appearance of rocks here, or for part of the Great Smoky Mountains.

Union City *Obion County (seat).* This place-name is believed to have been given in honor of the union of the states in the United States of America. Eighteen sixty-one marked the city's incorporation.

Union Grove *Blount County.* The earliest mentions of this community date to just subsequent to the Civil War. It is speculated the name came about as a result of efforts to bring about "union" after the war. The Union Grove Methodist Church dispatched a delegation to a meeting of laypersons in 1868.

Union Hill *Clay County.* This may have been the scene of a Union army encampment, or Union forces may have taken the hill during the Civil War, as battles are known to have been fought in this vicinity.

Union Ridge *Bedford County.* The name derives in part from the topographical feature, and for the fact that the first church that located here was a Union Church.

Unionville *Bedford County.* *Goodspeed's History of Tennessee, 1886,* reports that the community gained its name from the uniting of two unnamed post offices. The claim made by some that the name owes to Union sentiment during the Civil War is probably erroneous; Unionville seems to have been so named thirty or more years before the war. There was, however, a Union campground near Unionville. The town is believed to have been founded in 1827 on property owned by James Roy and Meredith Blanton.

Unitia *Loudon County.* Prior to 1770, the site was a Cherokee encampment. Another name for the place was Unity. Exactly what inspired the designation is unclear.

Upchurch *Greene County.* In 1880, Harrison and Silus Upchurch resided near this site, probably accounting for the place-name. Harrison was 44 at the time, while Silus was 70.

Upper Shell Creek *Carter County.* The hamlet of Upper Shell Creek is located about a mile from the community of Shell Creek, located on the stream of the same name. (See entry for Shell Creek.)

Upper Sinking *Hickman County.* Two creeks that drain the area are named Upper Sinking Creek and Lower Sinking Creek. This community is named for Upper Sinking Creek. The "Sinking" part is a result of the way in which the stream—when settlers arrived—receded into a cane bottom, then disappeared into the mouth of a large cave.

Uptonville *Madison County.* In earlier times, this location may have been referred to as Orange Grove due to an orangish hue to the soil in the area. At some early year, a number of Upton families settled the site, resulting in the name. An elderly native of the hamlet states specifically that the town was named for "Mr. Joe Bill Upton." Other early families here had the surnames Holloman, Parlow, Anderson, Jones, Glenn, Hailey, Foote, Fuller, Miller, and Burton. At one time, residents were fond of lamenting, "Upton Town, Jones Street, Parlow's Hotel, and nothing to eat."

Utah *Decatur County.* According to *American Place-Names,* a report by the explorer John Fremont popularized this name, which traces to the Ute Indian tribe. Uta was another early variation. The reason that it was applied here, in Tennessee, is unclear.

Vandever *Cumberland County.* At the time of the 1870 census, James C. Vandever resided in Cumberland County, possibly at this very site. When the 1880 East Tennessee census was recorded, in addition to James, three other Vandevers were listed as residing near here. Their names and ages: Nicholas, 34; Thomas, 32; and George, 39.

Van Dyke *Henry County.* An early (1870) resident of the county, Elizabeth Van Dyke, was probably responsible, directly or indirectly, for the naming of this place. Her last name may have been styled Vandyke or VanDyke.

Vanleer *Dickson County.* Wagen Vanleer resided in Dickson County during the 1850 census. He is likely connected to this site in some manner. A second—and possibly more reliable—explanation traces back to 1825, when Anthony Wayne Van Leer bought the Cumberland Furnace from Montgomery Bell. (Before that, Van Leer had leased the Tennessee Iron Works from Richard C. Napier.) The town's development was spearheaded by the Vanleer Land and Development Company. It was platted in the early 1890s and incorporated in 1915.

Vannatta *Bedford County.* A family with the Vannatta surname resided at this site, endowing it with its name.

Vann Town *Lincoln County.* A Vann Town native contributes the following information, distilled from text her mother, Belle Vann Gardner, compiled for the town's 1988 *Precious Memories* booklet. This passage explains the place-name: "The nearest telephone was Delap's Gin near Lincoln. Papa built a telephone line from there to the store. I remember one day the phone rang and Sheila Powell answered it, 'Vannville,' which was probably the origin of the name Vann Town." Belle Gardner recalled that it was early in 1916 when her father (William Aaron Vann), Lee Clemons, and Johnny Morton, all of Boaz, Alabama, came to this area to purchase farmland. W. A. Vann bought 520 acres for $7.50 an acre, but the others decided not to buy any. Mrs. Gardner specifically recalled, "On the first Monday in February 1916, we came from Boaz to Plevna, Alabama by train. We were met by George and Dave Woods, who carried us in a wagon to the house Papa had rented behind Lee Hazelwood's. Papa began building a new home for [us, but] we were forced to move into the house with only one room finished, since Mr. Hazelwood had previously rented the house we were living in." Between 1920 and 1925, Mr. Vann constructed a grocery store, blacksmith shop, gristmill, and barber shop, and owned two sawmills. He sawed the lumber free for a new Baptist church that was to be built. He made a deed for a school in 1925, to be called Vann Town, and in 1929 built a gin that was pulled by a steam engine. Later, he acquired additional acreage and built many houses. The Vanns had five other children besides Belle. Mr. Vann died in 1941 after contracting tuberculosis.

Vasper *Campbell County.* This community began to grow in about 1898. A family named Cross was one of the largest landholders. But the Vasper Mines began to expand their operations and grow in size; so the site became known as Vasper.

Vaughn's Grove *Gibson County.* This tree-shaded location may trace its roots to local 1870 citizens Fanny, Joel, and J. H. Vaughn. Their respective ages at the time were 60, 34, and 46.

Vernon *Hickman County.* Vernon was the original county seat, established as such by legislative act in 1809 and given its name in honor of Mount Vernon, George Washington's home. Proprietors of the parcel were Joseph Lynn and James Wilson. The county seat was moved to Centerville in 1822. Vernon sustained considerable damage during the Civil War.

Verona *Marshall County.* At one time, the site had the name Tyrone. Because there was another Tyrone in the state at the time, the Post Office Department required this one to change its name. The current name is thought to have been suggested by Captain William M. Robinson, a lover of Shakespeare who at the time was reading *Two Gentlemen of Verona*. Although the founding year is listed as 1859, the place was settled much earlier.

Vervilla *Warren County.* The term is said to mean "green village," and is made from parts of *verdant* and *village*. It is in the midst of a rich agricultural area. Dr. Thomas Springs is credited with naming the community in the 1870s.

Vinson's Crossroads *Warren County.* At one time, a prominent local family was surnamed Vinson. Little other information about them was available. The intersection here accounted for the "Crossroads" part.

Viola *Warren County.* The initial designation for the community was Blue Springs, suggested by a freshwater spring located on the Sam Ramsey farm. However, by 1872, postal authorities had discovered a second Blue Springs in the state, which had had the name longer. It is said that Greek Brawley, the postmaster here, had just read a book in which a character named Viola was the heroine. So he suggested that as the new town name, and it was accepted.

Vonore *Monroe County.* Vonore was incorporated in 1965. It is believed that the first postmaster here, Dr. W. B. Campbell, named the post office in 1893, with the town assuming the same identity. The name was reached by combining *ore,* for that found in the foothills in the vicinity, with *von,* a reference to local native General Crawford Vaughn. Previously, it was known as Upton.

Waco *Giles County.* This locality may have been named after Waco, Texas, for some unknown reason. There, the label originates from a tribal name often spelled Hueco, according to *American Place-Names*. But in the Southeast, it may derive from the Muskogean term for a heron.

Walden *Hamilton County.* Some historians credit the name to a 1700s explorer, Elijah Walden. Another account states that the community's name is a misspelling of the surname of a circa 1810 area farmer, John Walling. The community was chartered in 1975.

Walden's Ridge *Bledsoe County.* The village was incorporated in 1975. It owes its name to its founder, Elisha Walden. (Some sources give his surname as Wallen.)

Wales *Giles County.* In the 1830 census records for this area, two persons with probable or possible connections to this designation are listed. One is Jonathan Wales, and the other Jonathan *Wale*. It is not known which spelling is correct; both may be.

Walkertown *Hardin County.* Charles R. Walker was a county citizen in 1840. He is likely the individual to whom this place-name traces.

Walland *Blount County.* A company operating here was named the Schlosser Leather Company. The parent company was the Walton Company, located in England. The name Walland is a combination of *Wal*ton and Eng*land*. (An alternative source states that Walton and England were the names of two of the chief men in the company.) The place-name traces to 1902.

Walling *White County.* The place-name in all probability is tied to one of the many Wallings who were early citizens in this area. Eleven marriages involving Wallings are listed in the *White County, Tennessee, Oldest Marriage Book, 1809–1859*. Several of these were performed by Jesse Walling, Esq.

Walnut Grove *Campbell County.* This locality was populated by rugged individuals who enjoyed such pastimes as log rollings. The site was heavily timbered with black oak and black walnut, and assumed the name Walnut Grove. It was settled as early as the mid-1700s.

Walnut Grove *Dickson County.* The community at this stand of trees took its name from the black walnut trees present here. The black walnut grows throughout Tennessee.

Walnut Grove *Hardin County.* See preceding entry.

Walnut Grove *Meigs County.* See explanation for Walnut Grove, Dickson County.

Walnut Grove *Montgomery County.* See explanation for Walnut Grove, Dickson County.

Walnut Grove *Robertson County.* The owners of a large mill here named the business Walnut Grove. In time, the surrounding area also took on this label.

Walnut Grove *Sevier County.* See explanation for Walnut Grove, Dickson County.

Walnut Grove *Sullivan County.* See explanation for Walnut Grove, Dickson County.

Walnut Grove *Sumner County.* See explanation for Walnut Grove, Dickson County.

Walnut Grove *White County.* See explanation for Walnut Grove, Dickson County.

Walnut Hill *Crockett County.* This elevation was characterized by black walnut trees, which occur throughout Tennessee.

Walnut Hill *Sullivan County.* See preceding entry.

Walnut Shade *Macon County.* The shade here was provided by majestic black walnut trees.

Walter Hill *Rutherford County.* This place-name is sometimes seen styled as Walterhill. In the deeper past, it was at times known as Black's Shop, Black's Crossroads, and Abbott's Mill (or Abbot's Mill). (Later, the mill went by the name Pierce's Mill.) Sometime before 1830, the Major Abbott family erected a mill here, with a tiny collection of homes growing up in the area. Various accounts also are advanced for the current name. One states that a person named Walter Hill, a local storekeeper, was named postmaster in 1895 and submitted his own name as the place-name or postmark. But some believe that a Dr. Coleman named a hill at the location after his son, Walter. The term "Crossroads" in one of the earlier names referred to an intersection with the Lebanon Pike.

Ward Chapel *Coffee County.* Although no connection to a church could be readily made, several Wards conducted business in the Tullahoma area, only four miles from here, during the 1870–1880 period. These included one involved in the Ward & Powers store and at least two operating the Ward Bros. Livery Stable.

Warren *Fayette County.* Some assume that the site utilizes the surname of early families residing nearby. It is known that, in 1850, James L. and Henry Warren were Fayette County citizens. A second source indicates that a Henry Warren of Fayette County died that year, at the age of 67. This source identifies him as a Methodist clergyman and states that the community was named for him.

Wartburg *Morgan County (seat).* The city of Wartburg, Germany, inspired the name of this site. Many of its streets also were assigned the names of cities in Germany. It was chartered in 1851 and incorporated in 1968.

Wartrace *Bedford County.* Native American war parties were believed to have used a trace (path) through the wilderness at this location. A local stream is known as Wartrace Creek. Wartrace was incorporated in 1903.

Warwick Town *Union County.* In the late 1800s, John Perrington Warwick owned a large tract of land in this vicinity, which he divided among his five sons so each of them had enough for a farm. A general store was operated by Elvin Warwick and his son, Freeman. One of the churches was known as Warwick Chapel. Church picnics were held at the Alec Warwick farm. At least one map styles the name as Warwicktown.

Washington *Rhea County.* Establishment of the town of Washington was commissioned by an act of the state legislature in 1809. Historical sources state that it is in "some dispute" whether it was so christened in honor of the first president or for a local resident. However, more credence is placed in the belief that the name honors George Washington, the first president. Primary organizers of the community included Daniel Rawlings, Robert Patterson, Jesse Roddy, David Campbell, Alexander Ferguson, and Azariah David.

Washington College *Washington County.* The site is named for the Washington College Academy, which was named in honor of George Washington. Samuel Doak is referred to in a source as the founder, but it is unclear whether the reference is to the community or institution.

Washington Ferry *Rhea County.* This landing on the Tennessee River was previously known as the John Locke Ferry, or John Locke's Landing. The current name probably owes to its proximity to the town of Washington. It was first used in the 1820s but was later discontinued. In 1874, William R. Henry was permitted to reactivate a ferry at this location. His wife was Rachael Locke Henry, who inherited the land in 1872 from Newton Locke.

Watauga Flats *Washington County.* Apparently, this was a level location. (See following entry.)

Watauga Point *Carter County.* Some scholars feel the literal meaning of this Native American term is not known. Others claim it is Cherokee for "beautiful river," with versions of it appearing as *watogo* or *wattaggee*. It was the name of at least two Cherokee settlements.

Watertown *Wilson County.* Round Lick Creek converged from three branches here, resulting in a previous place-name of Three Forks. However, when citizens obtained a post office, they chose a name that included the surname of the first postmaster, local storekeeper Wilson L. Waters. The Watertown name gave them a designation that could refer both to the creek and the individual. Incorporation came in 1905. It is now a city.

Water Valley *Maury County.* This name is thought to have been suggested by Thomas Pigg when he observed the creek here at high water level, and noted the broad expanse of adjacent land that was inundated. Pigg is said to have commented that the site should be called Water Valley. It is fed by several smaller branches, creeks, and springs.

Watkins *DeKalb County.* A school built here about 1900 was labeled Watkins, apparently because the land was donated by Dr. J. N. Watkins, who was born in Kentucky in 1846. The school provided an alternative to the school held in the Jacob's Pillar Methodist Church. Dr. Watkins and his family appear in the 1900 DeKalb County census rolls but not in the ones from 1910.

Watson *Rutherford County.* In 1870, several Watsons were local residents, and probably provided the site with its designation. Albert, age 50; David, 58; Cap, 24; Violet, 46; and another David, 23, were among the resident Watsons.

Watson *Williamson County.* When the 1830 Middle Tennessee census was taken, Daniel, John, John M., William L., and Peter Watson lived in the vicinity. In all probability, one or more of them was identified with this place and led to its naming.

Watts Bar Dam *Rhea County.* According to articles in the *Chattanooga News-Free Press* in 1956, this site takes its name from the Watts family, who established the Watts Bar Landing. John Watts traded among the Cherokees in the mid-eighteenth century. His son, also named John Watts, became a Cherokee Indian chief. Chief Watts signed a treaty with Tennessee Governor William Blount in Knoxville in 1791. The dam itself is a facility of the Tennessee Valley Authority (TVA).

Wauhatchie *Hamilton County.* A Native American is believed to have given his name to this site, which became a station on the N&C (probably Nashville & Chattanooga) Railroad. One source identifies him as a chief of the "Lower Towns."

Waverly *Humphreys County (seat).* The town was incorporated in 1837. The current name probably dates to 1814, or shortly thereafter. In that year, Sir Walter Scott's popular first novel, *Waverly,* appeared. In the same time frame, a local citizen, Stevenson (or Stephenson) Pavette, became enamored of Scott's writings and persuaded locals to name the site Waverly. Now a city, the town was laid out by Isaac Little.

Wayland Springs *Lawrence County.* The seven renowned mineral springs here drew folks from other counties and states who desired to benefit from their supposed healing qualities. A resort prior to the Civil War, much of it was destroyed during the war. The name stems from Simon Harvey Wayland, who arrived about 1850. Some restoration work was done beginning in 1940, when Dr. B. H. Hardwick Sr. sold bottled water from the springs, calling his enterprise the Wayland Springs Mineral Company. The business declined after Hardwick's death in 1964.

Waynesboro *Wayne County (seat).* Like Wayne County and many other U.S. sites including "Wayne" in their names, this community honors the memory of Revolutionary War General "Mad Anthony" Wayne. The general served at Yorktown, with Washington at Valley Forge, and elsewhere during various conflicts. Now a city, Waynesboro was incorporated in 1827.

Wayside *Warren County.* An earlier name of the location was Falling Water, inspired by a nearby creek. When, in 1893, a one-room school was established "along the way" of the Faulkner's-Bluff Spring Road, it was labeled Wayside.

Weakley *Giles County.* This site is probably named after the same person for whom Weakley County was named, Robert Weakley (1764–1845). In 1796, he served in the Tennessee House of Representatives.

Wear Valley *Sevier County.* A North Carolinian, William Crocoson, immigrated to this site in 1793 with Aaron, his son. It became known as Crocoson's Cove. Forty years later, when David Cunningham was the local postmaster, he renamed the community Wear's Cove in honor of Colonel Samuel Wear, who in the 1780s had established Wear's Fort near the confluence of Walden's Creek and the Little Pigeon River. Colonel Wear was a veteran of the Revolution, the Indian wars, and the War of 1812. Decades after Cunningham changed the place-name, it was changed once again—to Wear's Valley.

Weaver *Sullivan County.* Weaver was a very common name in this area in 1880. Among those listed in early records were Rosanah, John P., Isaac, Jacob E., Jennie, William, William R., David G., David H., Conrad, David, Sarah H., two named Henry, Samuel, and Martha. Conrad, at 86, and Rosanah, 75, were the eldest of those listed, while the youngest was Jennie, at 18.

Webbtown *Macon County.* At the time of the 1870 census, Josiah Webb, age 58, resided near here. He or his family is probably responsible for the place-name.

Weber City *Lawrence County.* There are variant explanations for this place-name, which is sometimes seen styled as Webber City. One holds that it traces back to a Dr. Roland Weber, who lived in the vicinity. A second version states that the name refers to a community mentioned on an old *Amos 'n' Andy* radio program. And the least plausible explanation is that it was given its name when residents noticed an unusually large number of cobwebs on the bushes one year. (These were probably nests of the gypsy moth.)

Welch Crossroad *Union County.* A local grocery store was operated by Joe Welch, whose surname was taken to label the intersection.

Wells Hill *Lincoln County.* In 1825, Peyton Wells came here from Virginia. A well-to-do engineer, he purchased land, took up residence at the foot of the hill, and guided the hamlet's development. A daughter, Mrs. Theo Wells Harris, became the first schoolteacher here.

Well Spring *Campbell County.* A deep spring was discovered here—seemingly "as deep as a well." This fact inspired the name. The water source was located on Clyde Claiborne's farm, and according to one authority was seventy feet deep.

Wellsville *Blount County.* Stephen Wells purchased a gristmill and tanyard here in 1809. The designation of a post office called Houk was later changed to Wellsville (in 1894), after Stephen Wells had served as postmaster for some years.

West *Gibson County.* The town's namesake is Alex West, who founded it in the latter part of the nineteenth century. The site is sometimes referred to as West Station. West helped to lay the dirt bed for the rail track passing through the community.

Westbourne *Campbell County.* This hamlet is believed to have been named in about 1905 for the local Westbourne Coal Company, which was owned by R. Campbell and Alex Bonnyman.

Westel *Cumberland County.* In *Cumberland County's First Hundred Years,* an account of the naming is set forth. In the late nineteenth century, Westel Powell owned a great deal of property at the location. In the summers, he would bring his family here. As the story goes, one year he offered neighbors a proposition that anyone who named a child Westel would receive a tract of land. Miss Westel Burns was born about 1900, qualifying her family for the gift. It is unclear whether Powell had already applied the name to the place, or whether it assumed the designation after Miss Burns's birth.

West Fork *Overton County.* This site was one of the earliest settled places in the county. The name refers to the west fork of the Obey River. (A second source states that reference is to the west fork of the *Wolf* River.)

West Harpeth *Williamson County.* This hamlet is situated some three miles northwest of Harpeth. (See Harpeth entry.)

West Miller's Cove *Blount County.* This hamlet is southwest of East Miller's Cove. A cove was carved out of the shoreline here by the Little River. (See East Miller's Cove entry.)

Westmoreland *Sumner County.* The town derives its name from the county of the same name in England. Earlier names for the site included Coatestown and Staleyville.

Westover *Madison County.* The place-name *may* trace back to someone with the West surname. An individual named John West is described in one source as a leader in the southwest quadrant of Madison County. The hamlet of Westover is barely in the western side, and centrally located north to south. John West was active in the county in the nineteenth century. Possibly the same person, J. T. West is described as a first corporal in Captain Murchison's Company D of the Fifty-first Regiment of Tennessee Volunteers. In World War I, Ira West, of this county, served in the armed forces.

West Robbins *Scott County.* West Robbins is nominally west of Robbins. (See Robbins entry.)

West Shiloh *McNairy County.* West Shiloh is just across the county line, west of the Shiloh National Military Park, in adjoining Hardin County. (See entry for Shiloh, Hardin County.)

Wetmore *Polk County.* A local estate was owned by a family having the Wetmore surname, from whom the place got its name. The Wetmores were from New York.

Wheel *Bedford County.* The site apparently acquired this name in the late 1880s. It may have been so named because it was an agricultural "hub," or for local families named Wheeler—or both.

Wheelerton *Giles County.* Four Wheelers can be traced to this area using the 1830 Western Tennessee census records—Samuel, Nancy, James H., and James W. The place-name probably relates to this family. The 1850 census rolls show a Benjamin Wheeler still residing nearby.

White *Shelby County.* Cemetery records reveal that persons with the White surname proliferated in this area. In all, twenty-eight Whites are listed in one source alone.

White Bluff *Dickson County.* Early explorers in this area took note of the whitish appearance of the bluffs at the site. They probably had a high limestone content. Quarrying was practiced for many years in the county. Some credit the name to the White Bluff Iron Forge, which closed in the 1850s. The town was platted by A. Myatt in 1867 and incorporated in 1879. The first home was erected by Alexander Carr just after the conclusion of the Civil War, while the first store was constructed in 1865 by Morton & Wright.

White Chapel *Warren County.* In about 1900, a white building was erected here to serve as a Church of Christ. Thus, the place assumed the name White Chapel.

White City *Grundy County.* Charles T. White, age 43, and Betty White, age 44, were Grundy County citizens at the time of the 1870 census. It is likely they resided at this site, and the hamlet took its name from their surname.

Whitehead Hill *Carter County.* Apparently, the topography rose at this juncture, accounting for the "Hill" segment of the name. In 1840, local persons with the Whitehead surname included two named James, two Thomases, Larkin L., Charity, and John. One source spells the surname as Whitehaed, probably a simple mistaken transposition of letters. In 1880, Whiteheads answering the census roll call in Carter County included James, age 60; James, 80; John, 51; Thomas, 56; Andrew, 30; William C., 48; and Charles, 21.

White House *Robertson and Sumner Counties.* A local landmark evoked the name that remains with this site. A two-story dwelling that served as a stagecoach inn featured clapboard siding that was painted white. William Griffin managed the business, and guests are said to have included Andrew Jackson, Jenny Lind, and Sam Houston. White House is now a city, having been incorporated in 1893.

White Oak *Campbell County.* Local white oak trees inspired settlers in the 1800s to dub the place White Oak.

White Pine *Jefferson County.* Petitions to obtain a post office were circulated by Captain W. P. Nichols, who had come here in 1869. It is said that, during a meeting to find a name for the post office, various suggestions were submitted. Finally, one participant, believed to have been Esquire White, looked out the window and remarked that the tall white pine tree on the hill would serve as a landmark for the location. So White Pine was accepted as the name. One source states that white pine groves were present in this vicinity. The specific pine for which the site was named is said to have been felled by lightning in 1897. Incorporation came in 1893.

Whitesburg *Hamblen County.* At one juncture in the 1800s this area was home to numerous Whites. Some of them were George, Alfred, Washington, Wyley, Leannah, Levi, Jameson, Rebecca, Samuel, Joseph, William G., William, and John. Wyley was an African American.

Whiteside *Marion County.* A prominent attorney who became president of the East Tennessee Iron Manufacturing Company, James A. Whiteside, may be the person to whom this name is traceable. It is uncertain if he was the same person as James Anderson Whiteside (b. 1803), or a scion of that person. Glenn M. Whiteside (b. 1859) and William Mowbray Whiteside (b. 1856) were two other prominent Whitesides of the area.

White's Landing *Lake County.* Danny White, a fisherman, frequented this locale in crossing from Obion to Lake County, and vice versa, via Reelfoot Lake. As a consequence, his surname became affixed to the place.

Whiteville *Hardeman County.* The name traces back to the person honored with the name of the first post office here, Judge Hugh L. White. Subsequently, the community that grew up around the post office assumed the same name. Incorporation occurred in 1901. The first settler may have been E. D. Tarver, who arrived in 1820.

Whitleyville *Jackson County.* Andrew and Thomas Whitley resided locally, according to the 1830 Middle Tennessee census records. It is likely that their surname became associated with the place. Also mentioned in ancient references is an Edward Whitley, who in circa 1795, had Revolutionary War land warrants that may have brought him to this area. (There are eleven Whitleys mentioned in the index of this particular source.)

Whitlock *Henry County.* Whitlock was the surname of a farmer prominent in the area. A former designation was Chester, assigned by the Paducah, Tennessee & Alabama Railroad in 1889, but it was changed because of another Chester in Tennessee.

Whitwell *Marion County.* A Welsh industrialist and coal mining financier, Thomas Whitwell, immigrated to this area to exploit its coal reserves. One source identifies Whitwell as the inventor of the Whitwell stove. At various times, the place had been known as Cheekville or Liberty. Whitwell is a city.

Wilder *Fentress County.* Virtually deserted today, Wilder was once a thriving town. The first mining camp here was established in 1903 by a Union army geologist, Brigadier General John Thomas Wilder. Wilder had discovered an outstanding vein of coal in the highlands situated among Monterey, Livingston, and Jamestown, the site that became known as Wilder. During World War I, he had five hundred men employed in mining and mine-dependent jobs.

Wilder Chapel *Franklin County.* An original Ninth District settler in this county, John Wilder, donated the land for construction of a church at this locality. The place of worship, and later the community, took on his surname.

Wild Plum *Cumberland County.* This area did indeed feature a tree known as the American plum growing wild, undoubtedly accounting for this place-name.

Wildwood *Blount County.* The name was bestowed by the Reverend C. B. Lord, probably because of its situation in the "wild woods." Lord came to this place in 1870 from New York. As early as 1794, a schoolhouse was constructed here by Henry McColloch.

Wilkinsville *Tipton County.* In 1850, William Wilkins was a local citizen. It is probable he was in some way related to this place-name, but no further details could be located.

Williamsburg *Sevier County.* A store was operated at this location in the latter half of the 1880s by John H. and Eli Williams.

Williams Crossroads *DeKalb County.* This label identified a school located near an intersection where a Williams family lived. The small community that arose became known as Williams Crossroads.

Williamsport *Maury County.* A boat landing and flatboat ferry were operated here on the Duck River by Edward Williams, starting in 1807 and continuing for many years. A story is related in Goodspeed's county history of a slave lad, Judson Gantt, having rescued the Williams family from a great flood. Gantt was given his freedom as a reward for his bravery. He is buried locally, and his descendants resided here until very recent years. Town platting and incorporation took place in 1817.

Willis *Hancock County.* Larkin and Wilson Willis were local citizens at the time of the 1850 census, leading some historians to believe they gave their name to this site. By 1870, David, age 33; Elizabeth, 57; William, 24; William, 64; Leonard, 28; Manerva, 8; Melville, 25; and Thomas Willis, 26, populated the locale.

Williston *Fayette County.* Williston was incorporated in 1970 and is now a city. From its inception, it was known as Walker Station (from 1848 until sometime after the Civil War). This original label traces back to those who first settled the site—the Walkers—Sarah and Job. The Walkers had come from North Carolina. There was a core of residents who had to trek a short distance to Henry Willis's store, and would have preferred the store be in their midst. So they asked Mr. Willis if he would relocate the store to the place where his customer base resided. He said he would do so . . . with one condition: that they rename the site Williston. This was agreed to; so the move—and the name change—were made.

Willow Grove *Clay County.* Willow trees formed a grove here, providing the site with its name. It was quite a thriving and sprawling community. One source claims Willow Grove School and community are now flooded beneath the waters of Dale Hollow Lake.

Willow Grove *Haywood County.* The black willow and coyote willow grow in this region. A grove of one or the other must have inspired the person who named this location.

Wills *Johnson County.* The 1880 East Tennessee census records reveal a number of Willses residing in the county, one or more of whom probably influenced the placename. Among them were Adam, age 58 at the time; Elizabeth R., 53; Baxter, 18; Caleb, 66; David W., 44; John D., 71; Mary, 24; James H., 55; Norman R., 32; and Albert, 35.

Wilmore *Macon County.* The place-name may be a corruption of the surname Wilmourn. Thomas Wilmourn resided in this neighborhood when the 1850 census was recorded.

Wilson Station *Monroe County.* The index in the *History of Sweetwater Valley, Tennessee,* mentions James Wilson, W. Y. Wilson, and W. P. Wilson. At the time of the 1880 East Tennessee census, the following Wilsons resided in the county: Samuel, Samuel R., Thomas, Thomas J., Solomon, Sarah, Isaac N., J. H., J. D., George, and two named William. The label on this site probably traces in some way to one or more of these individuals.

Wilsonville *Cocke County.* Once called Ogdenville, this community traces its name back to Major William Wilson. His Wilson Tavern is said to have been visited by Presidents Johnson, Polk, and Jackson.

Winchester *Franklin County (seat).* An early legislator in the state was General James Winchester, a pioneer who had gained notoriety as an Indian fighter. This place-name traces back to General Winchester, who was born in Maryland in 1752 and died in Tennessee in 1826. General Winchester's son, Marcus Brutus (1796–1856), laid out Memphis with the assistance of William Lawrence. Today, Winchester is a city. Eighteen twenty-one was the year of incorporation.

Windletown *Overton County.* In 1850, Robert J. Windle and S. W. Windle were county residents. The place-name probably relates in some way to these individuals or other members of their families.

Windrock *Anderson County.* This was a mining community located at a higher elevation, where the wind swirled among the rocks.

Windrow *Rutherford County.* Nelson, age 40; Travis, 60; David, 26; and Byers Windrow, 63, probably played a role in this place-name. They resided nearby in 1870. Or, the designation may have been inspired by a possible ancestor of at least some of these individuals—Jonathan Windrow—who was in the county as early as 1830 or before.

Winfield *Scott County.* This community probably uses the given name of the man for whom the county was named, Winfield Scott (1786–1866). When the Civil War began, Scott commanded the Union armies. Previously, in 1841, he was general-in-chief of the U.S. Army. Today, Winfield is a city, having been incorporated in 1983. In an earlier time, it was known as Chitwood. The current name is believed to have been conferred by the Southern Railway. (Also see Scott in county listings.)

Wingo *Carroll County.* John and Dabney Wingo were local citizens at the time of the 1840 census, probably accounting for this place-name. By the time of the 1850 census, several other Wingos were listed as local residents, in addition to the aforementioned two. They included Nancy M., Sarah, T. F., James W., and Thomas G. Later still, in 1870, the census recorded Moses Wingo as being age 40, Thomas as 44, Godfrey as 60, and John J. as 45.

Winkler's Crossroads *Macon County.* Samuel Winkler may be this place's namesake. It is likely he lived at or near the intersecting roads in 1850.

Winn Springs *Hardin County.* Gideon B. Winn was listed in both the 1840 and 1850 census records as a citizen of Hardin County. It is likely he resided near the springs at this site and gave the place its name.

Winton Town *Coffee County.* John and Stephen Winton resided in this vicinity in 1850. It is highly likely that they are somehow directly related to this designation on maps.

Wirmingham *Overton County.* The site was heavily settled by members of the Winningham family, beginning in about 1816. For a time, it was known as Winningham Crossroads. When the postmaster requested (in his handwriting) that the place be officially named Winningham, someone in Washington read it to be Wirmingham, and the name stuck.

Withamtown *Sumner County.* On the occasion of the 1850 census, James Witham was a resident nearby. He or his family was probably responsible for the name of this location.

Witt *Hamblen County.* The name probably traces back, directly or indirectly, to Joel Witt, listed as a taxpayer in 1799. Another local person, Mary Witt, was the daughter of Charles Witt.

Wolf Creek *Cocke County.* Wolf Creek became a post office in 1859. Some claim the name was adopted because of numerous wolf packs that frequented the area. Another version states that the name was given by the Wolf tribe of Native Americans. Still another account attributes the label to the presence of a family with the surname DeWolf. At one point, the name became Allendale, but the Reuben Allen family had it changed back to Wolf Creek. The Allens operated an inn at the place at a later date. The third account may have credence, as one source states that a Mr. Wolf, or deWolf, received a land grant for the site in 1738 (this year seems extremely early). He apparently built a cabin nearby.

Wolf Hill *Sumner County.* In 1850, when a census was taken, James R. Wolf was a local resident. He is probably the individual identified with this hillside hamlet.

Womack *Warren County.* Census records of 1850 reveal several Womacks as having been local citizens. Among them were three named Abner, William R., Samuel, R. P., Mary J., Arsey, Burgess, Thomas, and two others named William. One or more of these individuals was probably responsible for this place-name.

Woodbury *Cannon County (seat).* Andrew Jackson's secretary of the navy, General Levi Woodbury, is the person for whom the town was named. Woodbury and Jackson were longtime friends. Woodbury was incorporated in 1843.

Woodland Mills *Obion County.* A number of mills in the area and a heavily forested topography resulted in this designation. At least one of the milling operations—perhaps the first at this locale—was established by W. G. McFettridge and C. W. McFettridge. One source states that the McFettridges operated both gristmilling and sawmilling businesses. Woodland Mills is now a city. The year of incorporation was 1968.

Woodlawn *Wayne County.* A local historian claims that this site was named for the Woodlawn subdivision in Birmingham, Alabama. (The Tennessee boundary with Alabama is immediately south of Wayne County.) The Wayne County Woodlawn was laid out in 1918 and is a subdivision of Collinwood.

Woods Valley *Dickson County.* A local history expert believes the name refers to a "densely timbered valley," rather than a resident family named Woods.

Woodville *Haywood County.* A number of Woods can be placed at or near this "ville" in 1870. They included Pat, age 48; Wash, 24; Sim, 35; Crais, 24; Elizabeth, 50; Stewart, 44; George, 22; and J. S., 25.

Woody *Cumberland County.* Individuals having the Woody surname living in this area at the time of the 1880 census included Alexander, age 44; Ellison, 30; Severn, 33; Wade, 35; Teril, 47; Harrison, 40; and James, 89. The name of the community probably traces to this family or these families.

Wooldridge *Campbell County.* This name evolved from the Wooldridge Coal Company, which operated locally in the 1880s and of which Colonel S. L. Wooldridge was president.

Worley *Hamilton County.* The individual or family to whom the name refers is vague. The reference is probably to a local landowner having the Worley surname. The site was once known as Worley's Switch, having a siding on the railroad.

Wright *Knox County.* A number of Wrights populated this neighborhood when the 1850 census was taken. Included were three named William, in addition to Paul D., Jeremiah, Isabella, and Charles A. In 1830, William, Elizabeth, and John Wright were listed as county citizens.

Wrigley *Hickman County.* According to *A Patchwork History of Hickman County,* Wrigley was built in 1919 from pre-cut lumber. A plant known as Bon Air Chemical Company, a subsidiary of Tennessee Products Corporation, operated a blast furnace that produced Wrigley semi-cold blast charcoal pig iron. A wood distillation plant stood nearby, furnishing select hardwood for blast furnace fuel and numerous by-products for industrial markets. An early officer of Tennessee Products Corporation was William Wrigley; the town was named for him. William Wrigley belonged to the family famed for its chewing gum products.

Wyatt's Chapel *Stewart County.* A descendant of the Wyatt family advises us that the community surrounding Wyatt's Chapel is known to many as "Big A." John Wesley Wyatt contributed the land for the church and school, the former of which then became known as Wyatt's Chapel. On some contemporary maps, Wyatt's Chapel is the place-name for the town. As a note of interest, a regional census recorded in 1830 lists John, James, Vinson, William, and Robert Wyatt as residing in Stewart County. By 1850, Christopher, James, Zachariah, Nimrod, Thomas, Gilbert, and James Wyatt resided locally, plus two named John and three named William. The label "Big A" is said to have been conferred by Bob Gafford, and was inspired by the **A** shape formed by intersecting roads at the site.

Wyly *Benton County.* At the time of the 1850 census, C. K. and James Wyly were local residents. The place-name likely was inspired by them.

Wynnburg *Lake County.* The Chicago, Memphis & Gulf Railroad was given a right-of-way and a parcel of land for a freight depot and passenger station at this location by a Methodist minister, Samuel Francis Wynn. Wynn had the community platted, and in 1910 obtained a post office under the Wynnburg name.

Yager *Warren County.* In post–Civil War years, a store was operated here by E. N. Yager. This site undoubtedly takes its name from him.

Yateston *White County.* The spelling of the surname portion of this place-name is probably an error, due to a phonetic similarity. The label is believed attributable to Washington Yeats, an 1830 resident.

Yell *Marshall County.* The name probably honors a distinguished gentleman who once resided in this area, later moving to Arkansas, where he "made a name for himself." Archibald Yell became governor of Arkansas and also a colonel. In 1847, he died at Buena Vista, Mexico.

Yellow Creek *Dickson County.* From the book *The Primal Families of the Yellow Creek Valley* comes this quote: "It is not known who gave Yellow Creek its name, but certainly a more appropriate name could not be found. Some names come naturally and anyone who has ever seen old Yellow Creek on a rampage during high water would instinctively call her 'Yellow' because of the great amount of fine yellow silt filtered into the stream by its many tributaries."

Yokley *Giles County.* Listed in the 1830 census records for the county was A. Yokley. Rightly or wrongly, the surname is also seen styled as Yokely. There is probably a distinct correlation between the person and this place-name. This inference is supported by current Giles County sources, which reveal that an Andrew Yokley and his family emigrated in the early 1800s from Davidson County, North Carolina. Other families who settled here in early times had surnames such as Cross, Hubble, Parish, Bledsoe, Trice, Hickman, Duncan, Lovell, Sands, Dunnavant, Hindman, Pinkleton, and Gibson.

Yorkville *Gibson County.* The city's founder, John C. Kuykendall, is said to have hailed from Yorkville, North Carolina (one source says South Carolina), and labeled this site with the designation of his previous home. Kuykendall founded Yorkville,

Tennessee, in 1830. Incorporation came about in 1850, but the charter later was lost or surrendered, and in 1964 it was reincorporated.

Young Bend *DeKalb County*. A bend of the Caney Fork River at this site became known by the surname of local residents John and James Young, who were brothers. They arrived from Rockingham County, North Carolina, settling here prior to 1820 and marrying sisters Jany and Rachel, the daughters of Aaron Cantrell.

Young's Crossing *Madison County*. This name likely traces to one or more of the local Youngs in 1840: Deaverly, Franklin Y., Josiah, William, Martin, or James.

Youngville *Robertson County*. This place-name probably traces to one or more of the Youngs who populated this (Red River) area during an early period. Included among them were those with given names or initials of Missouri, Jacob, and F. G. By the time of the 1870 census, area Youngs included Tabbott, age 56; two named Sam, ages 30 and 32; F. L., 45; Jerry, 32; Isaac, 43; J. R., 26; W. B., 36; and Thomas, 22.

Yuma *Carroll County*. The *Illustrated Dictionary of Place Names* suggests that this term may translate roughly as "sons of the river." It may trace back to an Indian tribe of Yuman linguistic stock, indigenous to the American Southwest, according to the source quoted. (A well-known city in Arizona also bears the name.) However, a Yuma, Tennessee, source states the term is locally accepted to mean "good, peaceful, and progressive, in an Indian language." Thus railroad officials changed the name to Yuma in 1895, from Grovewood, which had been inspired by the large grove of oak trees that shaded the settlement. According to local lore, a group of railroad officials stepped off the train, surveyed the acres of level land covered with corn crops, and remarked, "That looks good." Accordingly, as the tale is told, they changed the name to Yuma.

Yum Yum *Fayette County*. The town is referred to locally as the Garnett community. John H. Garnett had opened a general store in 1879 and wanted the town to have a post office. According to traditional lore, the name resulted when Garnett's friend, U.S. Senator Kenneth McKellar (who in 1886 helped get the post office authorized), asked what name Garnett would like for the office. He is said to have replied, "Just call it Yum Yum. There won't be another name like that." ("Yum-Yum" is the name of the woman Nanki-Poo is in love with in *The Mikado*. See Nankipoo entry in this volume.)

Z

Zion *Maury County.* The biblical term refers to a hill in Jerusalem or the city itself. It was generalized from that source to refer to the Chosen People, or a "new Jerusalem." It was often applied to a church or to a place by those with strong religious convictions.

Zion *White County.* See preceding entry.

ZuZu *Fayette County.* A clue to the inspiration for this name was discovered purely by chance during a casual browsing in 1997 of an Ohio antique mall. On the back wall of a booth featuring advertising items could be seen a sign with a listing for "ZuZu ginger snaps." Apparently, this was the name of a cookie available in the 1800s or early 1900s. Possibly some early settler, "stuck" for a name for his or her hamlet—and after downing a number of the snaps—thought ZuZu would be the perfect name for the community.

County-Names

Anderson. For five years prior to 1797, Joseph Anderson wore the title of judge of the Territory South of the River Ohio. He became a U.S. senator and served from 1797 until 1815.

Bedford. The county's name traces back to Thomas Bedford Jr. of Virginia. He came to Tennessee in 1795 and assisted in the development of Bedford County. Previously, he had served in the Virginia Assembly and the Revolutionary War.

Benton. The county is named for David Benton, an early settler in this region. A farmer who helped develop the county, Benton was a member of the Tennessee Militia during the Creek Indian wars.

Bledsoe. The county name refers to Anthony Bledsoe, who served in the Colonial Army of Virginia, rising to the rank of captain. He was also a major during the Revolution and a colonel in the Tennessee Militia. In 1789, he was killed by Indians near his home.

Blount. Knoxville's founder, William Blount, inspired the name of this county. At one time or another, Blount held a number of prominent positions, including governor of the Territory South of the River Ohio, U.S. senator, member of the Continental Congresses and the Tennessee Senate. He also served in the North Carolina legislature.

Bradley. The county is the namesake of Colonel Edward Bradley, of Shelby County, Tennessee. Important positions that he held included colonel of the Fifteenth Regiment of Tennessee Volunteers in the War of 1812, and colonel of Hale's Regiment.

Campbell. Colonel Arthur Campbell is believed to be this county's namesake. During the Revolutionary War, Campbell commanded the Seventieth Regiment of the Virginia Militia, and later, in 1781, was commissioner of Indian Treaties. He had served as a member of Virginia's House of Burgesses.

Cannon. The county takes its name from a former member of Congress (1814–1817 and 1821–1827), Newton Cannon. Cannon served in the War of 1812 and both Creek Indian wars, and was elected governor of this state in 1835.

Carroll. William Carroll, who served as the state's governor from 1821 to 1827 and 1829 to 1835, was the source of this county's name. He served as an officer in the War of 1812.

Carter. Landon Carter gave his name to this county. He held a number of positions, including militia officer of the Washington District, treasurer of the Hamilton and Washington Districts, speaker of the first state of Franklin senate, and secretary of state for the state of Franklin.

Cheatham. From 1855 until 1861, the Speaker of the House in the Tennessee legislature was Edward S. Cheatham. It was in honor of him that the county was so named.

Chester. Robert I. Chester (1793–1892) was the person for whom the county was named. He held many prominent positions, including quartermaster in the War of 1812, state legislator, U.S. marshal, and colonel in the Texas War of Independence.

Claiborne. The county was named for an early judge of the Superior Court of Tennessee, William C. C. Claiborne. At various times, he served as governor of Louisiana, governor of the Mississippi Territory, and, at the time of his death, was senator-elect from Louisiana.

Clay. Henry Clay (1777–1852) is the county's namesake. Clay served as a U.S. senator and congressman and as a member of the Kentucky senate and state house. In 1815, he was the commissioner for treaty with Great Britain, and at another time served as secretary of state.

Cocke. A former leader of the state of Franklin and a Revolutionary War officer, Senator William Cocke, is the county's namesake. He was elected to the Senate in 1796, 1797, and from 1799 to 1805, and had been a member of the legislature for the Territory South of the River Ohio.

Coffee. Major General John Coffee gave his name to this county. A close friend of Andrew Jackson, General Coffee commanded Tennessee troops during the New Orleans campaign in the War of 1812. He was known as a surveyor, as well as for his military exploits.

Crockett. Frontier soldier, humorist, and author David (Davy) Crockett was the individual for whom the county was named. Crockett lived from 1786 until 1836. He also served as a state legislator and congressman. In the Texas War of Independence, he became a casualty of the struggle at the Alamo.

Cumberland. The county attributes its name to the local Cumberland Mountains. In turn, the mountain range was named by Thomas Walker for the duke of Cumberland, who at that time was prime minister of England.

Davidson. A colonial soldier, William Lee Davidson (ca. 1746–1781), was the person who gave his name to the county. A Revolutionary War officer, Davidson served in North Carolina's Third, Fourth, and Fifth Regiments and died in action at Valley Forge.

Decatur. The county was named for Commodore Stephen Decatur, who distinguished himself during the Tripolitan War, and to an even greater extent in the War of 1812.

DeKalb. The county's namesake is Baron Johann DeKalb, a confederate of the Marquis de Lafayette, who in 1777 accompanied Lafayette to America. Appointed a major general in the Continental army and placed in command of soldiers from Maryland and Delaware, DeKalb was fatally wounded in the Battle of Camden in 1780.

Dickson. A Nashville physician, Dr. William Dickson, gave his name to this county. Dr. Dickson became prominent in politics, serving in the state legislature from 1799 to 1801 and later becoming Speaker of the House of Representatives.

Dyer. Robert Henry Dyer was influential in the formation of Dyer and Madison Counties, and Dyer County was named for him. Dyer served as a state senator and was an officer in the War of 1812. He also served as a cavalry colonel in the Seminole War (1818).

Fayette. The county, like many other places in the United States, was named for the Marquis de Lafayette (1757–1834). The French statesman, soldier, and nobleman was commissioned a major general for his service with the Americans during the Revolutionary War.

Fentress. James Fentress was a four-term Speaker of the Tennessee House of Representatives. The county was named in his honor.

Franklin. The county is named for Benjamin Franklin. Among the many high points in Franklin's career were playing an influential role in the treaty with England which resulted in independence for the colonies, and his role in drafting the Declaration of Independence. He also represented the colonies at the court of France, and was an inventor and scribe.

Gibson. Colonel John Gibson is this county's namesake. During the Natchez Expedition of 1812–1813, he distinguished himself in service under General Andrew Jackson. He also served during the Creek Indian wars.

Giles. The county was named for Senator William B. Giles (1762–1830). Giles served as a U.S. congressman and senator from Virginia, as well as governor of that state. He was a proponent of Tennessee statehood.

Grainger. The county was named in honor of an early first lady of what was then the Territory South of the River Ohio, which later became Tennessee. Her name was Mary Grainger, daughter of Kaleb Grainger of North Carolina. Born in an unknown year, Mary married William Blount. She died in 1802.

Greene. The county's name honors Nathaniel Greene (1742–1786), who served as commander at Trenton during the Revolutionary War. Greene succeeded Horatio Gates in command of the Army of the South, and is credited with forcing the British out of the Carolinas and Georgia.

Grundy. President Van Buren's attorney general, Felix Grundy (1777–1840), gave his name to the county. Other capacities in which he served were U.S. senator and congressman from Tennessee and chief justice of the Kentucky Supreme Court.

Hamblen. An early settler, attorney, and landowner, Hezekiah Hamblen (1775–1854), inspired the county's name. During one period, he served on the Hawkins County circuit court and county courts.

Hamilton. The noted statesman Alexander Hamilton (1757–1804) was this county's namesake. He served during the American Revolution, and in 1787 was a member of the Constitutional Convention. He became secretary of the treasury under George Washington.

Hancock. The county's namesake is John Hancock (1737–1804), who served in many prominent positions. He was a governor of Massachusetts, president of the Continental Congress, an officer in the Revolutionary War militia, and the first signer of the Declaration of Independence.

Hardeman. The county's namesake, Thomas Jones Hardeman (1788–1854), was virtually a career soldier. He held the rank of captain in the War of 1812, and fought in the Battle of New Orleans as a Tennessee Militia colonel. The year 1830 found him fighting for independence in Texas. As a commissioner in 1825, he had helped found the county seat of Bolivar. At one point, he served as a congressman from the Republic of Texas.

Hardin. This county was named for a veteran of the American Revolution, Colonel Joseph Hardin (1734–1801). When the short-lived state of Franklin was created, Hardin was named Speaker of the state assembly. Later, he served as a member of the first territorial assembly and as a justice from Greene County. In the second territorial assembly, he became Speaker of the House. A son, Joseph Hardin, led a settlement party to this area in 1816.

Hawkins. The deed of cession that transferred the Southwest Territory (now the state of Tennessee) to the Federal government was signed by Benjamin Hawkins. Hawkins served as a U.S. senator (1789–1795) from North Carolina and as a member of the Continental Congress.

Haywood. Judge John Haywood (1762–1826) was honored in the naming of this county. From 1816 until 1826, Judge Haywood served on the state's Supreme Court of Errors and Appeals. He has been called the "father of Tennessee history."

Henderson. Prior to the Battle of New Orleans, the county's namesake, James Henderson, was commander of the Tennessee troops. During the Natchez and Creek campaigns, he served as staff officer to Andrew Jackson.

Henry. The Revolutionary leader, patriot, and statesman from Virginia, Patrick Henry (1736–1799), was the person for whom the county was named. Among other positions in which he served were governor of Virginia and member of the Continental Congress.

Hickman. In 1791, explorer-hunter Edwin Hickman was killed by Indians near the current county seat of Centerville. The county assumed his surname.

Houston. Sam Houston, the county's namesake, held many important posts. At various times, he was a governor of Tennessee and a U.S. congressman, president of the Republic of Texas, and a U.S. senator from Texas. He served as a commander during the Texas War of Independence. Houston was born in 1793 and died in 1863.

Humphreys. Judge Parry W. Humphreys (1778–1839) served the Superior Court of Law and Equity and was Circuit Judge of Law and Equity for the Fifth District. In 1813, he served as a member of Congress.

Jackson. The county name honors the seventh president of the United States, Andrew Jackson. At various times, Jackson served as a senator and as a representative in Congress, as well as a member of the Tennessee Constitutional Convention. He gained fame as a military leader—especially at the Battle of New Orleans—and died at The Hermitage, in Davidson County.

Jefferson. The county is named for Thomas Jefferson. Jefferson was the principal author of the Declaration of Independence and became the nation's second president. At various times, he also served as Virginia's governor, the nation's vice president, and secretary of state.

Johnson. One of the county's prominent citizens, Thomas Johnson, was honored in the naming of the county. He settled on the Doe River in an early year, after having come from Carter County. Johnson served as one of Johnson County's first magistrates.

Knox. Major General Henry Knox (1750–1806) was honored in the naming of this county. During the Revolutionary War, he served as General George Washington's chief of artillery. Later, after Washington became the first president, Knox served under him as secretary of war. Knox was a founder of the Society of the Cincinnati.

Lake. Lake County was named for a body of water formed by a series of earthquakes in 1811, Reelfoot Lake. The earthquakes changed the course of the Mississippi River and dammed the Reelfoot River.

Lauderdale. The county owes its name to Colonel James Lauderdale. According to the *Tennessee Blue Book,* Lauderdale was killed leading troops against the British a few days before the Battle of New Orleans on December 23, 1814.

Lawrence. The speaker of the words "Don't give up the ship" is honored by this county's name. At the time, Captain James Lawrence, in command of the *Chesapeake,* was engaged in a War of 1812 battle with the frigate *Shannon.* Lawrence died as a result of wounds incurred in that encounter.

Lewis. This county's namesake was the noted explorer of the U.S. interior and Northwest, Captain Meriwether Lewis (1774–1809), who died in this county.

Lincoln. Major General Benjamin Lincoln (1733–1810) was the county's namesake. Lincoln served the Confederation as secretary of war from 1781 until 1783. A leader during the Revolutionary War, he became chief commander of the Southern colonies. In 1787, he commanded the forces that suppressed Shay's Rebellion. At one time, he was lieutenant governor of Massachusetts.

Loudon. During the French and Indian War, the commander in chief of the American and British troops in the Southern colonies was the earl of Loudoun. The British Fort Loudoun, established in 1756, was named for the earl. The county took its name from the fort.

Macon. The county takes its name from a well-known political figure who was prominent in North Carolina, Nathaniel Macon. Macon served in that state's house and senate over a thirty-seven-year period. He was a state senator fourteen years, two of them as president pro tem, and was Speaker of its house for six years.

Madison. President James Madison gave this county its name. A Princeton graduate, Madison served eight years as secretary of state before his election to the nation's highest office in 1809, where he also served two terms. Earlier, he had been a member of the Constitutional Convention, the Continental Congress, and House of Representatives. Later, he served ten years as president of the University of Virginia.

Marion. The county was named for the "Swamp Fox," Francis Marion (1732–1795). Marion earned the nickname for his guerrilla tactics during the Revolutionary War.

Marshall. The county traces its name to Federalist leader and Revolutionary War soldier John Marshall (1755–1835). He also served with distinction as secretary of state, U.S. congressman, and chief justice of the U.S. Supreme Court.

Maury. Abram Poindexter Maury Sr. (1766–1825) inspired the county's name. Maury laid out the town of Franklin and served as town commissioner. He was also known as a state senator, farmer, civil engineer, and attorney.

McMinn. In 1796, Joseph McMinn served as a member of the state's Constitutional Convention. For four years, he served as Speaker of the state senate. He was governor of Tennessee from 1815 until 1821.

McNairy. John McNairy (1762–1837) was the individual from whom the county took its name. Among the posts he held during his career were delegate to the 1796 Constitutional Convention, North Carolina Superior Court judge, trustee of Davidson Academy, and U.S. district judge for Tennessee.

Meigs. The county was named for Return Jonathan Meigs (1764–1824). From 1808 to 1810, he was a U.S. senator from Ohio. From 1810 to 1814, he served as governor of Ohio. He was U.S. postmaster general from 1814 until 1823. Meigs had served as a colonel in the Continental army and distinguished himself in the Battle of Sag Harbor. Earlier, at Quebec, he was captured and later exchanged. At Stony Point, he took part in the victory. In 1810, Meigs was appointed Indian agent for the Cherokee tribes.

Monroe. The country's fifth president, James Monroe, was honored by the naming of this county. Before becoming president, Monroe served six years as secretary of state. Earlier posts included a stint as minister to France (1794) and minister to England (1803–1804). In the interim, he was governor of Virginia from 1799 to 1802. Monroe also served as an officer in the Continental army.

Montgomery. As early as 1777, Colonel John Montgomery entered the Cumberland region of the state for purposes of exploration. He became the district's first sheriff and signed the Cumberland Compact. Montgomery was involved in several campaigns against the Native Americans of the region, including Nickajack and Dragging Canoe. One of the state's largest cities, Clarksville, is said to have been founded by Montgomery.

Moore. An early settler who served as a justice of the peace in Lincoln County and as an officer in the War of 1812, William Moore, was the namesake of this county. Moore was born in 1786 and died in 1871.

Morgan. Brigadier General Daniel Morgan gave his name to this county. Morgan was a veteran of many military campaigns, including the French and Indian War and the Revolutionary War. In the latter, he defeated Banastre Tarleton at Cowpens, and during the former was second in command to General Benedict Arnold at Quebec.

Obion. Opinion is divided on the origin of the county name. One explanation holds that a French-Irish officer who may have explored parts of western Tennessee gave his name to the area. Another possibility is that the name comes from a Native American term believed to mean "many prongs."

Overton. The name traces to John Overton, a pioneer who became an attorney and was closely identified with Nashville. Overton, General James Winchester, and Andrew Jackson co-founded Memphis. From 1804 until 1809, Overton served as a judge of the state supreme court.

Perry. Like numerous other U.S. sites, the county was named for Oliver Hazard Perry (1785–1819), who forced the surrender of the British fleet in the War of 1812. His flagship, the *Lawrence,* was damaged, but Perry continued to fight from the *Niagara,* and ultimately was victorious.

Pickett. In its naming, the county honored Howell L. Pickett, a state representative from Wilson County. Later in his life, Pickett immigrated to Tombstone, Arizona, and practiced law there.

Polk. The county was named for a governor of Tennessee and the eleventh president of the United States, James Knox Polk (1795–1849). Polk also served in such capacities as Speaker of the U.S. House of Representatives, member of the Tennessee house, and state senate clerk.

Putnam. A major general in the Revolutionary War and a veteran of campaigns at Bunker Hill and Harlem Heights, Israel Putnam, is this county's namesake. He also commanded forces at the Battle of Long Island, and was a commander in the Detroit Expedition against Pontiac during the French and Indian War.

Rhea. John Rhea, an early advocate of higher education, inspired the county's name. Rhea also fought during the Revolution, and was a veteran of action at Vinge Mountain.

Roane. A member of the Constitutional Convention and for a time a federal court judge, Archibald Roane, was the county's namesake. He also served as governor of Tennessee.

Robertson. James Robertson, founder of Nashville and the Watauga settlements, gave his name to this county. Robertson (1742–1814) was also a state senator, soldier, pioneer, and surveyor. Many consider him the "father of Tennessee."

Rutherford. President Washington appointed the county's namesake, Major General Griffith Rutherford, to a post as a member of the legislature of the Southwest Territory. The territory later became Tennessee. Rutherford became a hero during the Revolutionary War.

Scott. A War of 1812 veteran, General Winfield Scott's military service spanned several conflicts. He was a commander in the Mexican War, and in his later years served as a military adviser to the president. At one point, he was Army chief of staff.

Sequatchie. The county is thought to have been named for the Sequatchie Valley in which it lies. The valley gets its name from a Cherokee chief. In the early 1700s, the Cherokee leader traveled to South Carolina and signed a treaty with representatives of the colonial government at Charleston.

Sevier. The county derives its name from Colonel John Sevier, who served during the American Revolution and Indian wars. He commanded forces at Kings Mountain, among other venues. Sevier became the governor of the state of Franklin and the first governor of Tennessee. He also served as a congressman.

Shelby. Isaac Shelby helped arrange the purchase of the western district from the Chickasaws in 1818. He was appointed U.S. commissioner along with Andrew Jackson.

Smith. The county's namesake, Daniel Smith, at various times served as a senator from Tennessee and secretary of the Territory South of the River Ohio. He surveyed much of the region, and made the first map of the state. He achieved the rank of colonel in the Revolutionary Army.

Stewart. An early settler of this area —Duncan Stewart—inspired the county's name. He was a veteran of the Revolutionary War. Stewart was born in 1752 and died in 1815.

Sullivan. An officer in the Revolutionary War, John Sullivan (1740–1795), inspired this county's name. Sullivan also served as lieutenant governor and surveyor general of the Mississippi Territory, attorney general, member of the Continental Congress, and legislator.

Sumner. An officer in the French and Indian War, Major General Jethro Sumner, is the person for whom the county was named. He also helped defend North Carolina against Cornwallis, fought to defend Charleston in 1776, and was involved in struggles at Brandywine, Valley Forge, and Germantown.

Tipton. The county is named for Joseph Tipton, who lost his life while leading an attack in 1791. He had organized a band of soldiers for the purpose of defending the Northwest Territory against Indians.

Trousdale. A one-time governor of the state, William Trousdale (1790–1872), is honored by this county's name. He served as the state's chief executive from 1849 to 1851. His biography also reveals that at one time he was the nation's minister to Brazil, and served with Andrew Jackson at New Orleans and Pensacola. In the Mexican War, he commanded the Fourteenth U.S. Infantry, and reached the grade of brigadier general. Trousdale was nicknamed the "War Horse of Sumner County."

Unicoi. This county name is probably taken from a Native American term, *u'nika*, translating as "white" or "fog-draped." The reference was to the Southern Appalachian Mountains in the vicinity.

Union. The county may have been named Union because of strong eastern Tennessee sentiments favoring preservation of the (federal) Union. However, some believe it may have been so named because it represented the "union" of the five counties from which it was formed—Anderson, Knox, Grainger, Campbell, and Claiborne.

Van Buren. The county was named for Martin Van Buren, who served as the nation's president from 1837 to 1841. Among his earlier offices were U.S. senator from New York, New York governor, and secretary of state under President Jackson. He also became vice president before becoming president.

Warren. A Revolutionary War patriot, General Joseph Warren of Massachusetts, is this county's namesake. General Warren died at Bunker Hill in 1775.

Washington. One of the older Tennessee counties (est. 1777), this entity honors the nation's first president, General George Washington, recognized as the "father of our country."

Wayne. Major General Anthony ("Mad Anthony") Wayne is the county's namesake. Hailing from Pennsylvania, Wayne executed many clever tactics during the Revolutionary War. A great many U.S. places attribute their names to him.

Weakley. The county takes its name from Robert Weakley, who in 1796 served in the state's House of Representatives. At various times, he was also a member of Tennessee's State Constitutional Convention (1834), a militia colonel, and Speaker of the state senate. He also had been a member of the North Carolina Constitutional Convention.

White. The county's first settler, Revolutionary War veteran John White, is the source of the name.

Williamson. The county was named for a colonel and surgeon general of the North Carolina Militia, Dr. Hugh Williamson. A signer of the Constitution, he also served three terms as a representative at the Continental Congress.

Wilson. The county's namesake was David Wilson, a distinguished veteran of the Revolution, who at other times also served as Speaker of the House (1794) and member of the Territory Assembly.

Acknowledgments

Marcie Ainsworth
Howard E. Alderson
Harbert Alexander
Alberta Kitchell Allen
Mary Evelyn Allen
Eddie Archer
Angela Barclay Arnold
Margaret D. Ashton
Elizabeth R. Atkinson
Mr. and Mrs. Olen E. Bailey
Pansy Nanney Baker
Peggy Balding
Sara A. Barnes
Oliver A. Bayless
Blanche Beaty
Lonetta Beshears
Sara W. Bigham
Allan C. Birdwell
Alpha Black
Marie Bradford

James H. Brady
J. Roger Bragdon
Martha O'Shell Bridges
Christopher D. Brown
Mona Moore Brown
Bettye J. Broyles
Ruth R. Broyles
Jimmie Lee Bryan
Ernest Buck
Sandra Buckner
Inez E. Burns
Rachel H. K. Burrow
Edgar D. Byler III
David Cagle
William L. Calahan
Edith Killian Caldwell
Campbell County Historical Society
Bernice Cargill
Julia Herod Carnahan
Martha McKenzie Carpenter
Blanche Carver
Joe M. Casey
Mollie Chapman
A. B. Chitty
Jeneva Walton Connor
Mack H. Cooper
Julie Cromwell
Leo Croy
Margaret Davis
Peggy Davis
Donald Davison
Ned Denton
Katheryn Frye Dickens
James A. Dillon Jr.
Sara E. Dollar
William ("Dale") Donegan
Edward Dotson
Rose E. Duke
Elizabeth Duncan
Bobbie Dunlap
E. Ennis
J. Rice Evans

Larry Allen Faulkner

Jessie Felknor

Mary Sue Floyd

Henry Foote

Bill Fox

Annette Francisco

Clyde Franklin

Ethel Freytag

Ruth Fulton

Wilma Holland Fults

Janet E. Gann

Jill K. Garrett

James E. Gentry

Evelyn Glass

Perry E. Goad

Josetta Griffith

Lary Hagood

Julia Hamlin

Wanda Hance

Cora Harper

Mary Eunice H. Harrell

Mary S. Harris

Gladys Ousley Hassell

Floyd and Violet Hatmaker

Levenda Hatmaker

Effie Dalton Heiss

Annie Henderson

Mary Ann Hendrikson

Timothy R. Henson

Frances Hickle

Suzanne Hill

Nancy K. Hillis

Elva Hodge

Lorinda Killian Holder

Mr. and Mrs. William Hood

Freeman Hopper

Robbie Houston

Margie G. Howard

Imogene S. Huffstutter

Robbie Hughes

Mary R. Hurley

E. Jackson

George B. Jackson
George E. Jackson
Ronald Vern Jackson
Buford Jennings
Erlene Lewis Jernigan
Nancy Butts Johnson
Keith Jones
Jessica Keen
Elizabeth Kelley
Nancy Kennedy
Judy King
Knox County Public Library System
Susie Kries
Albert Lane
Betty Lankford
Susan Lauver
Florence Robinson Lawson
Margaret Earley Lee
Joseph Paul Lewis
Kae J. Lewis
Sue Ann Lewis
Marise P. Lightfoot
Beulah Linn
Joe D. Little
Mildred Littrell
H. A. Longmire
John N. Lovett Jr.
Evelyn L. Luckett
Shirley W. Manuel
Ann L. Marks
Tim Marsh
Maryville *Daily Times*
J. D. Matthews
Emily McClellan
Gene and Earlene McDaniel
Winnie Palmer McDonald
Elizabeth McGee
David McGregor
Robert B. McKinnon
Frances L. Meek
Irving W. Meek Jr. Public Library
Donald B. Miller

Sayde Miller
Wilma J. Miller
Dorothy Moore
Elizabeth J. Moore
Elizabeth Morgan
Kathy Morris
Dorothy R. Morton
John Mulvihill
Mrs. Paul Neal
William J. Nesbitt
Kathy Niedergeses
Wayne Odle
Bonnie M. Page
Clara M. Parker
Billy Parks
Mack Parks
David Patton
Bonnie Heiskell Peters
Roberta Plant Poyner
Marian Bailey Presswood
Tim Pulley
Claude Ramsey
Vanessa Razzano
Rita Read
Yolanda G. Reid
Fern Reynolds
Kathleen West Robbins
H. B. Roberts Jr.
A. J. Robinson
Phillis Robinson
Doris Wiley Rollins
Joy Rosser
Kata C. Rowland
Marvin Scott
Hilda H. Sharp
Byron R. Sistler
Kay Smith
Michael G. Smith
William R. Snell
James Southerland
Joel Shane Spears
Gus A. Steele

Ken Stephens
Terry Stephens
Jennie Beth Stokes
Phyllis A. Strunk
Seth Tallent
Elizabeth Taylor
Emmett Taylor
Paul Taylor
Thomas Edwin Todd
Phillis M. Uehlein
Virginia Clark Vaughan
W. H. Vaughn
E. R. Walker III
Mary Ellen Martin Walker
Jan Wallace
Ron Warren
Ethel and Lizzie Warwick
Bill Webb
Thomas G. Webb
Brittany M. West
Frances West
Ricky James West
Elizabeth W. White
Betty Williams
V. Wisdom
Faith and Billy Young
Fran Young

Larry L. Miller, an Ohio native, is an advertising copywriter based at Brady Lake. His previous publications include *Ohio Place-Names* (Indiana University Press), numerous fact articles, books on local history and nostalgia, columns, photo spreads, and poetry.